Shocked and Appalled

To Peter
Best wishes
Jack Kapica
June 26/85

Shocked and Appalled

A Century of Letters to
The Globe and Mail

Edited by Jack Kapica

LESTER
&ORPEN
DENNYS
PUBLISHERS

FIRST EDITION

Canadian Cataloguing in Publication Data

Main entry under title:

Shocked and appalled:
a century of letters to The Globe and mail

Includes index.
ISBN 0-88619-062-2.

1. Newspapers – Sections, columns, etc. – Letters to the editor.
I. Kapica, Jack. II. The Globe and mail.
PN4914.L4S54 1985 081 C85-098174-3

Design by Thornley Design Associates Ltd.
Typesetting by The Coach House Press, Toronto.
Set in 11 pt. Bembo

Printed and bound in Canada by
John Deyell Company for

Lester & Orpen Dennys Ltd.
78 Sullivan Street
Toronto, Ontario
Canada M5T 1C1

Acknowledgements

For all their valuable assistance, in various and sometimes unconscious ways, I would like to thank the following:

Globe and Mail editor Norman Webster and features editor Ed O'Dacre, whose belief in this project made them so generous in giving me the time to accomplish it;

Chief *Globe and Mail* librarian Amanda Valpy, whose trust in me was admirable; and librarians Paul Paré, Rick Cash and Lisa Anderson, for their patience;

Erling Friis-Baastad, whose help with microfilm saved my eyes, and perhaps my sanity;

Stanley and Nancy Colbert, for their continuing and invaluable help;

Alberto Manguel, the godfather of so many projects, and ultimately of this one;

Dave Billington, for having been there when I needed him the most;

All the letter writers past and present;

My predecessors at *The Globe and Mail,* for their judicious tastes;

My editor, Gena Gorrell, who can make manuscripts sparkle;

And my wife, Eve Drobot, whose support, encouragement and understanding are infinite. It is to her that all this labor is lovingly dedicated.

Contents

Foreword

Newspaper readers are not passive consumers. They hold to the splendid notion that their paper belongs not to its owners or its editors, but to them, and they take their responsibilities very seriously. They monitor the staff's performance daily, frequently taking pen in hand to point out lapses in grammar, thump mistaken opinions, and raise matters of public interest ranging from the national debt to the proper plural of hippopotamus.

Shocked and appalled they may be; reticent they are not, and the wise newspaper sets aside prime editorial real estate for this correspondence, letting readers occupy the space in their own way and refraining from adding those cute quips to the bottoms of letters which make the editor out to be so much more clever than his correspondent. The bonus is that the editor ends up with one of the liveliest, best-read pages in his paper.

Jack Kapica's selection from a century of letters to *The Globe* makes the point perfectly. Mazo de la Roche pleads for the lives of the pigeons at city hall. Eugene Forsey eviscerates the hapless post office. One "M. St. J." attacks the newspaper for advocating a distinctive Canadian flag – in 1901.

Letters in 1920, and again in 1979, marshal thoughtful arguments for a flat earth. A reader in 1885 asks mercy for Louis Riel. Another, in 1984, uses modern physics to explain the previously inexplicable: "The spinning of the dryer creates a black hole that sucks single socks into nothingness." Of course.

Shocked, appalled, exultant, dyspeptic, or just doing their duty as they see it, the readers write. It is, after all, their newspaper.

Norman Webster
Editor-in-chief
The Globe and Mail

Introduction

There are moments in the life of a letters editor which are special.

To be fair, the letters page of a newspaper must be a forum dedicated to its readers, a page where their opinions can be heard, their honor defended, their spleen spilled. But occasionally, in the deluge of pompous letterheads, florid stationery, and odd scraps of paper that flood the editor's desk each day, there will be one which leaps out from the rest, an opinion so outrageous or a rebuke so witty that the editor must pry open a space between two more sober writers to relieve the tension. No one – not even the editor of *The Globe and Mail* – can take relentless earnestness for ever.

These are the correspondents who write for the sheer joy of writing, who treasure the spirit of debate for its own sake.

The majority of the 15,000 or so who write to *The Globe and Mail* each year are one-shot writers, prodded to seek their moment at centre stage when the limelight falls on their own expertise. A few are "professionals" in that they are official spokesmen for some group or cause and part of their duty is to ensure that their interests are shown in the best possible light – politicians, doctors, lawyers, butchers, bakers, and presidents of the Amalgamated Candlestick Makers.

The genuine recidivists – those who continually hone their quills while contemplating the editor's jugular – are a bit more difficult to explain. Some start off as "professionals", but their talents quickly transcend the merely functional purpose of writing. The best example of this sort is the redoubtable Eugene Forsey, who published his first letter to *The Globe* in 1948 and is still going strong. As Canada's foremost constitutional expert, he has a justifiable mission to correct points of law and political practice. But Forsey's keen ear, sharp eye, and love of the written word have also allowed him to indulge in his avocation as one of the most ferocious guardians of grammar *The Globe* has ever known. A letter from his Senate chambers or law office is just as likely to contain a stinging elucidation of the laws of the language as of the laws of the land.

Although the letters editor must be non-partisan, there inevitably develop some favorites among the regular correspondents. Since I started editing the letters in 1979, I have nurtured a few perennials (they alone know who they are), but I must allow that some of the all-time greats simply came with the territory. Such was the case with Eugene Forsey, and Austin Small, whom I inherited from my predecessors.

The editorship of the letters column is an exception in the practice of journalism in that it carries with it a singular lack of curiosity. Other than being aware of correspondents famous in their own right, it is not part of the editor's duty to know the writer's age, trade, or motives for writing. But, inevitably, the arrival of a letter from Austin Small was an occasion for the heart to beat a little faster. Usually explaining human failure as the obvious result of the flatness of the earth, his letters from the other side of the Looking Glass were short, to the point, and wonderfully funny. It was obvious that I was dealing with a studied craftsman. But for all the pleasure I took in midwifing his musings, it never occurred to me to search out the man behind the postmark.

It was gratifying to learn that others also appreciated Austin's writing. A couple of years ago, CBC's *Sunday Morning* produced a documentary on chronic letter writers and, not surprisingly, sought out Austin Small. On the radio, his voice sounded as I had expected: warm, thoughtful, and thoroughly mischievous. His approach to writing a letter, he revealed, was to treat the task with great care. A thought would surface in reaction to a story; he would write it down, polish it, let it sit overnight, and only mail it if he felt it passed muster in the cold light of dawn.

The respectful distance between us lasted four years. Then a relative of his called to say that Austin was in hospital. On an impulse I put together a package of *Globe and Mail* stationery and pens and sent them to his hospital room with a note. He never answered. A couple of weeks later, I received a letter from the same relative, saying that Austin had died.

Austin's chief rival for the title of resident wit, H.W. Somerville, happened to phone shortly after Austin's death and I told him the news. The next day, *The Globe* printed a letter from Somerville that echoed the sentiments of innumerable readers:

> *The Globe and Mail*'s editorial pages will be a little greyer with the recent passing of your Oakville irregular, Austin Small, whose gentle whimsy and real erudition so often brightened a day.

Some letters spring from highly distinguished sources. There was, for instance, the case of the most awesome letter never printed by *The Globe and Mail*. Reporter George Bain, long a thorn in the side of the Liberal Government, left *The Globe* in 1973. And despite an announcement of the move, the post shortly delivered the following letter:

Sir:

Where's Bain?

P.E. Trudeau
Ottawa

Who decided against printing the letter, and why? No one will admit to remembering.

Other letters are simply moments of sheer frivolity. After a particularly rainy period in 1961, *The Globe* printed the only non-letter it ever received. A considerate reader had mailed an umbrella to the editor, with only his name and address appended on a brown tag. What else could the editor do but faithfully photograph the gift, and run it nestled in the appropriate column?

Of course, not all letters (or umbrellas) are charming. Every newspaper receives its share of unprintable mail from writers who have more on their minds than debate. There have been death threats against visiting royalty (promptly handed over to the proper authorities) and imprecations from outraged correspondents who, instead of seeing their names in print, received a gentle note saluting the "Dear Correspondent" and expressing regret that space limitations make it impossible to "publish all of the many thousands we receive each year." One rejected writer entered *The Globe*'s offices several years ago and, after harassing the nearest reporter for ten minutes, began to emphasize her point with her umbrella, on his head.

In 1844, when George Brown founded *The Globe,* the distinction between letters and news stories was hazy. Many of the "stories" were in fact lengthy letters that amounted to compendiums of gossip from far-flung Kingston and Hamilton, reporting on the latest gavottes of pukka society, and requiring five headlines to describe.

It was a small world then, one in which everyone knew everyone else's name and profession and was familiar with all the current issues of debate – or perhaps *The Globe* was merely directed at those who did. (George Brown and his heirs had targeted their audience quite specifically; the paper was fondly called "The Scotchman's

Bible".) Letters contained few references to first names or issues, and relied for their impact on florid Victorian syntax.

The Globe continued to lavish space on its loyal readers. By 1889, zealous letter-writers had almost taken over the paper as their private forum, and correspondence had to be moved off the editorial page lest its sheer volume drown out the sober contemplations of the editor. Often a full page was devoted to one topic alone (the Imperial Federation League thrashing out reciprocity with the United States, for instance, or later, doomsayers insisting that trolleys running on the sabbath heralded the end of the Empire and Christianity). The more individualistic writers had to content themselves elsewhere in the paper.

But Sir John Willison, editor between 1890 and 1910, put an end to that. He grew savagely selective, demoted letters to filler material, and scattered them throughout the paper where space could be found – jostling sporting results, elbowing gossip columns, or squatting under the weight of enormous advertisements for cancer cures and electric hernia belts.

Sir John's action raised an outcry, and he was forced to relent somewhat. In 1903 he created "The Mailbag", a column of letters restricted to no more than 750 words (still hefty by today's standards) which he crammed into five inches of the smallest type he could find. But his standards were too stilted and the structure was too stifling for genuine inspiration, and the resulting dullness of the column forced its demise in a matter of months.

By 1910 the letters had found their way back to the editorial page, where they have remained since, and it was then simply a matter of what their assembled chorus would be called. "Voice of the People" was a long-time favorite, despite its Latinate pretension; the chatty "Readers Discuss Current Topics" found an equally regrettable vogue. It was not until the forties that "Letters to the Editor" emerged as the straightforward consensus.

After their reinstatement on the editorial page, the letters soon recovered their vitality. In the twenties and thirties, for instance, letters on the subject of baptism and religious intolerance became so furious and long-winded that it was a relief when the editor exercised his italic prerogative: "With this letter, correspondence on this subject is closed."

In the early years, many writers hid behind preposterous pseudonyms – "Fidelis", "Civitas", "Veritas", "Pro Bono Publico" were popular. Perhaps these writers felt their ideas were more important than their own modest identities, or perhaps they feared social retribution for unpopular views. It was the savagery of the religious debates that forced *The Globe* to insist, on March 18, 1930, that henceforth all letters on the subject of religion be signed with the writers' real names; on September 26, 1940, the edict was extended to all subjects.

History plays a part in the letters page only as it is manifest in the readers' minds. Popular invective does not always attack incidents that will some day be considered historic, but may instead go howling off after another, more electrifying debate. This explains the curious absence of letters, for example, on the assassination of the Archduke Ferdinand at Sarajevo in 1914, and on the collapse of Wall Street in 1929; each of these events preceded by a few days an Ontario election fought on the issue of temperance, a more thoroughly satisfying topic for debate.

Of course the greatest number of letters come from Cabinet ministers shoring up shaky budget proposals, labor leaders condemning arrant management, insecure churchmen fine-tuning a Sunday sermon and ordinary mortals interpreting the world with bone-chilling sincerity, and it is necessary to print these letters to present a truly balanced view of the readership. But the letters editor also finds poets discussing turtle soup, choleric old gentlemen expressing special feelings about cats, spinsters spilling over with complex theories about astronomy, and astrophysicists writing limericks. These irresistible letters punctuate the litany of worthy opinion with sheer flights of fancy, exquisite nonsense, and brilliant facetiae.

This collection is a sampling of those moments which the letters editor cherishes. It is not meant to be a sober record of issues vital to national and international interest. Rather, it is a compendium of bulletins on the tenor of the day, sometimes startlingly prescient and sometimes just so succinct that they are a delight to read with the hindsight of history.

These letters are therefore presented virtually intact, printed as they were first published. Every effort has been made to preserve their original venom, character, and piquancy. On rare occasions typographical errors have been corrected, or a first name or title inserted for clarity, or a repetitive preamble cut short.

Shocked and Appalled covers the period 1885 to 1984, a neat century's worth of letters. A hundred years ago, Canada was testing its mettle as a nation. Sir John A. Macdonald was embarking on the last six years of his governance over a financially troubled land; Wilfrid Laurier was biding his time in Quebec; Lord Strathcona would soon go to the lonely village of Craigellachie in British Columbia to hammer in the last CPR spike; Louis Riel was plotting the Northwest Rebellion which would plunge the youthful country into its first test of maturity; and *The Globe*, which had five years earlier lost its founder George Brown to a bullet fired by an addled former employee, had already proved it could survive without its visionary creator.

What has not changed since those dramatic days has been the readers' reverence for the power of the letter to the editor. Whether written by eminent names or by those whom history has forgotten, their words are as treasured today as they were then. It is in their honor, and that of my predecessors at the letters desk, that this volume is offered.

Jack Kapica
April, 1985

Shocked and Appalled

Chapter 1

The Art of Writing Letters to the Editor

October 30, 1937

There are certain great occasions in the life of man. There is baby's first tooth, his first word, then much later his first pair of long trousers. The major event is yet to come – the first shave. From here follows in rapid order his first drink of hard liquor and its subsequent implications – "I dare do all that may become a man; who dares do more is none." By this time he has convinced himself and the State that he is a man, so he polls his first vote. But our hero has yet to cross his Rubicon. Oh, joy! Oh, bliss! his first letter to the editor.

Once upon a time I read a letter to your paper that ran something like this: The world is made up of two classes of people, sensible ones and those who write letters to the editor. This letter, then, is to shed some light on the question, Why letters to the editor? or to be more explicit, Why this letter?

To begin with, I've got nothing better to do, which explains at least 75 per cent of the letters you receive, Mr. Editor.

Then again, people are always asking this rather rude question, And what do you do for a living? Now, instead of saying, "Livin' on the ole man," I shall assume an air of importance and reply in an offhand manner, "Journalism! I write for The Globe and Mail."

Those who don't wish to go to the bother of taking their soap boxes down to the street corner to revolutionize the order of society merely write a letter to the editor, and the Government remains as usual.

The real underlying reason for this letter is not to predict the end of the world or advocate closing the beer parlors, or even to settle that much-debated question of how to spell "buses." My reason is not of such a lofty nature, and while it may seem insignificant to you, Mr. Editor, I assure you it is of no small import to me. This problem which is close to me is how to eat breakfast in bed without sliding around on toast crumbs the rest of the day. Any answer will be gratefully received, with the exception of "Get up," or "Quit having toast for breakfast." A grand prize of two bent pins will be awarded to the one sending in the best solution. All may compete, with the exception of your columnist J.V. McAree, who, it is assumed, would have an unfair advantage.

To be complete, a letter to the editor must have a pungent comment at the top. May I suggest – "The Light That Failed," since it is absolutely irrelevant to the contents of irrelevancies: therefore quite appropriate. I have no hesitation in predicting a brilliant literary future for myself. If your publisher George McCullagh started his career as a mere newsboy, what possibilities the future must hold for a full-fledged writer like myself!

Since letters to the editor are a chronic disease, my next journalistic gem will take the form of how I would run The Globe and Mail if I were in Mr. McCullagh's shoes (assuming his shoes would fit me). The results, as well as astonishing, are guaranteed to bankrupt the publisher and his sponsor within at least six months. I eagerly await the opinion of the world at large. Have I a promising future writing letters to the editor or is my literary genius doomed to languish where it began, sliding on toast crumbs?

Wee Willie
Belleville

◆

April 16, 1970

With regard to the letters written to and published by The Globe and Mail may I ask this question: Why do so *many* people write so *many* words to say so little?

T.S. Reddy
Niagara Falls

◆

May 12, 1979

You recently printed a letter of mine that was considerably shorter than the one I wrote. I can only assume that portions of it must have been lost in the mail.

Tom Hunter
Don Mills

April 10, 1982

You publish so many long stupid letters that it occurred to me you might like this short stupid letter as a filler.

Henry Hindley
Ottawa

◆

January 4, 1984

Although I have been a reader of The Globe for more than 50 years, I cannot recall an occasion when both the editorial and letters pages have been eliminated, as in your Dec. 24th issue.

On reflection, it proves to me that we could just get along without the punditry of your omniscient Cassandras. But it put a blight on the day before Christmas to be denied the almost deathless prose of those chosen to represent the vox populi.

There were all kinds of other features on which the axe might have fallen. One hopes that this dismal omission will not become an annual event.

Stanley R. Redman
Midland, Ontario

Chapter 2

Riel and His Times

The telegraph lines which had just been strung up across the prairies had their first severe test on March 26, 1885, when Louis Riel tore down the wires prior to taking Duck Lake. Newspapers in the East were forced to rely on eyewitness reports from those who returned from Saskatchewan, and the first news was not received in Toronto until ten days later. But when General Frederick Middleton captured Batoche on May 12, the lines were set up again, and the news – and public response – was swift.

May 23, 1885

It is not to be wondered at that just now there should be a bitter feeling among Canadians against the hostile Indians in the North-West.

When once happy homes have been turned into desolation, it is very difficult to take a philosophic or even a Christian view of the Indian question. But the people of the Dominion must be hopeful not to let their feelings get the better of their reason or philanthropy. I see that some of the North-West papers, and certain correspondents of eastern journals, indulge in the most bitter invectives against the Indians for their outrages round about Battleford. Now, without attempting to deny or minimize those wanton acts, there are, it seems to me, many things we must bear in mind. Apart altogether from the provocation the red men have had in the way of hunger, loss of land and game; apart from the palliation which their ignorance and paganism offer, we should recollect that white soldiers have again and again committed equally ruthless outrages. It is only a century since the Revolutionary war, and yet in many instances during that struggle, quarter was denied, and massacres were openly perpetrated by white troops. In that war, the peaceful and cultivated Indian settlements of York state were reduced for many miles to a blackened waste. In the later Indian wars of Florida hounds were employed by white soldiers to hunt the Indians from the swamps.

In the Sepoy mutiny orders were given to spare no man with arms in his hand, and the soldiers themselves grew sick of slaughter.

In the late war between the North and the South General Sherman marched a Northern army of 65,000 men from Atlanta to the Sea, laying waste a country three hundred miles long and sixty wide. In this vast tract, although life and limb were spared, cotton houses, barns, and unoccupied dwellings were indiscriminately destroyed. Not only were the requisite food and forage taken – this was perfectly justifiable – but women and children were left in an absolutely starving condition. Jewels, money, and other portable valuables became, with the sanction of the officers, the property of the soldiers, while those thing which could not easily be removed or converted into money, such as books, pictures, furniture, etc., were destroyed beyond recognition. In one instance at least the horses of the cavalry were led into the parlour and library, upon the floor of which books and ornaments were scattered; and the horses were then made to stamp these household treasures beneath their feet, and this in a country from which the enemy's forces had departed, and under the eyes of the officers of a Christian army. The highest races are, after all, but little removed from barbarism. It needs but the excitement of battle or the rage of passion to bring out the old savage instincts.

And although acts such as those of the Indians at Battleford seem to us not only brutal, but also absolutely childish, yet to the Indian the pianos and pictures and books of the white settlers were the symbols of the power and wealth of those who had robbed him of his land and driven away the buffalo, the special gift of the Great Spirit. A decisive defeat will probably do Chief Poundmaker good; but after that, after the superiority of the white troops has been clearly shown to the Indians, the Canadian people will insist that justice, pressed down and running over, be done to the red men, who for more than a century have remained loyal to British rule, and the great majority of whom have remained loyal even during the present crisis.

J.H. Long

◆

September 1, 1885

I have been a good deal surprised to see that some of the Liberal papers are arguing that Riel's sentence should be carried out in its extreme form, without paying any attention to the jury's recommendation for mercy. If there is one thing of which we have been strongly assured during the past months, by these very papers, it is that the Government by its culpable negligence is mainly responsible for the Rebellion and all its sad results. In one of your recent editorials, you express the opinion that Mr. Dewdney and his masters are responsible for all the lives lost and money wasted on the late deplorable Rebellion. If so, it is scarcely consistent to urge that the lesser culprit should meet a felon's death, while the greater ones, in the nature of the case, meet with no penalty whatever!

I neither desire to defend Riel, to make him out a hero, nor even to prove him insane, *i.e.,* in the sense in which we consider a man's mind so far unhinged that he is incapable of transacting business. But it is easy to see that, with a considerable strain of foolish vanity, he is, on the whole, a political fanatic, a hare-brained enthusiast full of dreams and fancies. It is easy to understand how a man of an excitable and fervid temperament, worked upon by brooding over his people's wrongs, which we are told were real enough, and by feeling that he was regarded as the only possible deliverer, should have fancied that he had "a mission" to raise the standard of revolt which he regarded as the standard of freedom. Of course his conduct in doing so was rash, misguided and mischievous to the last degree, as too many Canadian know to their cost. But in this he is no more and no less culpable than any other revolutionary leader, – as, for instance, Jefferson Davis, or our own Papineau or William Lyon Mackenzie; and we know that no such harsh meed was meted out to them. It is true, sadly true, that the rebellion led by Riel cost Canada dear enough in money, in destroying the budding prosperity of a new settlement, ruining the hopes of hard-working settlers, and, worst of all, the sacrifice of many precious lives. But Riel did not desire any of these things for their own sake any more than did the Government in sending troops, bullets and Gatlings, to check the rebellion. It is very doubtful, indeed, whether he expected fighting at all. His former experience naturally gave him reason to hope for gaining all he wanted without bloodshed; and but for what seems to have been the *contretemps* of the Duck Lake encounter, a peaceful settlement might have been accomplished.

But every man who provokes a war may be called, in just the same way, the proximate cause of all the misery and the heavy loss it involves. Probably no one man has caused greater havoc and loss of life than the first Napoleon, – called "The Great," and this without even the excuse of righting the wrongs of the oppressed. Yet the combined wisdom of Europe – after his second assault on her peace – decreed him no harsher sentence than his confinement on St. Helena. No man of our own day has sacrificed the lives of so many thousands of brave men, under the influence of "an idea," as has Bismarck, and it seems that he himself often remorsefully feels this; but I do not suppose his bitterest opponent would desire his execution as a felon. Arabi Pasha instigated far greater slaughter and far fouler barbarities than any that can be laid to the charge of Riel, yet even he was allowed to retire in peace to Ceylon, and finds those who defend his conduct on the same grounds on which Riel bases his defences. The point at which an appeal to arms ceases to be treasonable, and becomes heroic, is extremely vague, and seems to be largely determined by the after success. And political executions – unless in very aggravated cases, such as assassination – have come to be pretty generally regarded as a mistaken policy. As things go, and have gone, even in Canada, the execution of Riel would be a politic blunder, as well as a political wrong, throwing us back about half a century, and recalling the unfortunate military executions of 1838. If Riel, by one section of the people, is made a political scapegoat, by another he will be made a political martyr. Nothing could be more fruitful in the seeds of future disaffection. Ireland is still suffering from the mistake which sent Emmett to the scaffold. Living in exile or partial confinement, with a death penalty imposed on his return, Riel could do little harm – especially with moderately good government in the North-West. Dying on the scaffold, he would leave in the hearts of the people – whom with all his faults he loves – a bitter memory, and a name that would for generations be a rallying cry for sedition and sectional animosity. It would harden our present antagonism of race and religion, and postpone indefinitely the fusing and consolidating process we all desire. His death cannot bring back one precious life, nor make restitution for the slightest wrong. Nor do I think it could bring balm to any mourning heart to know that the widow and children, now waiting in torturing suspense, should also be deprived of their earthly stay.

Let Riel be served with the same measures he wants to mete out to "the clergy," and placed on an island in the Atlantic, or elsewhere, where he can declaim to the rocks and waves as harmlessly as did Demosthenes! Ontario – next to the North-West the chief sufferer – has a noble opportunity of showing herself magnanimous and binding to her her fellow subjects in a tie of gratitude not easily broken. If, in a blind outcry for vengeance, she throws this away, our Dominion may be, for generations, "a house divided against itself." This is a matter that concerns every true Canadian, and I speak for many who hold the same views.

Fidelis

Riel was hanged November 16, 1885, and was indeed made a martyr. The following letter shows to what lengths the martyrdom was carried out.

March 3, 1972

I read with interest the story Lock Of Hair Believed Riel's Sells For
$600.

The lock of hair is probably authentic. After Riel's death the
coroner's jury was empaneled by Dr. Dodds, and a verdict of death
by hanging was rendered. The hair of the deceased was cut off one
side of both head and face. All the buttons torn off the coat, the
moccasins removed from the feet and even the suspenders cut into
pieces for persons to obtain mementoes of the deceased.

Today one can visit the RCMP Museum in Regina, Sask., to
view a portion of the rope used to hang Louis "David" Riel. Have
we improved much since 1885?

Peter F. Frank
Oakville

The Servant Girl

December 7, 1885

That ill-treated class, the servant girls, are under a debt of gratitude
to The Globe for bringing their case forward. What has been said
regarding endless toil, bad food and cold and cheerless lodgings, is,
in too many cases, not a whit overdrawn. For several years after the
writer came to Canada she suffered inconceivable hardships, ill-
usage, and insults as a "general servant." What made the treatment
appear so harsh was her inexperience among rough people. Her service in dear old Ireland and England had been under ladies. "Put a
beggar on horseback," etc., is just as applicable here as in Ireland;
and, of course, in a new country like Canada, where the greater
number of employers of labour are not "to the manner born,"
decent treatment of servants is naturally the exception. Maggie
———, a Scotch servant girl, who crossed the Atlantic with me about
ten years ago, married a bricklayer in Toronto a few years ago who
made lots of money at Corporation work. She asked the writer to
live with her as a "general servant," which was done. She treated
the writer worse than her dog. It was ever thus, "a silk purse cannot
be made out of a sow's ear." My old sweetheart, a soldier in old Ireland, God bless him, used to tell me his colonel rose from the ranks,
and that was why he was such a tyrant. He told me none of the soldiers liked to be under any but bred gentlemen. Such statements
were unintelligible then, but my Canadian experience has made the
matter plain. I am now in the service of a lady, and shall not be soon
tempted to leave her. Cheer up, poor heart! and when you get a lady

for a mistress stick to her. It would pay us, as a class, to subscribe some of our wages towards the education and refinement of those under whom we must serve. Ignorance is always associated with coarseness and brutality. Can we combine for improvement and protection?

Kathleen O'Neil

The Women Vote

January 7, 1886

I am not particularly enamoured with the idea of female suffrage, which identifies women with the turmoil attending municipal and political contests, but inasmuch as that privilege has, so far, been accorded them, they have the right to require that they be provided with separate polling places for their own exclusive use. My observation at one of the polling places in St. Thomas ward fully justifies this suggestion. It must have been exceedingly mortifying for ladies to have their votes challenged, and sworn before a room full of men, which ungallant conduct was evidently resorted to with the view of deterring the timid from recording their votes.

John MacLay

> *Unmarried women with property were given a vote for municipal bylaws only in 1882; the next year, the vote for women was extended to municipal elections.*

A Word from D'Arcy McGee's Ghost

In a lifelong battle with the Fenians, Thomas D'Arcy McGee had managed to alienate the British in Ireland and the Roman Catholic bishop of New York before he found favor in Canada as an eloquent proponent of Confederation. He won election to Sir John A. Macdonald's first Canadian Parliament, advocating full Irish support for Macdonald's cause. But he still made his enemies – once again taking on the Fenians, he was assassinated in the early hours of April 7, 1868. Patrick James Whelan, a Fenian, was hanged for the shooting on February 11, 1869.

August 11, 1887

Now that the question "Who shot McGee?" is being discussed anew in courts and journals, an autograph from Ghostland may be interesting to listen to.

9

A certain prominent Irishman in Ottawa, lately deceased, was an old friend of McGee, and a devote believer in spiritualism. Not long before his death I heard him tell, at a friend's dinner table, a strange tale, of which the following is the substance:

"When I was in Boston a few years ago I went to see a lady who professed to be a 'writing medium.' I said to her, 'I want to consult the spirit of D'Arcy McGee.' 'Who was he?' 'Oh, a Canadian politician whom I used to know.' She went into an apparent trance and soon began writing, rapidly, but fitfully. When she handed me the result my hair began to rise. It was McGee's own handwriting from beginning to end! It was in the ordinary form of a letter addressed to myself and dated – with the day of the month and the year only. I won't speak of all that was in it, but I'll tell you part of it. He said:– 'It was not Whelan who shot me – it was so-and-so,' naming a man I knew well, who has since died in a lunatic asylum. 'Whelan was there with him, but it was not he that fired the shot.'

"When I came home I went up to see Sir John, and showed him the letter, folded so that he could see neither date nor signature. I said, 'Do you know the handwriting?' 'Of course I do! That's poor McGee's.' 'Now look at the date and signature.' He did so and then said to me, with a very queer look, 'My God! What does this mean?' Then I told him all about it, just as I've told you. And we both felt very queer about it, too, I can tell you."

And so did the whole dinner party; for poor ——'s sincerity and agitation were as evident as possible – and no mundane explanation occurred to anybody.

Outaouais

More Letters

August 1, 1888

An article recently published in The Globe on the number of words used in ordinary conversation and writing revived in my mind what from time to time I have often thought of in somewhat the same direction. The writer in question says:– "Every well-read man of fair ability in conversation and writing will use not less than 6,000 or 7,000 words." Again:– "Common people use from 3,000 to 4,000 words, according to their general intelligence and conversational powers." Again:– "An illiterate man will use from 1,500 to 2,000 words." The great mass of our people must be classed among what are here called "common people" – those who have had but small educational advantages or of improving what they have. This class, in my opinion, would derive great benefit if they would write more letters, but that is the very thing they are most reluctant to do, because they are not good spellers, and they dread having their ignorance in this respect made so manifest. This class in writing a letter would only use such words as they knew the meaning of, consequently in this respect a dictionary would be of no use to them. Of the 3,000 or 4,000 words at their command they could correctly spell all but perhaps 50 or 60, and perhaps not more than four or five of these would occur in a long letter of 40 or 50 lines. A dictionary contains some 90,000 words, consequently few own such a book, and those who do seldom or ever refer to it on account of its size. Now, the question is this, Could not a small, cheap dictionary be got up for this class, containing say some 1,000 or 2,000 words? The meaning only of such words as have the same sound – such as principle and principal, etc. – need be given. A small book of 20 pages, with two columns of 25 words each, would give 1,000 words; or say 20 leaves and 40 pages, would give 2,000 words. I cannot but think that such a book would be in great demand and meet a "long felt want."

A.B.C.
Brantford

The Mighty Province

January 18, 1889

I have been trying to realize the vast extent of the Province of Ontario from The Globe's descriptions thereof, and I think all of Ontario's sons should rejoice on the new and brighter era about dawning on this great Province.

Encircling on their Northern shores the four most magnificent lakes in the universe, and while six States to the South border thereon, they kiss the shores of Ontario alone on their northern shores, and this mighty Province still extends hundreds of miles to the west of Lake Superior. I am afraid that the following lines will give but a very faint idea of the natural resources and wealth of this fine Province.

There doth arise a sweet aroma
From great spruce forests of Algoma
And from the poplar birch and pine
Thereto is wealth in many a mine

Ontario she doth take pride
In her vast lakes so long and wide
Several States approach Lake Erie
Each one claiming it for deary

But our fires of love do glow
Alone for Lake Ontario
Round it our Towns and Cities cluster
O'er it Toronto sheds her lustre

And this fine Lake's southern beaches
They are famed for grapes and peaches
Mong choicest fruits you ramble on
From Niagara to Hamilton

Ontario north is land of pines
A land of lakes and rocks and mines
And beneath the dark pine trees shade
How happy is the youth and maid

For here in summer you keep cool
And fish for trout in sparkling pool
In great northern hunting ground
There both fish and game abound

Nature this Province doth endow
With hearty sons to guide the plough
In south we have the fruitful soil
Where nature doth reward for toil

And travellers all they do adore
The lovely isles near Huron's shore
Superior makes a grand display
All 'round her shores to Thunder Bay.

James McIntyre
Ingersoll

> *Five years earlier, a cheese factory in Ingersoll, Ontario, had created a cheese for exhibition that weighed a staggering 7,000 pounds. Its size so moved James McIntyre that he wrote a poem, much in the manner of the above, titled "Ode on the Mammoth Cheese," thereby earning him for ever the title of Canada's Cheese Poet.*

No Canadian Literature

January 25, 1889

There is not a Canadian literature because there is no Canada. The Dominion has not yet cast aside its swaddling clothes and evinced the courage to announce its own majority. Too timorous and indolent to adventure upon the stormy seas of national responsibility, it sits at the feet of its foster mother and lets the reign of progress sweep on. The magnificent provinces encompassed within its borders resemble a mechanical, as contradistinguished from a chemical, union, being held together by circumstance and not by affinity.

In our present dependent relation to Britain, our eyes are set towards London; our culture, our aspiration, our capacity for high achievement gravitate towards that greatest capital, while the struggling literary life which remains with us is permitted to languish and die for lack of encouragement and appreciation. It will be readily conceded by all thoughtful minds that, while one section of our populace is clamoring for Imperial Federation, another enthusiastically espousing the inconceivable theory of Annexation, and a third is expressing its sublime satisfaction with our present degrading Colonial condition, without name or nationality; while so much irrational inter-Provincial jealousy and discord are kept alive by unscrupulous politicians, and while there is no profound national love and devotion to alleviate the baneful extremes of partisanship and to knead and assimilate the various Provincial types into one united Canadian nationality, the cultivation of a distinctive Canadian literature is, in the nature of things, impossible. History affords no single instance of a distracted dependency producing a literature of its own, but the annals of every literature illustrate the truth, that national development and consolidation have ever been the fruitful parents of intellectual effort and attainment.

Reason and reflection should teach Canadians that there is but one remedy for our present dearth of intellectual life. Let Canada assert her national independence, which is her legitimate birthright. Independence will beget self-reliance and national virility; self-reliance, in its opposition to external pressure or interference, will promote federal unification; from national assimilation will spring a sincere and devout love of country, which will burst forth in the wild-flowers of poetry, in the soldier's battle-hymn and the woodman's carol; it will proclaim itself from platform and pulpit; it will echo from the million-tongued press; it will transform the politician into the statesman; it will consecrate to its service the highest talent and the most exalted genius; it will evolve a new nation whose legislators, seeking only the welfare of the State, will, by just and equal laws, recognize literary distinction as a necessary part in the make-up of a great nation; it will impress itself upon every feature of our national life, and reach its highest aspiration in the creation of a typical national literature. While we tolerate a derivative existence we need expect nothing higher than a derivative literature.

A.M. Taylor
Toronto

Small Balls of Fire

May 6, 1890

The appearance last evening for the third time of a luminous ball of fire in the streets of this village induces me to ask yourself or some of your scientific correspondents a few practical questions. But, in order to explain myself, I will first give a short description of the last appearance of this phenomenon, as described by a reliable gentleman living near the Baptist church in this village:– "On the evening of the 29th inst., as I was in a rear room of my residence without a light, I was surprised by the sudden illumination of the room to an extraordinary extent. I looked out the window, and, seeing a bright light a few rods up the street, seized my hat and ran out to ascertain its cause. On nearing it, at a distance of about a rod, a luminous ball about the size of my closed hand appeared lying on the ground and bounding along the highway in front of me, making a hissing noise and sparkling each time it struck the earth and bounded along. I followed it and approached it, but, when within about two yards of it, it suddenly moved away northward at a very rapid pace, as fast or faster than a running horse, leaving a peculiar odor not unlike burning powder, and disappearing over the hills north of the church. The centre portion of the luminous body was of a very white color, like the calcium or electric light, and appeared to be without substance. This was surrounded by a bright red light, which in turn was enveloped by a voluminous smoke. The wind was blowing strongly from the north at the time, and this went rapidly against the wind as I approached it. It was followed by both pedestrians and horsemen, but could not be overtaken."

The locality where these balls have appeared three times within ten days is of a sandy loam and gravelly soil, about forty rods from the cemetery, and about fifty rods from a spring coming out below the knoll on which the church and cemetery are situated.

Can it be possible, Mr. Editor, that the phosphorated, carbonated, or sulphurated hydrogen gases have travelled around or through the base of the knoll a distance of forty or fifty rods without being disseminated; and, becoming ignited, spontaneously produc-

14

ing the ignis fatuus so much dreaded by the superstitious of the olden times; and would either of these gases or a mixture of them produce a light of sufficient brilliance to illuminate the side of the church to enable people to count the clapboards at a distance of a quarter of a mile away?

Again, could a fireball of that description travel in the face of a strong wind at that speed? Or might there have been a strong undercurrent under the hills in a contrary direction to that of the main superstratum above?

I take it for granted, Mr. Editor, that the fact of none of the three appearing to have material substance or to have fallen from above precludes the idea of their being of meteoric origin.

Apologizing for trespassing on your valuable space, I am, yours very truly,

J.R. Malcolm, M.D.
Scotland, Ontario

The Vow to Obey

June 27, 1891

The fact that the word "obey" has been dropped from a large number of marriage services has given to the world many of its truest wives and noblest mothers. It is no small thing to ask a woman who is capable of thinking and feeling to promise "before God and these witnesses" to "obey" him with whom she is to spend whatever may remain of her life; and no woman who has a proper conception of marriage will make such a promise. "It doesn't amount to anything after all," people say, but it should amount to something. Promises made so solemnly should not be broken. There is many a woman, good, kind, generous and unselfish, whose heart is brim-full of mother-love that longs to find its centre, but who will never marry because the service of her church demands a promise of obedience. How can she make such a promise without foreseeing the future? And so she lives alone, saying, with a suppressed sigh, "O, no! I could never be happy married; I am too independent." Dear soul! She is just the one who could be happy, and just the one who could make someone else happy, too. With a love that knows no limit and a courage that knows no lessening, she would place herself by her husband's side ready to share his joys and his sorrows; and, if I know anything about human nature, he would never turn and miss her.

But that troublesome little word of four letters – which, no doubt, had its place in social economy long ago – is going to deprive these two good souls of all this happiness; is going to deprive the world of grand results that come from united effort; and, saddest of all, is going to rob the world of what might be lives of inestimable value. And just here some of my dear orthodox friends are holding up their hands crying "O, what a false doctrine!" I ask no one to accept it, but I firmly believe that there are children that have never been born, and so a link is dropped out here and there in the great chain of life, or is supplied by one that does not fit and was never intended to be there. God forgive the mistakes and sins of a blind people!

If our beloved Queen – God save her – had never been a mother, it would be impossible for me to give her the homage that I give to the humblest woman of our land who meets my ideal of a mother. There is nothing so honorable as true womanhood. But is it not a sad condition that she whose habits of thought and of life make the men and women of our country – affecting as they do the mind and manner of the child to be born – must put a restraint upon her soul and a shade of sadness into her life by making a promise of obedience – in she knows not what – to him whose life is to blend with her own.

The millennium is not to come to us through the influence of the church, but the influence of the home – the home with its freedom, its love, its loyalty, its unity and its peace. Then let the way be made easy to such a home.

When I remember that there are but two denominations – one besides the Church of England – that have not dropped the word in question I grow impatient for them to follow. For I think of how much the word would have cost me – the honored name that I bear, a sacred memory for nearly a dozen years, a greater love for and confidence in humanity because of the unexampled life that went out too soon, a link from earth to heaven; and a quiet joy that must surely follow pain as the still morning follows the dark night.

Eva Rose York
Toronto

The Poetic Obituary

Sir John A. Macdonald died on June 6, 1891.

July 17, 1891

We have had to endure a great deal since the death of the late Premier. We have listened in wondering silence to adulation which

16

would have made the angel Gabriel blush for himself. But there is a limit to human endurance; and with the obituary poetry that limit is reached. Take the poem The Song Of Our Children's Children, for instance. Whatever Sir John's failings may have been he did nothing awful enough to deserve that obloquy. Besides, the man is dead and his memory at least ought to be protected. As a personal friend of the eulogized departed I feel that I must enter a protest. Examine the above-mentioned poetical effusion and be thankful you are not dead. It reads: –

'Tis well that we solemnly bore him along.

On hygienic grounds mainly we are prepared to agree with the author that "'Tis well" he is buried, so we can let this pass.

With the bells of his Canada throbbing
Their sorrowful tales forth with tremulous tongue,
And the heart of his Canada sobbing.

The lightly inconsequent way the preposition "forth" gambols around the line is what first takes our attention, and we are in a measure prepared for the information that bells can throb tales with tongues. But why "his Canada"? "His" by right of possession? No, that cannot be. I know a man up north who has been able to hold on to his farm and I own a few corner lots myself. "His" by right of creation? If this is the meaning, it is sheer blasphemy, and I would refer the author to Genesis 1:1.

'Tis well that he rests in Canadian earth
And in good British soil he reposes.

Now unless we suppose Sir John to be divided in death, by way of keeping up with his party, Canadian and British are evidently one and the same. This is Anglomaniacism carried out to its last resting place.

With his loving old head, thank God for its birth,
Fast asleep in Canadian roses.

The delicate appropriateness of this elegant and ladylike burial must strike even the most casual observer as strangely pathetic. This couplet is the gem of the collection. It is a stroke of genius. Who but a poet would thank an already overburdened providence for the birth of a loving old head?

He fought like a hero; he fought not for gold
He fought not for self, nor for glory;

17

Are we to understand that the late leader of the Government fought for the pure love of a row?

He died in the harness, undaunted and bold –
A Patriot, Briton and Tory.

The last line unfolds a thrilling climax. From the insignificant and ambiguous "patriot" to the great and glorious title of "Tory"! Could feeling rise higher?

He found us in winter, he left us in June
With a bountiful harvest before us.
And bosoms inspired by the thrill and the tune
Of the birds of the forest in chorus.

The orchestral effect of the last two lines is only dimly marred by the religious veneration the author displays for the truth. It is not in his opinion a thing to show any great familiarity with. Nor do considerations of metre interfere with the working out of his grand central idea – whatever it may be. Thrill and tune is good and reminds me of Lord Dundreary's delightful asininity. "One feather to a whole flock. Kind of lonely for that feather." One thrill for a forest of birds!

'Tis well that we cherish the magical name
Of fair Canada's father and chieftain;
For shall not Sir John A. Macdonald's great fame
Be the song of our children's children.

Because the author has dropped a few feet here and there out of the other verses it is not fair to try and make up in the last verse by throwing in some extra feet in this promiscuous manner. It is not exactly clear at first how a name can be magical or fame a song, but the man who can reconcile it to his conscience to make "children" and "chieftain" rhyme can do anything. However, he is no more guilty than half a hundred of others.

But what I want to know is this – is there no way of stopping the deluge? Is it a case for the Humane Society or the Young Woman's Temperance Union?

A Sufferer

Curiously, it is a habit among otherwise perfectly normal people to burst into poetry upon hearing of the death of a beloved public figure; see the poem supplied to The Globe on January 26, 1901, on the death of Queen Victoria. Needless to say, The Song Of Our Children's Children did not appear in The Globe, which left all post-mortem adulation to the Tory papers; The Globe's letter-writers did not see fit – or perhaps were not permitted – to write jeremiads on the death of a Tory premier.

How to Tickle a Trout

February 3, 1892

Many Canadians ridicule the idea and few believe that a trout can be caught by the hand by a process known as tickling, yet such is the fact, well known in England and Scotland, but to what extent followed to the present day I am unable to say. When a lad I was shown by other boys how to catch trout by hand in a river in Devonshire. You select places where any bend or projection in the river is the cause of the water being almost undisturbed by the current; there trout can be found motionless in the water towards the surface. You stealthily approach the fish, getting your hand quietly under the water and under the fish, then you slightly disturb the water with your forefinger pointing upwards toward the fish, and this it is that tickles or causes a sensation in the fish, holding it satisfied to remain until your hand working slowly upwards can easily grasp and capture it.

It would appear that John Bunyan was no stranger to this mode of fishing: –

Yet fish there be that neither hook nor line,
Nor snare, nor net, nor engine can make thine;
They must be groped for, and be tickled too,
Or they will not be catched whate'er you do.

Geo. Fred. Jelfs
Hamilton

Chief Sequoyah's Alphabet

April 9, 1892

Perhaps one of the most wonderful achievements of modern times is that of "the Indian Cadmus," Sequoyah, the inventor of the Cherokee alphabet and written language.

As the first alphabet and so the fountain of all language is supposed to have originated with Cadmus the Phoenician, so the first Indian alphabet and the source of written language and literature among the red men of America is traced with absolute certainty to the famous Cherokee Sequoyah.

Although scarcely half a century has elapsed since his death, a mist of uncertainty already surrounds his birth and life. But somewhere very near the beginning of this century this remarkable personage was born in the Cherokee nation and educated in its customs. In fact he never knew any other than the Cherokee language, which, until he began to record it, was like the other Indian dialects – purely oral.

Sequoyah's grandfather is said to have been a white man; but there was no evidence of it in the appearance of the grandson.

The story goes that at a council of Cherokee chiefs in their town of Saunta, an old reservation east of the Mississippi, there was a debate on the comparative strength and future of the red and white men. The strongest argument advanced in favor of the white man was his ability to use the "talking leaf" and so send messages at a distance. Sequoyah listened silently and then burst out as if by an inspiration:

"You are all fools! The thing is easy! I can do it myself."

Thereupon he is said to have picked up a flat stone and with a charred twig from the council fire to have made certain marks upon it, each of which, he told his fellows, represented a certain word; he also told them that tomorrow or a month from then he could and would tell them those words without hesitation as soon as he saw the characters on the stone.

From this beginning Sequoyah conceived and perfected the Cherokee alphabet, utilizing the cries of wild beasts, the call of the mocking-bird, the shrill exclamations of children, the softer sounds of the squaws and the rotund notes of the organ of the adult brave for his vocal sounds. When he thought he had gathered all the different sounds, he attached to each a pictorial sign or image – birds and beasts and inanimate objects alike furnishing him these signs.

And so the Cherokee alphabet was finished, the vocal sounds were reduced to writing and in an incredibly short time the entire Cherokee nation learned and used it.

There are 85 characters in Sequoyah's alphabet, and by appropriation from the Cherokee Legislature a newspaper called The Advocate is now printed and circulated in that language.

John Paul Bocock

Overworked Students

May 12, 1893

A paragraph in your issue of today tells us that some of the students at Toronto university are reported to have broken down from overwork. I venture as an old student from my own experience and observation to give the young student two pieces of advice. My first advice is to avoid over-reading. Remember that the mind is not a passive receptacle like a pint pot, and that when its active powers are exhausted, however long a student may sit over his books and follow the characters with his eye, his mind can assimilate no more. Cramming before an examination, therefore, is almost useless. It is worse than useless, because it impairs energy. I always deemed it best, instead of lengthening, to shorten my hours of reading as the examination approached, feeling that my freshness would stand me in greater stead in that ordeal than the small addition of knowledge. I remember that once when I was a fellow of a college at Oxford a student rushed into my room at night and implored me to tell him what he had best do for his examination, which was coming on the next day, and for which he was ill prepared. I told him decidedly to go to bed, and, if I remember right, he passed.

In the second place, I would say, read early in the morning and not late at night. Reading late at night, which shortens or disturbs sleep, is fatal. I happened once to meet Lord Westbury, then Sir Richard Bethell and attorney-general, in consultation about a bill which was going through parliament, and, knowing what a burden of labor, legal and political, he was bearing, I could not help congratulating him on his evident vivacity and freshness. "Yes," he replied with the air of pious self-complacency characteristic of him, "I do bear my work well, and I owe it, under God, to my habit of working early in the morning instead of late at night. I set out in life with many dear friends – he laid a tender accent on the 'dear' – I have buried them all." Lord Russell, though a man of frail constitution, went through a long and laborious public life, nor did his powers fail him till he had reached a great age. Lady Russell told me that only once during their married life did she remember his having called for candles in his library after dinner. I believe that general experience will be found to bear out what I say.

Goldwin Smith
Toronto

Goldwin Smith had been a don at Oxford. His erudition mesmerized Canada, although his calls for an economic union with the United States went largely unheeded. He moved to Toronto in 1871, anointed himself Canada's resident intellectual, and founded several journals of note: The Canadian Monthly and National Review, The Bystander, The Week, The Weekly Sun and, with John Ross Robertson, the Evening Telegram in 1874.

The Woman's Submerged Name

June 22, 1893

If a woman upon marrying is to lose her own name entirely, and be henceforth known only as Mrs. (equivalent, not etymologically but in usage, to "wife of") So and So, what valid objection can be urged against the consummation of the absurdity in her taking his professional title as well? It is more expedient, and just as easily defended. For "Mrs. James Smith" means just the wife of James Smith, while "Mrs. Dr. Smith" means Dr. Smith's wife; and if James is a physician, and known as Dr. Smith, the latter is more praise than the former. So with "Mrs. (Rev.) Jones," which we often see, too. It has everything to recommend it that "Mrs. Edward Jones" has, and no more is said against it, for if the lady is not "rev." neither is she Edward. Why should any one take complaisance in one and shiver at the other?

The fact is, the custom of the wife's taking the husband's name is a mere survival from the time, not so long past, when she lost all rights to, and capacity for, holding property; and, in a great measure, lost also personal liberty in marrying. She was, in the legal phrase, "merged," so it was no wonder her name was submerged. Her rights to property are now, however, on the way to being fully recognized, and her right to her name will follow, for more things are wrought by property than this world is at first sight apt to dream of.

The whole argument for a woman being known by her husband's name, to the extinction of her own, is based on the idea of her inferiority. Eliminate that, and the arguments reversed are just as strong for the husband taking the wife's name. True, many women, who have no longer a realizing sense of their own inferiority, cling to it, but that is only an illustration of the fact that "old phrases are slow to go."

Why should a woman's preference for her own name argue any disrespect, any want of affection, for her husband? Husbands can love and respect their wives while retaining their own names; so can wives their husbands. A woman's respect for her husband has no tendency to decrease because she also respects herself and her rights to individual recognition; because, in a broad word, she asserts her equality. True, her growth in intelligence does impose upon him the condition of deserving respect if he is to have it; it shifts the burdens of "seeing that she reverences him" from her shoulders to his.

Katherine Ballantine Coutts
Thamesville

The Egyptian Dancer

January 6, 1894

I was on my way from Australia to England by the handsome steamship Orizaba. Everyone knows the weariness of a long sea voyage, when the eye becomes tired of the sight of "water, water everywhere," and the increasing thumping of the huge engines makes one's head ache.

It was with a feeling of relief that I stepped ashore at Port Said, that interesting – if wicked – port, the only place in the world where such a heterogeneous mixture of all nations of the earth can be found. After visiting the Mohammedan mosque and the money changers – of whom we read in the time of Solomon, for nothing changes in the unchanging East – it was growing dusk, and, noticing a crowd gathering about a building, I joined it and waited for the doors to open. After the doors had opened there was a mad rush for seats, and soon the place was crowded almost to suffocation. It was a low, dingy building, and the first part of the entertainment was of the music hall type, poor singing and still poorer playing, but it was evident the people had not gathered there to hear this. From different parts of the house came impatient cries of "dancer," "ballerine," "tanzer," from dozens of foreign tongues. The noise was confusing, and I was just about to leave the place, thinking the dancer was probably on a par with the performances just witnessed, when the sudden silence of the audience surprised me. There was not a sound in that crowded building, but a silence like the stillness of death. I turned quickly to the stage. A young girl was standing there motionless as a statue, looking not at the people, but beyond them. The eyes were unnaturally brilliant and her long, black hair reached nearly to the floor. My sensations were those of a paralytic, a feeling of numbness came over me, and I was conscious of a great desire to sleep, like one partly under the influence of a mesmeric trance. It may have been five minutes that she stood in that position, absolutely motionless; then slowly she began to dance, but no dance which I had ever before seen was like this, and never before had I seen such a figure, except in my dreams. She was clad in soft shimmery stuff that clung to her shapely limbs as though it liked the contact. Her arms were bare and perfect as the arms of Venus, and as she moved to and fro the white skin on her beautiful limbs glistened like snow on the window pane. I use the simile advisedly, for there was nothing glowing or warm in the flesh tints, but cold and beautiful as a statue. The face, had it been carved in marble, could not have been more colorless and could not have been more

23

beautiful had it been one of Canova's matchless marbles. There was nothing sensuous in her movements, it did not set the pulses tingling, neither did it appeal to the intellect, but seemed to deaden both senses and intellect. As I looked I forgot her beauty, her youth, her grace and saw only motion, and was again conscious of the feeling as of mesmeric influence, and, looking around, I saw many people following the movements of her lithe body by similar movements of head or arm, and evidently unconscious of the fact. Again this strange influence almost overpowered me, and, half sleeping, half waking, I watched and was again conscious only of motion. What was the motion? Not the waves of the ocean, nor the swaying of trees, nor the motion of birds in their flight. Her beautiful arms, as she raised them and stood swaying to and fro, seemed something apart from a human body, and as I looked at her beautiful hair the heavy braids seemed to writhe and twist themselves about her body.

I sprang to my feet with an effort and forced my way through the crowd into the street. When I reached the open air I began to ask myself if it were not all a dream. Soon the people began to leave the building and the graceful figure of the danseuse appeared. There could be no mistaking that figure, with its graceful, undulating movement. As one in a dream I followed her, unconsciously keeping step and watching the swaying of her body. She might have been in a somnambulistic sleep, so little attention did she pay to anything around her. The eyes seemed to be fixed and staring, but no change took place in the peculiar motion of her body. I took no note of time or place until she turned and entered a house with no sign of life about it. As in a dream I noticed the house had an air of decay, tangled vines half hid the entrance. The moon at that moment emerged from a cloud and one room of the house was sufficiently lighted to enable one to see any object within. I walked mechanically to the window, and shall I ever be able to banish from my sight, either sleeping or waking, what I there saw. Like a body without a soul that beautiful creature entered the room and began crooning a low, mournful chant. From out the darkened corner came gliding toward her a huge snake, and now for the first time the lovely creature seemed to have life. She stood with arms upraised and body bent slightly forward, while the snake came towards her swaying, swaying its horrible body to and fro. She bent forward until her eyes were fastened upon those of the monster, then she stooped until her beautiful mouth touched the slimy folds, and then it drew its body up and around her, coiled its shiny folds through her hair, and, with its horrible head close to her face, she began

24

again the rhythmic motion, gliding into a darkened corner, out into the moonlight, and again into obscurity.

How I reached the ship I cannot tell, but during the remainder of the voyage I was under the doctor's care with brain fever.

Lydia Leavitt
Toronto

Canada's Peril

January 19, 1894

Our country has weathered many a storm, but is now threatened as never before.

Traitors within and enemies without have sought to overturn her political institutions; ferocious bigots, orange and green, have threatened internecine war; greedy, grasping, grinding monopolists have sought to devour a helpless people; labor combinations have assailed our industries; the hated Gaul has attempted to fetter British institutions with his language and his customs; the cruel Saxon yoke has oppressed our Celtic brothers to desperation; a foreign potentate would break, if possible, the proud spirit of the free people of Canada; a tyrant Provincial Premier would make us vassal slaves to illiterate marksmen, his near kinsmen, by reason of the tie of residence in our common country.

But, sir, great as have been these threatened disasters, they at least recognized as sacred our modern civilization. Now, however, our cup of bitterness is full, for the son of a bare-legged Scot has audaciously dared to claim equal rights, political and religious, with the noble descendant of a U.E. Loyalist. Let such a claim be for an instant tolerated, and what will be the limit of pretensions of the descendants of the clannish Scots?

The abandonment of the immodest kilt was a triumph to the centuries of effort to bring the savage Highlanders within the influence of modern civilization, but already the sanction of the law, wrung from a coward Parliament, has been given to a return to his primitive simplicity, and now refined sense is being daily offended by the appearance of bare-legged Scotchmen on the public streets of this good city, and that in broad daylight, too. Such is the beginning, but where will the end be? Shall it be said that savage instinct shall be allowed to assert itself, and that Canadian Scotchmen shall flaunt their bare legs in our sacred streets, and that it may yet be said of him as of the red Indian: —

Lo the poor Indian, whose untutored mind
Clothes him in front, but leaves him bare behind.

Again, I demand, shall *lazzaroni* uproot our modern civilization, and with pibrock and claymore undo the efforts of generations?

No, for the spirit of St. George lives still in the breast of one great man – the sterling Ryerson of ancient lineage – and Providence has selected him to command the new St. George's own regiment and which cannot too soon take the field and lead his invincible forces against the bare-legged Kilties, worthy representatives of an ignoble race, and, that task performed, let him, *vi et armis,* rescue our Protestant majority from being devoured by the miserable little Catholic minority of this Province.

War to the Death
Toronto

An Uncommon Bird
September 12, 1895

A mistaken idea prevails among many people that to give a bird the power of articulation it is necessary to split his tongue. No more mistaken or absurd notion could possibly be. The splitting of a bird's tongue would, I believe, ruin the power of speech, if it did not cause the death of the bird. I have in my possession a crow, with a beautifully shaped little tongue, which I have taught him to use to the astonishment of some persons and the amusement of many others, especially to the children. Some months ago you kindly published a brief description of this crow which I addressed to The Globe. Since that time I have succeeded in teaching him to say several other words. Altogether he has acquired eighteen distinct sounds of an imitatory nature. Among others he has learned to say cuckoo, and to cry like a cat, to bark like a dog, to quack like a duck, to sigh and to cry, to coo, coo, coo, coo, coo, to cackle like a hen, to answer "What" when called, to call one of the children by name, Flo and Florrie, and to make a peculiar noise which I can only describe as a laugh. From the children playing in the street he has learned to call at the top of his voice in a manner which I cannot describe. Just in the way children call to each other, between a shout and a squeal, and this noise he makes when any member of the family is seen by him from his daily place in one of the upstairs windows, which gives him an excellent view for a long distance around. By his warning voice, which is also one of welcome, we always know when one or other of the family is approaching in the distance. There is nothing harsh or at all disagreeable in his voice. Excepting in that caw, caw which is his natural cry, nearly all of the acquired and various noises which he makes are of a soft and pleasing character. So tame has this crow become by kind treatment that he will stand upon my hand and gently take a piece of meat from my lips, and he dearly loves a little play. To take my handkerchief from my pocket, or the pin from my scarf, or the studs from my shirt is a real pleasure which he cannot resist. But woe betide the stranger who ventures to approach him within pecking distance. His beak is strong and sharp, and many are they who know it. Sometimes the neighbors of children play upon the grass beneath his window, and now and again quarrel, and he gets excited and scolds, scolds loud and long. If one should slap me in fun upon the back two or three slaps in the presence of this, I may say remarkable, bird he will scold, spread his wings and fly to my defence. Some people say, "What a shame to keep that bird shut up in the house." But in this instance it would certainly be a shame to turn him out. He has become so attached to us and to the house that the only way of getting him outside at all is by carrying him out, and then he will not stay unless some one of the family remains with him. He is never caged up, but he loves his home too well to leave it. There are two large cats in the house, and only on one occasion did they attempt to molest the bird, and then it happened this way: There was in the kitchen at this time besides two cats a puppy dog, to which a bone had been thrown by one of the children. The cats, the bird and the dog all made a simultaneous rush for the bone, and then began a rough-and-tumble fight for a minute or two, when I picked up the bird none the worse but a little shaky, having his beak full of fur from one of the cats. They have never touched him since, they are in fact afraid of him, for he delights in making them cry aloud by seizing the end of their tails with his beak. A very noticeable thing about him is his power of quick perception or discernment. His eyesight is remarkably keen and he recognizes instantly any of our family a long distance away. Sometimes in play I throw to him from the ground some little thing to catch, and if straightly thrown he is sure to catch it in his beak. I hope that these few extended remarks on the crow will have the desired effect of deterring those of your readers, if there may be any among them, who are under the delusion that the splitting of a bird's tongue will enable him to talk, from doing so foolish and cruel a thing.

Sydney Smith
Toronto

Just As We Expected
July 2, 1896

Referring to your editorial in today's Globe in which you express the opinion that under the influence of a Reform Government the water in the lakes will rise six inches, allow me to say that since the elections the waters of the Georgian Bay have risen ten inches, as can be verified by inquiry of the harbormaster at this port. It is also a fact that during that time several refreshing showers have fallen, all during the night, thus not interfering with business.

A. Chellew
Collingwood

> *Wilfrid Laurier's magic worked quickly for Mr. Chellew and The Globe, which expected the waters to rise on Laurier's election. But Laurier was not yet even in power: the election had been held June 23, and it was not until July 9, a week after this letter was published, that Prime Minister Charles Tupper, who had been stubbornly clinging to power, was finally persuaded to resign.*

The Sky in January, 1897
January 5, 1897

The great scientific family can keep in her registers the year 1896, just passed, at least during its four months, September, October, November and December, so inauspicious to the fine spectacle of the azure sky, as having deprived us almost without intermission of the chance of bowing at the glorious arrival of the stars, the celestial worlds, the marvels of the heavens, and of all the curiosities of the wheelwork of perpetual motion.

In January Mars is the king of our evenings; Jupiter the giant world of our nights; La Belle Venus is the first to appear in the western sky, reflecting the light of the sun; then come the sparkling fires of the variable, multicolored, brilliant and scintillating white, red, yellow, orange, rose, green, blue and violet stars; of the fine, double-colored ruby, garnet, topaz, emerald and sapphire distant suns; of the most luminous couples and of the finest celestial diamonds.

We do not know of any spectacle more delightful, more enchanting, and at the same time more startling – we were going to say more ideal – and more sublime than the one presented by the divine sun. With a simple opera glass, provided with dark blue smoked glasses, so easily procured at the opticians, it is easy and without any danger whatever to the sight to pay our most ardent and grateful homage to the governor of the world, by the observation of his deep, gaping and frightful wounds. The sun-spots are the grey hairs of the king of light, the signs of the old age of the god of day.

The sun, now a single star, has been a nebula, then a multiple star, a quadruple, a triple, and only a double at the time when Jupiter, an extinguished sun, was himself giving light. The visible sun is composed of an invisible sun; the first burns and the second fertilizes and warms, like the principle of life in the flesh of man. The sun is the dazzling source of light, heat, movement, harmony and beauty. He it is who exists in the birth, life, breath, smile and voice, in sweetness, happiness, kindness, devotedness, study, science, singing, laughter, music, work, production, love, union, fecundity, repose, sleep, peace, and quiet, and flies away in the last breath of the moribund. It is the sun, too, in the wise Socrates, the eloquent Roman Cicero, the astrologer King Alfonse X of Castille and Leon, the Canon Copernicus, the noble thinker Giordano Bruno, the observer Tycho Brahe, the immortal Kepler, the unfortunate Galileo, the genius Newton, the philosopher Fontenelle, the illustrious Herschel, the learned Laplace, the celebrated François Arago, the astonishing Edison, and that great pair of travellers to the celestial worlds, Sylvie and Camille Flammarion.

The sun gives, the moon refuses, according to the immanent law of the divine power, that Greater Creator. The visible moon of an earthly cold is composed of an invisible moon to the eyes of flesh, but striking to those of the mind, because she sterilizes and cools. There is the genius of evil, ugliness and wickedness. Let those who have not undergone its influence cast stones at the authors of the finest, noblest and greatest astronomy.

The kings of eloquence in enduring the sufferings of others by this law rejoice with a joy equal to their sufferings, in dying martyrs for the sake of affirming the truth. Truth carries no mask, bows to no man's will, seeks neither place nor applause; she only asks a hearing in the light of the Sun of suns, King of the kings of light, and

God of the gods of day. By our will we can change the course of the moon. Let us see how much more we can do against her influence. She it is who is the cause of the rags of the poor, the draperies of the rich, the lunatic, the robber, the liar, the forger, the incendiary, the murderer; rage, hatred, sorrow, divorce, madness, jealousy, constraint, insult, mockery, famine, accidents, abuse, injury, injustice, patents, codes, trials, fences, frontiers and war budgets. She arms the brother against the brother, the father against the son, and the son against the father.

The earth is the moon of the moon, and for the lunarians the colossal luminary of dreams and mystery, the pale sun and the solitary globe wandering in their silent firmament. In the present state of optics, by means of a suitable instrument, giving a telescopic vision sufficiently clear, which would not cost over five million dollars, not only could we settle once and for all this question: "Is the moon inhabited?" but we could also measure the influence of our globe on lunar life by the direct application of the laws of force. At the present moment, in spite of our poor instruments and the small number of our senses available for the study of natural and terrestrial life, and for the universal and eternal creation, we find that God is so great that Mahomet cannot be his prophet.

It is the moon again which attracts the waters, inundates the land, funds kingdoms, creates republics, massacres innocents, makes martyrs of Christians, builds prisons, constructs dungeons, raises scaffolds, stirs up rebellion, sets kingdom against kingdom, tears Poland in pieces, sows Siberia with the bones of some of the noblest of the human race, butchers Cuba, robs a republic of New France and a monarchy of New England, and gags an Alsace so mournéd and a Lorraine so regretted, weeping and crying with rage.

Wilfrid Marsan
Director of Westmount Astronomical Observatory
Montreal

A Satellite of the Earth

May 1, 1897

A celestial body exists within our solar system which until the present time has not been recognized by modern astronomy. It is a globe formed of water and will rank as a satellite of the earth; it is placed at a distance of 240,000 miles from the earth, around which it revolves in a synodical period of 29 days and 12 hours. It travels in the same path as the moon and is always on the opposite side of the earth, hence it is in conjunction with the sun when the moon is in opposition, and it enters the sign of Libra about the same time that the moon enters Aries. It is the cause of the secondary tide of the sea. The moon draws the tide on only one side of the earth at one time. It is also the cause of some irregularities of long period to the moon's orbit and has some effect in keeping the reflective side of the moon towards the earth; it is a transparent body, and when near conjunction the sun's rays refracted through it form the Zodiacal light. It has not always kept its present position. Forty-three centuries ago it came within the sphere of the earth's attraction, when its waters covered our planet to the depth of more than one mile and remained for one year, and during that year all the waters above the snow line on all parts of the earth, except part of the continent of Asia, were frozen, and when the waters returned from off the earth the tropical icefields began to slide according to the elevation and incline of the land on which they rested and they melted, first, on the edge that was nearest to the equator and afterwards the parts towards the tropics where the icefield was thicker. In time the polar ice caps began to melt and break down and slide toward the line, and they have been breaking up and melting in sections ever since and will continue to do so until they disappear, and the frigid zones will in time be as clear of ice in summer as they were before the deluge, and the Arctic explorer of the distant future will have a simple walk over.

In the south polar zone the ice was kept in place 60 years ago by mountain ranges and had a very steep incline toward the line, and if it has not receded much since that time then to scale the southern ice cap will be a question of mountain climbing. As fast as the icefields melt the surplus waters find their way to the equatorial regions and are evaporated and are drawn above the atmosphere and regain that world of waters, which the early Egyptian and Assyrian astronomers called by a name that signified the Great Deep – the preglacial man of science is the antediluvian man of Revelation.

Joseph A. Armstrong
Toronto

Origin of the Word "Canada"

June 23, 1897

The origin of the word Canada has ever been disputed and is still in doubt. During my 40 years of Canadian life I've seen many attempts at a solution, notably one of a Scotchman, who, having been here over a century since, upon returning to Scotland described the (then) bibulous habits of our people by stating that they drank of whiskey, a "can a day," and hence Canada!

Apropos of the subject I append a clipping from a recent issue of an English church newspaper, which is new to me and may interest some Globe readers. It is dated at Ryde, April 24, and is signed A. St. A. P. and reads:– "one of the earliest discoverers of the new world was a Portuguese, who drew a map of the places he had visited in search of wealth, and on that part of his map which would now bear the word Canada, he wrote two words, 'Ca nada,' which are the Portuguese for 'nothing here,' by which the worthy shipper intended to convey that there was nothing there worth taking away, no gold or silver or other loot. Succeeding chartographers, copying from the said man, and not knowing Portuguese, took the two words for one, supposing this to be the name of the country, and so established the name which has since become singularly inappropriate as nobody in Canada would for a moment admit that there was 'nothing here.'"

H.C.
Collingwood

Wild Pigeons

John James Audubon once reported flocks of passenger pigeons – or wild pigeons – numbering between one and two billion, and one flock in Michigan covered twenty-eight miles in length by three to four miles in breadth. The last known passenger pigeon died in the Cincinnatti Zoological Garden in 1914.

February 4, 1899

I noticed a short item in yesterday's Globe by G. C. T. Ward saying it would be a matter of much interest to many if, through The Globe, anyone who has seen wild pigeons in recent years would make it known. Well, Mr. Editor, I had the pleasure of seeing nine of them in a wheat field near the village of Glencoe last fall, and they are the first I have seen in 25 years. They did put me in mind of the olden times. When I was a boy I used to spend a great deal of my time trying to strike them with sticks. They have often taken over half a day crossing over our farm, flying very low, as they seemed to be very tired. They would make for the townships of Stephen and Hay on Lake Huron shore, among the hemlock and pine trees until the hatching season would be over. They could be plainly heard cooing three miles away. They would flock together by the thousands and after the young were able to fly they would return south until next spring; but where they are gone I would like to know. To see a few of them is to me as seeing a dear old friend.

D.C. Black
Appin

Chapter 3

The Question of the Century

January 6, 1900

To decide a bet, please inform me if today, January 1, commences another century.

H. Maloney
Amherstberg

♦

January 6, 1900

In case a child was born on January 1st, 1801, the first day of the 19th century, what was his age on Monday last, January 1st, 1900? Ans. – 99 years. He will be 100 years of age on January 1st next, 1901, and on that day we shall enter upon the twentieth century. The claim being made by many that we are now in the twentieth century is certainly an error.

Geo. J. Barclay
Toronto

♦

January 6, 1900

... you are correct if the first year of the present Christian era was called the year "one." The whole question hinges solely on this. If the opening day of this first year was called simply 1st of January, and the next year commenced as the 1st January, A.D. 1, then we have now really started on the new century. The closing days of each year of the era would run thus: 31st Dec., 31st Dec., A.D. 1; 31st Dec., A.D. 2; 31st Dec., A.D. 3, etc., until 31st Dec., A.D. 99, when the first century would be complete, and thence onward to 31st Dec., A.D. 1899, when the nineteenth century would be complete....

Andrew T. Drummond
Kingston

January 6, 1900

… If in the date January 5, 1900, the "1900" refers to a year gone by, why not be consistent and say that "January" refers to a month gone by, and the "5" to a day gone by? Surely our chronology is at least consistent! If this is not the year 1900, then this is not the month of January, but the following month, and this is not the fifth, but the day after. Have we not made a mistake after all, and did not the century really begin 36 days ago? Are we up to date or are we behind the times? …

Tempus Fugit
Toronto

♦

January 13, 1900

(With bearing on the century question.)

> A Scotchman bet five hundred pence
>   That he and Jean could shear
> One hundred sheep and set them free
>   By daylight bright and clear.
>
> So in a pen the sheep were put,
>   Ten times ten wethers fine.
> But Sandy said one hundred sheep
>   When clipped meant ninety-nine.
>
> They led them forth and rightly clipped,
>   As Scotchmen only can,
> And thrust a mark upon the fence
>   As off each wether ran.
>
> Then as the evening's shades drew nigh
>   And sun had ceased to shine,
> The Scotchman kissed his wife and said
>   We've finished ninety-nine.
>
> Jean said, "Gude mon, I hope you're richt,
>   But aye I dinna ken,
> Howe'er the wager you can claim,
>   Wi' ane still in the pen."

J.A. Gibson
Strathroy

Riders of the Plains

February 3, 1900

My attention has been called to a communication in your columns dated January 13, and signed "Ex-Trooper," wherein I am accused of crediting myself as being author of a poem I recited recently in Massey Hall, called "The Riders of the Plains," which poem "Ex-Trooper" declares was written by the late Thomas T.A. Boys. My good friend "Ex-Trooper" (for he surely is a friend of mine if he has ever been a member of that splendid force, the Northwest Mounted Police) is, I fear, confounding my poem – which by the way most certainly is my poem – with one written many years ago by another person altogether. I had not, when I wrote my verses eighteen months ago, heard of the poem he refers to, nor did I know that the title "The Riders of the Plains" had been used in literature otherwise than in Mr. Gilbert Parker's delightful works, and I felt that I had in part thieved his right to the title until I found after many months in the Territories that the name was in common usage amongst the settlers and the ranchers, and therefore not exclusively the literary property of Mr. Parker. Recently, however, when I visited Edmonton, a gentleman there, whose name has for the moment escaped my recollection, called my notice to the poem, "The Riders of the Plains," written by an erstwhile N.W.M. Policeman by the name of McKay. I read the poem – it was in manuscript, and I was under the impression, from what the Edmonton gentleman said, it had never been published. In this, however, I may be wrong. The poem consisted of some 25 stanzas. It would take quite a half-hour to recite it. At the time it was written, Miss Maude Earles' world-famous picture, "What we have we hold," had not been painted. If "Ex-Trooper" will kindly remember, my poem of five stanzas is entirely based upon that picture. I regret that my use of the title has led to any confusion. It will greatly please me if "Ex-Trooper" will graciously assist me in obtaining a copy of Mr. Boys' poem. I would like to know if it is the same one that was attributed to McKay.

E. Pauline Johnson
Ottawa

Emily Pauline Johnson (1862-1913), also known as "Tekahionwake," was a celebrated poet, performer and star of the recital circuit.

The Queen's Soliloquy

Queen Victoria died on January 22, 1901.

January 26, 1901

I

Hark! I hear the ripple, ripple, ripple,
As I ride upon the sunset sea,
Whisp'ring welcome o'er the shimm'ring deep,
Floating thro' the gloaming o'er and o'er,
While the Pilot tenderly doth keep
All the path along the distant shore.
Jesu, "Rock of Ages, cleft for me,
Let me hide myself in Thee" – in Thee!

II

Ay! I hear the ripple, ripple, ripple;
Pearly gates ajar now greet my sight.
Calm, I wait the King of kings' command;
Robed in white, thro' His atoning blood,
Clasp in faith the Everlasting hand,
Guiding me each step o'er deep'ning flood.
Haste, eternal day! fast sinks the night;
Nearer gleams the border–land of light!

III

Wait, my soul! As ripple, ripple, ripple,
Wafts this weary coil to longed rest,
Let me reach one parting last embrace,
One farewell my wedded nation give.
Glorious realm! death giveth perfect grace;
I with thee in memory e'er shall live.
Keep the faith! my loving last behest –
Now, farewell! I to the goal am blest!

IV

Nearer still! sweet ripple, ripple, ripple,
Ebbs the tide! I reach the golden shore.
Saviour, let me to Thy bosom fly!
Albert! Consort! come I safe to thee!
Children clasping in my home on high!
Jesus, Thou didst grant the victory –
Fadeless crown I wear, tho' thorns Thou wore –

37

Heaven's light! with Thee for evermore!

Agnes Grote Copeland
Toronto

Fifty Years Ago

June 22, 1901

Your daily publication of extracts from The Globe of 50 years ago must be of considerable interest to all readers of the paper, but especially so to old subscribers. As, for instance, the publication on the 5th inst., giving an account of a motion made in Parliament by William Lyon Mackenzie on June 5th, 1851, reminds me that I have been a constant reader of The Globe for 50 years.

The death of David Thompson, M.P. for Haldimand, in the fall of 1850 or spring of 1851 rendered an election to fill the seat necessary. William Lyon Mackenzie had been lately amnestied and had returned to Canada in time to announce himself as a candidate at that election. Besides Mr. Mackenzie there were some five or six other candidates – George Brown, Amsden of Dunnville, McKinnon and Decew, both residents of the county, and one or two others whose name or names I have forgotten. Mackenzie received less than one-fourth of the votes "recorded," but as he had 28 more than the next highest on the "poll books" was duly elected.

At least one incident worth telling occurred during that contest. Mackenzie's first address to the electors was delivered at the Village of Dunnville, and, as almost every man there at the time was a Tory, and, of course, violently opposed to Mackenzie and all his ways, his reception was very warm, but not by any means cordial. The meeting was held in the open air, Mackenzie standing on an empty barrel. When he attempted to speak, the crowd would not allow him to do so, and for a time he was in danger of being roughly treated, if not killed. He managed, however, to say that he had by his own efforts saved the country the payment of a large sum of money. On being permitted to explain he drew from his pocket a large printed handbill, issued by the Government, offering 1,000 pounds for the taking of William Lyon Mackenzie, dead or alive. "Now," he said, "I have saved the people of Canada all that money by keeping myself out of the reach of arrest." This novel claim put the crowd in somewhat better humor, but even then he might not have been allowed to speak without further interruption had it not been that just then the head of the barrel on which he was standing fell in, carrying him down into the barrel. Mackenzie being short of stature and having on his head a broad-brimmed felt hat, he was almost hid from view. The effects of the amusing incident were such that he was then allowed to address the people there and at other places in the county without further interruption. Mackenzie's expulsion by force several times from the House to which the voters of York had elected him before the rebellion of 1837-8 was then fresh in the memory of the people, and consequently on his election for Haldimand many were led to expect some lively scenes at the meeting of Parliament then approaching. This caused many to subscribe for The Globe for the session, and I, although then only a mere lad, also subscribed, with the result that I have been a constant reader of The Globe ever since.

P.B. Owens
Toronto

Canada and Canadian Women
October 12, 1901

A review appeared in The Globe of Sept. 7 upon an article in a recent number of the Nineteenth Century by Mrs. Staples. It suggests the necessity, or at least the desirability, of inducing upper-class women of England to emigrate to Canada, for the purpose, as far as the reader can make out, of importing sweetness and light, and civilization generally, into our cruder Canadian homes, or, as the article in question has it, "to foster the aesthetic side of life, that the nation that is to be may be greater in mind, as well as famous for prowess in sport and war." Now, putting aside the absurd implication that Canadian enterprise is limited to "prowess in sport and war," this is rather unkind. Considering the undeniable fact that the public school system of Canada is one of the finest, if not the finest, in the world, and turns out an infinitely more broadly-trained boy or girl than any board school and most of the private schools in this country, it does not seem to me that England could undertake to supply Canada with any better variety of sweetness and light than is evolved here.

Mrs. Staples remarks, in a slightly disparaging way, that colonial life is too eminently practical, and that in the effort to meet the material demands of our western civilization "the softer qualities which make up the sum total of the charming person are likely to be eradicated." I have two portraits in my mind's eye, one of an

English gentlewoman, according to the foregoing definition, possessed of quite as much education as they supply women with over here, who runs her household of two with five incompetent servants of the usual English type; the other of a bright university educated Canadian girl, who can cook and make her own pretty gowns as well as she reads French and German. Neither of these is an exceptional type in the least. Canada does not want "charming women" and "women of birth and breeding" of the English type. Her own possess a high-spirited honor, an active and balanced mind, in comparison to which the other is insipid mediocrity.

As for criticizing the ultra-practical life of the west, one has only to live over here to realize how much broader our American civilization is. It does not exist for merely a few rich, who live in idleness and luxury. They are surrounded here by everything that this older civilization can give them in the way of culture, and every form of beauty, and, in addition, a servile servant class to stand between them and the actual strife of existence. In America the race is open to everyone, without other restriction than nature herself has made, and the fewer old world artificialities Canadians import the better for them. It is true that civilization in America, especially in the west, rests upon a more primitive basis than is the case here, and that mere birth and breeding, in the English sense of the phrase, count for very little in a land where all, professional man and laborer alike, must work for a living, and rightly so. It is true that the society class in our country is neither large nor influential enough to fix that petty, artificial standard of morality known as good manners. But as a matter of fact, the native courtesy of our people as a whole is practically an unknown quantity here. It is scarcely necessary to give the well-worn example of the almost universal kindly consideration of women by Canadian men. And as to that worship of the dollar, so often and so feelingly referred to in English press and pulpit, as characteristic of America, I never heard of a minister or official member of any church there holding shares in a brewery, as is notoriously the case in this country.

When Mrs. Staples talks of the necessity of educating women for pioneer life she is right, but she had better stay at home and preach that doctrine to the "Little Englanders." What Canadian women need to learn in that direction their own necessities and common sense will teach them. Canada does not need to import Government-bolstered "gentlewomen" from England for that purpose. Native Canadians with an ancestry of the sturdy Puritans who left their homes in old England for the sake of their religious opinions, and again left their homes in the New England colonies at the time of the American revolution, these sons and daughters of United Empire Loyalists have no need to go begging to England for birth and breeding. Canadians have the best possible, for their national purposes, at least, in fighting blood, and this aforesaid "ultra-practical mind," whose workings (though this is at present more particularly the case with the United States, perhaps), the average British business man has only too good reason for deploring, as his antiquated methods of doing business are being superseded too rapidly for his comfort in not a few respects.

Australia and South Africa can have the "lady pioneer," as Mrs. Staples names her, if they want her, but Canadian women are good enough for Canada.

Rubina Preston
London, England

Some Honorable Members

Richard McBride, Minister of Mines for the British Columbia government, resigned on September 3, 1901, over a dispute with Premier Dunsmuir about a Cabinet appointment, but won his seat back in a by-election. When the ninth B.C. Legislature convened on February 20, 1902, McBride entered the hall to discover his desk had been placed among the benches of the Opposition, among them former Minister of Mines Smith Curtis and former Premier Joseph Martin. An altercation was the natural result.

March 8, 1902

The trouble about the seat of the leader of the Opposition arose this way: The Government, in the first instance, refused to decide who should have the particular seat, which by custom and by long usage has always been accorded to the leader of the Opposition. Some time before the session began on Monday Mr. McBride's desk was placed in the position usually occupied by the leader of the Opposition. When he came in he found it so and took the seat. Mr. Martin came along and objected, but in place of referring the matter to the House to decide remained standing a little distance back of the seat. When prayers began and the members stood up Mr. Martin came forward, seized Mr. McBride's chair, pulled it back and stood in front of it. Immediately upon the conclusion of prayers, and not before, I pushed my seat forward for Mr. McBride to occupy – an act of courtesy which I had a right to do – thereupon Mr. Martin threw himself against my chair and against me, endeavoring to push the chair and myself back, whereupon I resisted and started to push Mr. Martin and his chair over, when a number of other members took part in a general scramble over the possession of the chair. There were two acts of aggression on the part of Mr. Martin before I interfered with him: first, in his seizing and pulling away Mr. McBride's chair, and, secondly, in his thrusting himself with great force against my chair and myself. In addition to my undoubted right to resist force with force, it had been made quite apparent that the Government was quite helpless, as it had not dared to decide the matter at the proper time, and it was therefore a case of every man being a law unto himself and protecting his rights as best he could. There was no attempt by any member to hit or injure any other member. So far as I know there was no real anger shown by anyone – on my part there was none; but I was fully determined not to allow bulldozing to prevail, as it would likely lead to other future attempts of it from the same source.

Smith Curtis
Victoria

Improved Spelling

April 26, 1902

I am greatly delighted to read the following closing line of a paragraph in the fifth column of page 26 – the prohibition page – of last Saturday's Daily Globe, namely, "you now license yet condem." I hope the omission of the "n" from the end of that final word was not an oversight. I do hope The Daily Globe is going to let that proofreader favor us with more common sense of the same sort. What a blessing to the rising generation if all useless letters could be omitted. But why should not the newspapers move along again on the line of the good sense they displayed about 25 years ago in cutting down telegraph and programme to telegram and program. Running my eye back over the article alluded to on page 26 I found in a space of nine inches of matter more than 40 useless letters. Just glance over the following list of words wherein the meaning could be as well expressed and understood without as with the redundant letters, all taken in due order from that nine inches of matter, viz: –

Usual way.	Improved.
appearing	apearing
emphatically	emphaticaly

strained	straned
necessity	necesity
coffee	cofee
question	qestion
will	wil
because	becaus
course	cours
highest	hiest
unguarded	ungarded
those	thos
earners	erners
opportunity	oportunity
possible	posible
have	hav
remunerative	remunerativ
strained	straind
license	licens
interrogation	interogation
continue	continu
till	til
success	succes
thoroughfare	thorofare
liquor	liqor
admitted	admited
young	yung
enable	enabl
guarded	garded
unfortunately	unfortunatly
temperance	temperanc
illustration	ilustration
discussing	discusing
narrow	narow
attempted	atempted
business	busines
cease	ceas
especially	especialy

There are 38 different words in the above list, and the 40 letters saved by this improvement would form nine or ten more words of average length. Thus there would be a very important saving effected on the cost of books and papers by using less silent letters. Now that the schools have adopted the phonetic method of teach-

43

ing our children to read, why do not other newspapers take the matter up as has been done by one Toronto daily, and give the movement a good lift forward?

William H. Orr
Toronto

The Dangers of Electricity

August 16, 1902

Two concurrent circumstances are occurring, the increase and use of electricity as a power and the violence and number of our storms. It may be contended that the action of man could not affect the atmosphere of the earth; but it may be remembered that the clearing away of our forests reduced our Canadian winters in Ontario from four months in old times to two months now. The press of today tells us the Egyptian Sphinx that is some 6,000 years old is now rapidly decaying, owing to alterations in the climate of Egypt, due to the irrigation works of recent years. The firing of cannon has in war times increased the rainfall. Thus experience proves that the action of man can affect the air, and the question is asked, Is electricity taken from the air and collected by the machinery used or is it an element existing in the air and turned into electricity by friction? If taken from the air, it follows the tendency should be to produce less violence and longer periods of calmness in the atmosphere by its absence. If it is added to the air, naturally our storms or wind and rain and changes in temperature will be greater and more violent. Electricity seems to be what life is to man, the cause of motion, and is life to what has been considered by man inanimate matter. Therefore, has anyone considered what may result if we continue making machinery for its manufacture, utilizing all power, natural and artificial, creating vested rights which later on may be found to be a source of danger to the many? The attention of the Legislature should be drawn to this by the press, and our men of science should collect facts and inform us as to the future consequences of unlimited production of electricity and using it as power.

Civis
Hamilton

Euclid and the Referendum

Following the announcement of yet another referendum on the question of temperance for Ontario.

44

November 29, 1902

The following on Euclid and the referendum may influence gentlemen of mathematical turn of mind: –

Axioms
(1) To drink whiskey does the drinker no good.
(2) Any man by working can make a useful article.
(3) No man will work to make a useless article.
(4) The wealth of a country is the sum of the wealths of the individuals.
(5) An article has value when a person wants it.

Proposition I. Theorem
If a man pays 50 cents for a pint of whiskey and drinks it, the wealth of the country is decreased by that amount.

Proof. – Let AB and CD be two men.

Now AB by working can earn 50 cents. – Ax. 2.

And CD by working can make a pint of whiskey. – Ax. 2.

And since AB wants the whiskey,

Therefore the whiskey has value. – Ax. 5.

And its value is 50 cents.

Therefore, by their work these two men have increased the country's wealth by $1. – Ax. 4.

Now, AB pays CD 50 cents for the whiskey and drinks it (Hypo.),

And since the whiskey does AB no good (Hypo.),

Therefore AB's labor has not increased his wealth;

But CD's labor has increased his wealth by 50 cents,

Therefore the total wealth created by these two men is 50 cents.

But before AB drank the whiskey the total wealth created was $1.

Therefore AB's drinking the whiskey has decreased the country's wealth by 50 cents. Q.E.D.

Corollary 1. – If a man by drinking whiskey renders himself to any extent incapable of working, that man cannot to the same extent increase the wealth of the country.

Corollary 2. – If AB does not want CD's whiskey, that whiskey will have no value (Ax. 5). Therefore CD will not work at making whiskey (Ax. 3), but will create wealth by making sugar or a coat.

Proposition 2. Theorem
If a man by drinking whiskey deprives his family of food or clothing, he is not in his right mind.

Proof:–

All animals give their young necessary care.

But this man does not.

Therefore this man is not an animal.

All men give their offspring necessary care.

But this man does not.

Therefore this man does not as other men.

But he is alive and has the shape of a man.

Therefore a man who drinks whiskey is not in his right mind. Q.E.D.

To cut off from a man a part of his whiskey equal to what he spends for it.

First solution:– Stop all men from making whiskey to drink.

Stop all whiskey from coming near the man who wants it (Dominion Postulate). Therefore in both cases a part of the whiskey is cut off from the man equal to what he spends for it.

Second solution: – Cut off from AB his right to buy the whiskey CD has made. And from CD cut off his right to sell the whiskey (Provincial Postulate).

Therefore, either AB cannot drink the whiskey, or they both will break the law.

And if they break the law they are criminals.

But no man desires to be a criminal.

Therefore AB will not drink the whiskey.

And thus a part of the whiskey has been cut off from AB equal to what he spends for it.

Proposition 4. Theorem

If it is the duty of the Government to prevent crime then the Government should prevent the drinking of whiskey.

Proof:– Since a man who is drunk is not in his right mind, and a man not in his right mind frequently commits crime;

Therefore a man who is drunk frequently commits crime.

Now the person who commits crime is not in his right mind and should not be punished, but should be taken care of.

But someone should be punished.

Therefore the Government who permitted the man to drink should be punished.

But the Government cannot be punished for crime.

Therefore, it is the duty of the Government to prevent the drinking of whiskey.

W.T.
Chatham

The Lightning Lunch

February 21, 1903

Your editorial, "An Impending Calamity," is very interesting, showing the advance of the times. I am afraid it will take a good deal of persuasion before John Bull foregoes his roast beef and plum pudding. The latest thing just now is the "lightning lunch." It is calculated that a practiced Chicagoan can "do" its prescribed courses "inside of a minute."

A Chicago man rattles ahead at a pace
At which a mere Chathamite reels,
And, in proof of his taste
For an ill-advised haste,
Has a habit of rushing his meals.
He esteems it bad form, and old-fogeyish, too,
To sit down at a table and munch;
In Chicago, you know,
It is quite comme-il-faut
To go in for the "lightning lunch."
There is nothing more chic,
Nor more Yankee-ly "slick,"
Than an up-to-date lightning lunch.

Their soup in the form of a capsule they bolt,
Their fish-course they suck from a quill;
Concentrated beefsteak
They're enabled to take
In the shape of a rather large pill;
Mutton chops are condensed into wafers with ease,
There is nothing to chew or to crunch;
And a lozenge completes,
If they're anxious for "sweets,"
What's comprised in a "lightning lunch."
And they're able to boast,
In a minute at most,
They can tackle the "lightning lunch."

None the less, let us hope that the plan will not spread;
For, whatever the Yankees may do,
We have not the least wish
To consume soup and fish
In the form of a pellet or two.
We should not be content with a tabloid for tea,
Though the notion seems funny at once,

And we firmly decline
Upon globules to dine,
Or to lozenges suck for our lunch.
If Chicago reveals
A desire for such meals,
Let her stick to her "lightning lunch."

There is not the least doubt that some time may be saved
When one's food in this way is obtained,
But, admitting 'tis so,
We should much like to know
What is done with the leisure thus gained?
Because, if it's spent in a sordid attempt
Further dollars together to bunch,
We can only deplore
"Filthy lucre" should score
At the cost of the maltreated lunch;
And shall do all we can
To keep under a ban
The cult of the "lightning lunch."

J.J. Wilde
Chatham

Old Friends of The Globe

*In celebrating its diamond jubilee, The Globe asked those among its
readers who had been its earliest subscribers to write in their recollections. A large party was held in their honor.*

June 14, 1904

Although only a reader of The Globe for fifty years, I doubt
whether many of your patrons have paid as much for it as I have, the
total being nearly $300. My name first went on The Globe books
for a weekly in February, 1857. I took it two years, then took the
tri-weekly for three years. For the next seven years I was in Cariboo, or in Victoria, B.C., the last four years having the weekly sent
from The Globe office. Since November, 1868, I have taken the
daily. The years I did not subscribe for it in British Columbia were
costly ones, as the price of the weekly in Victoria was 25 cents per
copy, while in Cariboo in '62, '63 and '64 it would average $1.50 per
copy. In '62 and '63 it often cost $2.50 per copy.
    Here is a summary of what it has cost me: –
        40 copies of weekly bought in Cariboo at $1.50   60.00

80 copies of weekly bought in Victoria at 25 cents	$20.00
6 years' subscription to weekly	$12.00
3 years' subscription to tri-weekly	$12.00
20 years of daily at $6	$120.00
12 years of daily at $5	$60.00
3 years of daily at $3	$9.00
Making a total of	$293.00

A.R. Carnochan
St. Catharines

◆

June 15, 1904

I noticed, in reading a short editorial in The Globe on Friday last, that I am debarred from participating in the festivities at your coming "jubilee" on account of not being a "first reader." However much I may regret not being eligible, it will not prevent me wishing you success and a very joyous time. If you go strictly according to the rule you lay down, how many are there on the list at the present time that will be in a position to receive an invitation? I fancy not one. I have been a subscriber – not at the head office – and a reader of The Daily Globe for the last forty-six years without a break, and intend (D.V.) to continue for some years to come, as I would feel lost without it. I am a fairly good hand at the "trough," but I'd rather go without my midday meal any day – Christmas excepted – than be without my Daily Globe.

At times I have thought that we old subscribers should be pensioned off and receive our paper free for the rest of our natural lives, which would not be for many years at most, but I suppose if you were to adopt that principle there would be so many of us applying that it would cut down your subscription list to such an extent it might cause you trouble financially, so I, for one, will not make the request at present. I wish The Globe the greatest success, and many more jubilees.

W.B. Nelles
Ingersoll

◆

June 16, 1904

As one who spent more than a decade in the service of The Globe, I desire to express my gratification at the progress that great daily has

49

made, more especially in recent years. More than twenty years have passed since I held the position of city editor, but my recollections of those days are but as yesterday. Well do I remember that morning on which Hon. George Brown was shot by Bennett, and I was the second man on the scene of the tragedy after the report of the pistol was heard. Mr. Alan Thomson, father of the present foreman in the news room, was ahead of me. Mr. Brown had Bennett's wrist firmly in his grasp, and so prevented him from again using his weapon. The wounded man was the coolest among the four persons then present, and called out, "Don't strike him (Bennett); I have him fast." It was an exciting moment for the rest of us.

Wm. Campbell
Toronto

> *On March 25, 1880, George Bennett, who had been fired from his job in The Globe's engine room for intemperance and released on bail after a charge of non-support of his wife, entered George Brown's office and demanded Brown sign a note certifying Bennett's employment record. Brown was brusque; Bennett drew a gun and fired. The shot entered Brown's thigh. Eventually, the wound became infected and killed Brown.*

Beware the Yellow Press

March 25, 1905

It is a distinct drawback to "Young Canada" that United States' newspapers, especially Sunday editions, have so large a sale in the Dominion. The craze is growing, especially in Montreal, where the flaring yellow journals of New York are on sale at every corner. We do not wish and cannot afford to have our ideals lowered to their superficial standard, and the narrow perspective, absence of structural fact and gross sensationalism of their news cannot fail to influence the readers. For years I have read and been influenced myself by some of the more responsible New York papers, and it has taken two years in the States and one in England to realize how erroneous my impressions have been under their tutelage. Chief of these had been the depreciation of all things British until, unconsciously, the untravelled drifts into the error of believing the United States heaven, all others far below, and British conditions Hades. One editor has for weeks been sneering at the deterioration of the British race. If they are not as big as their fathers, what a difference one finds in going, say from New York to a Canadian or English town, to leave the narrow-chested, wizen, commercial-worn and stunted hordes and find healthy, wholesome-looking and, often, stalwart men. Reading recent American jibes I contrast now the "kilties" or some of the strapping fellows of the London Scottish, the Honourable Artillery Company or Rifle Brigade, and the narrow-chested American youths that I saw shambling along in the National Guard during the inauguration. Recently all American papers have flared the figures that show a decrease in the English birth rate. But only one had the courage to print the greater decrease in the death rate, so low indeed that even London stands far below the high death rate of American cities, with their lack of municipal supervision.

"Young Canada Abroad"
New York

A Robin That Reasoned

March 20, 1906

In the interesting paragraph under this heading which appeared in Saturday's Globe, the statement is made that the process by which instinct becomes concentrated wisdom is not made known. While this statement is as true in this case as it is in all others that are not demonstrable by physical science, yet psychological science offers an explanation which fits all such cases, and hence has a just claim to be considered as true as any physical demonstration.

This is that all sub-human species have what may be termed "group or oversouls," analogous to the "subliminal selves" of humanity, expounded by Frederick W. Myers and Sir Oliver Lodge. This group-soul is common to all the members of a species, incarnates them and uses for their benefit all the experiences gained by the various individuals, and though these last are dying continually, yet the group-soul persists, and its content is continually being increased through the lives of its members. Equally each new member starts with that accumulated experience at its command which is known as instinct, but truly is concentrated wisdom.

W.H.
Toronto

A Memorial for Brant

May 19, 1906

Photographic representations of Joseph Thayendanegea Brant, General Brock and the old homely motto, "Home, Sweet Home," are before me by electric light as I write these words after having read the words of the Governor-General of Canada, uttered at the Pilgrims' dinner in New York.

Lord Grey says "that there are higher laws than the laws of possession." If the opinion be one of individual sentiment representing an Imperial view of empire worth, then I am quite in order to recall the chivalric character and place Joseph Brant holds in the early history of Canadian struggle for nationhood. He has been dead 99 years – the centenary of his demise is in the fall of 1907. May it not form a fitting season for some slight token of respect to this man and his people, who did much to uphold British interest a century and a quarter ago?

The Six Nations Indians, as a whole, are not an aggressive sort of people for these expressions of recollections of the past; indeed, their old Matriarchal system of government hardly demands any form of outward show of respect for the aged past. Therefore, if Brant be a worthy Canadian subject of respect, surely the centennial of his dramatic demise should commend itself to all as a fitting period for some form of national Canadian review. There is ample scope for the reflective mind as well as the man who would persist in thinking that the accumulation of wealth is the highest and the inevitable end of man.

Brant and his people built the first Protestant church in Ontario; close to the church live his descendants. They are good farmers. Another section of the Mohawks, who became Roman Catholics generations before the final migration north, live near Montreal. They are progressive.

There is a beautiful monument to the memory of Brant in the city of Brantford, erected some years ago. One man can do very little, even if he be a Mohawk, to inaugurate a grand scheme of "memorial" to a worthy character and his people, but many can do much. Shall anything be done?

J. Ojijatekha Brant-Sero
Bridlington, Yorks., England

> *John Ojijatekha Brant-Sero, a descendant of Joseph Brant, was an interpreter, poet and dramatist, and historian of the Six Nations. He translated "God Save The King" into Mohawk.*

A Wolf Story

March 19, 1907

The attention of the writer has been called to an item that has appeared in several Toronto, Montreal and local papers, viz., the tragic death of Robt. Ogelstein by wolves in the vicinity of Canal Lake, district of Haliburton. This is either a cruel hoax or a deliberate falsehood, as Robt. Ogelstein is working in one of the company's camps in the township of Lawrence. Ogelstein's story is that he was pursued by wolves, and only having a revolver and a few cartridges, he took refuge in a tree. Soon five wolves appeared and went on duty under the tree. Robert opened fire, killing two, which the three unhurt wolves immediately devoured. Not a bad meal for three wolves, especially as he had killed the largest two. Robert, having shot away all his ammunition at the two, looked forward to becoming the second meal, and seriously thought of starting on his toes and eating himself up rather than become food for the wolves. But his cramped position prevented this. The wolves in the meantime trotted off, and Bob descended from the tree, looked around for a tuft of hair or a stray toenail of the two departed, as a souvenir of the incident, but nothing remained. All had gone into and off with the three that allowed Bob to escape. I know this robs our district of what would have made a hair-raising story, but, belonging to the group with the little axe, we cannot lie.

Rolla
Rock Lake

Usurpers of the Roads

March 7, 1908

You say that somebody says that the horses on the country roads, now that they are growing accustomed to the appearance of automobiles, no longer show the same fear of them.

You have heard of the plea of the Eastern potentate, when admonished that he ought to forgive his enemies, that he had no enemies. They were, he cheerfully remarked, all dead.

The horses are not dead, it is true, but their drivers, moved by a fear that is not unreasonable, shun the roads that motorists seize upon for their special indulgence, to the exclusion of those that maintain them. Farmers' wives who formerly used the main roads for pleasure and business purposes will not now venture to drive on them during the automobile season. Men that have spirited, young horses only do so at their peril and in constant fear, ever ready, if they can discover an automobile coming, to escape into some convenient farmyard or up a side road, if fortunate enough to know of one available for the purpose. My work calls me out at night. I have had to buy a new horse. How he would act should we encounter one of these usurpers coming towards him at twenty miles an hour, with its blinding flood of light shooting 100 yards ahead of it, I do not know. I must accept the risk, and, of course, whether I meet one or not, I suffer all the while through fear of it. Is that right? An automobile built to run 30 miles and over has no right whatever to travel upon roads built and maintained for horse travel and traffic.

It is a mean piece of business, but quite characteristic of urban practice outside of city limits.

W.O. Eastwood
Whitby

The Lady with the Lamp

March 19, 1908

May I say a word on the above subject in reference to Miss Florence Nightingale's invaluable service? I remember, on regaining consciousness after an attack of typhus fever in the hospital at Balaclava, before the nurses arrived there, I felt as if I could take a little nourishment. I was presented with a hard ship biscuit and a nice piece of fat pork. I tried to take a piece of the biscuit, and broke a piece off a tooth in the attempt. A few days afterwards two nurses came with medical comforts, but I had lost all desire for anything, and wanted to be let alone. Having refused to partake of any of the delicacies which they carried with them, I was asked if there was anything I would like and they would get it for me. With a view to getting rid of their importunities, I said I would like some "parritch" and milk, thinking they could not get that. But in the morning there was a saucer of porridge and some condensed milk, of which I took a teaspoonful. It came regularly every morning (with other delicacies), until I was able to finish the saucerful. On becoming convalescent, while sitting in front of the hut which formed part of the hospital, I was grieved to see Miss Nightingale carried up the heights on a stretcher to a hut which had been erected, overlooking the sea, to accommodate her during her illness. And there was general rejoicing on her recovery. I am glad she has been made the recipient of the freedom of London, which, as the Lord Mayor said, should have been conferred on her half a century ago.

I may state when the I.O.O.F. lodge was instituted in Bowmanville, in considering what name should be chosen for the lodge, I had the honor to suggest the name of Florence Nightingale, which was accepted.

J.R. Brown
Late Sergeant Highland Light Infantry
Toronto

The Discovery of the North Pole

October 20, 1909

Cicero said: "Nisi utile est quod faciamus stulta est gloria" (unless there is some good or worthy object or act in what we have done, the glory is sterile). Benjamin Franklin said: "What signifies philosophy that does not apply to some use?" The only use that can be made of the Pole excitement is for each of the contestants to write a book, to tell over again the struggles of those who fought for a northwest passage, and failed; to illustrate with the same old engravings, and (though it will not be written) that if either had made a patent for a mousetrap either would have benefited the world more.

J.S.S.
Perth, Ontario

> *Robert Edwin Peary had reached the North Pole on April 6, 1909, only to discover upon his return to Labrador that Dr. Frederick A. Cook, who had been with Peary in an 1891 expedition to Greenland, claimed to have reached the Pole in 1908. Peary, upset by the news, rushed a book into print in 1910, but it was filled with printing errors and the inconsistencies did not help his cause. But his account was straightened out, he was promoted to rear-admiral, and by 1911 the general public finally accepted his version – see the letter of January 23, 1913.*

The Historic Three

November 10, 1910

I notice that in Friday's Globe my illustrious namesake has a poem under the above caption, in which he points out that three of the men most prominently connected with the recent reform of the land laws in Great Britain rejoice in the same name: the three being Henry George, Lloyd-George and His Majesty King George. I should like to pursue the subject a little further and call attention to the derivation of the word "George," which shows that it is a most appropriate name for men whose great interest is in freeing the land for the people. An apt illustration is found in the fact that Virgil's essay, preaching his version of "Back to the Land," is entitled the "Georgics." With your permission I would suggest the following as a fourth stanza to the poem in Friday's issue: –

The very name shows this should be
For "ge" in ancient Greek means "land,"

Compare our word ge-ology –
While "erg" is work we understand –
Vide en-erg-y. Then what more grand
Than men who righteous land laws urge,
    Should bear that name,
    That honored name
    Of George?

Elven Bengough
Toronto

Why the People Kick

December 14, 1910

Superintendent McCullough of the Toronto Railway Company wants to know what the people are kicking about.

Well, Mr. McCullough, here's why: –

We are kicking because the Toronto Railway Company deliberately holds empty cars in its barns while those on the street are jammed; on the principle that the most people crowded into the fewest cars pay the largest profits.

We are kicking because the passengers on the Toronto street cars are treated worse than the law allows cattle to be treated on the railroads.

We are kicking because we do not like to remove our gloves, unbutton our coats and hunt for tickets and change outside on a windy day, with the temperature below zero.

We are kicking because we hate to stand waiting for a car at a busy corner while a slow conductor makes out seventeen transfers, sells $3 worth of tickets, scraps with two men about the time punched on their transfers, and then rings the "go ahead" bell before we get on.

We are kicking because our feet freeze while the conductor holds the door open, sells his tickets, gives transfers, and attempts to enforce the most foolish and irksome set of rules ever inflicted on the long-suffering public.

We are kicking, dear Mr. McCullough, because strangers tramp on our toes in your cars when the conductor yells "Move up th' front."

We are kicking because we have more decency than the Manager of the Toronto Railway Company would allow us, and don't like to see our sweethearts, wives and daughters crushed in promiscuous contact with rich man, poor man, beggar man and thief.

We are kicking because we hate to fight our way through 40 feet of tightly packed passengers to get off through the front door when we could more easily get off the back.

We are kicking because you carry women passengers past their streets, and because you start your cars without regard to whether we are on or only half on.

We are kicking because we do not like transferring to your stub lines. What a rotten, stingy, little one-horse way of running the car service (71 people waiting to get on a bob-tailed car, actual count)!

We are kicking because the Toronto Railway Company is out after the last cent and the last drop of blood; we are kicking because the men who helped draw up the city's side of the railway contract have turned traitor, and now work for the railway company.

We are kicking because our tempers are worn raw by the high-handed policy of the Toronto Railway Company, because the Toronto Railway Company is the only public service corporation left which has not at least attempted to give courteous, efficient service to its customers.

We are kicking because you make women and children stand on a rocking, jolting platform, in constant danger of being thrown off, while the conductor gets ready to admit them to the car.

We think, Mr. McCullough, that even you will find from the above that we have reasonable grounds for kicking.

H. Addison Johnston
Toronto

The Causes of Bad Spelling

May 16, 1911

An instructiv study of the causes of errors in spelling has been publisht by Prof. William T. Foster in the current number of the Journal of Educational Psychology. A posse of five clerks tabulated the errors made in the writing of 10,000 short essays by college students from 140 different institutions in 15 different States of the Union. No one can dispute the claim that the results are worth more than if the students had written dictated spelling tests for it is clearly useless to be able to spell words that the speller never writes – indeed, it is worse than useless by the value of the time that he has wasted in learning to spell such words.

The errors in those 10,000 essays were classified, according to their apparent or most probable causes, into ten lists, namely:– Errors due to silent letters, 426 per thousand; errors due to carelessness, 233 per thousand; errors due to mispronunciation, 129 per thousand; errors due to obscure sounds, as "er," 83 per thousand; confusion of "se," "ce," "ze," 22 per thousand; confusion of "ai" and "ie," 16 per thousand; confusion of "ie" and "ei," 15 per thousand; confusion of "able," "ible," "ance," "ence," 14 per thousand; confusion of "ant" and "ent," 12 per thousand; causes not in above classes, 50 per thousand.

To illustrate – an error such as "government" woud be referd to mispronunciation, "crunb" for "crumb" to carelessness, "necesary" and "ocassion" to tripping over silent letters. The insertion of superfluous silent letters happend nearly as often as the omission of such letters – the proportion being 194 to 232 per thousand.

In examining the causes of error, with a view to discover means of avoiding or preventing them, Prof. Foster sees little help from more careful and distinctive pronunciation because dependence on the sounds of words, so irregular and often contradictory is English spelling, leads astray as often as it guides aright. He showed that many of the errors made more truthfully represent the spoken word then the conventional spelling do, and, further, they are supported by numerous accepted analogies. Many of these erroneous forms are preferable in every way, except that they are not in fashion. Most of the words checkt for superfluous letters were evident attempts to spell according to analogy. "But in English spelling, as a general rule, he who reasons is lost."

Prof. Foster shows that 76 per cent of the errors were clearly due to the exercise of reason as against fashion. He argues with good effect that, so far as his investigation can be made a basis for generalization, it proves that the majority of difficulties which confront intellectual people among grown-up spellers woud disappear with a conservativ extension of the principles of simplification advocated by the Simplified Spelling Board.

John Dearness
London, Ontario

An Age of Overeating

March 4, 1912

Why is it that we, in this enlightened and prosperous age, are not as efficient in church work, in social work and in everyday work as we might be or as many of us would like to be? Why is it we do not get as much joy out of life as we might get? Many answers might be given to these questions, but one answer may be given by asking two more questions: How many people do you know that have stomach trouble? How many different kinds of stomach remedies are there in use? Now, why do we have stomach trouble? Again, many answers might be given, but again let me answer by two questions:

Why do we eat so many different foods at one meal? Why do we generally feel tired and cross the day after a social or banquet? Have you ever dined at an hotel or restaurant and had already eaten a meal of potatoes, meat, beans, etc., when a waitress would come to you and recite mince pie, plum pudding, syrup, etc. Of course you would eat one or more of these tasty dishes. Have you ever attended a social gathering after having previously eaten a good supper, and filled your poor stomach again and then had someone bring around some angel cake and you ate it also?

Now why do we go to extremes by eating such a variety of food at one meal and in consequence of such a variety too much also? It is because there is so much hog, or rather animal nature, in our make-up that we eat nearly anything that is set before us. And why do the good and faithful housekeepers and hotelkeepers set such a variety of food before us? It is because they hate to set a poor table and hate to have Mrs. Neighbor get ahead of them by having more and better things to eat, and because we are willing to put up with it if not demand it and become inefficient, cross, and dope ourselves with stomach remedies in consequence of our indulgence. Now how are we to get our cooks to understand that we want good, plain food such as our grandparents used to have in the pioneer days? And why not have one central dish at each meal instead of such a variety of dishes, each one of which seems to be the central one by the way we devour them sometimes? I would like to see this important matter discussed through the press and in Women's Institutes, as it is the women whom we have to educate, or at least persuade, to feed us so that we may avoid stomach trouble and all its accompanying troubles or perhaps and more likely get cured of it.

Orloff Mallory
West Hill, Ontario

A Most Ungallant Man

May 7, 1912

With your remarks regarding the Queen street avenue all who have any regard for the beauty of the city must sympathise. But there is one point which to some extent accounts for its forlorn condition which you have failed to consider, and that is the rights which all women possess and which they exercise to the fullest extent of destroying the grass along the edges of paths which are provided for ordinary pedestrians.

This right arises out of another right which all women possess, which is to make their feet appear smaller than they really are. For instance, a woman with number four feet is entitled to wear "two" shoes. If she has "six" feet she is entitled to wear "three" shoes. Naturally a person with "four" feet in "two" shoes demands and is entitled to walk on the softest spots she can find, and walking along the streets, or in the Avenue or in the parks she asserts and exercises the right to walk on and destroy the edges of the grass. In the Avenue alone in one year, taking both sides of the east path, she will destroy a strip about a mile long and thirty-six inches wide, and next year she will destroy another thirty-six inches, and so on, until there is no more to destroy. Would it not be a good plan to try and effect a compromise with the women? They want to vote. Why not agree to let them vote, provided they will agree to give up their right to destroy the city's property?

A Mere Man

Cold Weather on the Way

January 23, 1913

On Saturday I sent the following telegram to Commodore Peary, discoverer of the North Pole, and Monday I got his reply – and Tuesday we got the weather: –

> To Commodore Robt. E. Peary
> Washington, D.C.
>
> Kindly use your influence with the North Pole, which you discovered, to ship us by your new parcels post system three weeks of zero weather, so that merchants can dispose of their winter goods. So far it has been the warmest winter in the history of Hamilton, Ont., Canada. L.R. Tobey

> Reply.

> Have ordered desired brand weather: look out for it. Peary

L.R. Tobey
Hamilton

Fit Persons to Marry

June 24, 1913

I beg to suggest, in the interest of reform, that, in future, marriage licenses be issued by medical men only, as they would be qualified to see from personal observation whether the applicants were fit and proper persons to become parents or not. By this ordinary precaution, the reproduction of degenerates might be sensibly checked. Yours for a normal world.

Garrett O'Connor
Bridgeburg, Ontario

The Burial Place of Tecumseh

September 3, 1913

In the latest "Story of Tecumseh" the writer says: "The faithful bodyguard of the great chief carried the body of their dead leader deep into the recesses of the enshrouding woods," and later the place of his interment was kept a secret by his devoted followers. No man other than they has ever known.

In 1908, through The Globe, I told the people of Canada that the place of Tecumseh's burial was known, and that under proper circumstances the same would be made public. The writer of the above knew of this statement, and the challenge contained in his work is hereby accepted. The story of Tecumseh's death and burial was told in my presence in September or October, 1851, by Joseph Laird of Florence, Ont., who claimed to have ferried Gen. Proctor across the Thames on his escape. It was then a matter of news; the detailed statement of the old scout Joseph Johnson having just been given to his wife, who had, of course, told others. Laird was convinced that Johnson helped to bury the chief, and that the story he told was true. This is a digest of the scout's statement, and many an old resident will recognize parts of it as current gossip sixty-two years ago.

Tecumseh fell, wounded, in the first minute of the fight. Johnson raised him and set his back against a tree. He would not be sheltered from the enemy's fire, nor would he cease for a moment urging his followers. On their right the Americans had overcome all opposition, and were turning their attention to the Indians when the war cry of the chief ceased. Tecumseh's head had fallen forward on his breast. There was a small bullet hole in his hunting shirt just over his heart. The Americans were forming for a cavalry charge and there was no time to lose. Between the chief's body and the enemy lay a giant whitewood that had blown down, and over this the falling leaves had drifted. Johnson dragged the chief's body to the log and covered it with leaves. The Indians who were near the chief had fallen, and the one killed by Col. Johnson of Kentucky was supposed to have met his death covering the scout's attempt to hide the dead leader. At any rate, the clash between these two enabled the scout to complete his task and escape. The remaining hour of daylight was spent in securing a fitting burial spot. At midnight Johnson and two Shawnee warriors returned to the battleground. A squad of Kentuckians were camped on the opposite side of the log where the body was hidden. It was raining, and a deep fog rested over the field. A sentry was on duty within twenty feet of the body, but the log lay between. The body was dragged slowly and stealthily till at a safe distance, then tied in a blanket, a pole inserted and placed on the shoulders of the two warriors.

At the spot chosen there was running water. Above, and on the same bank, stood a hickory and a basswood tree close together. Below and on the same side an oak had been torn partly out by the roots and lodged between the first-mentioned trees, the body of the oak having sent up sprouts along its entire length. The water was dammed above, and the obstructions remained below; then with their hands and knives, a shallow grave was made, and in it the body, stripped of everything that would aid in identification, was laid. When this was completed the obstructions were replaced below, the dam removed, and the falling rain obliterated every mark made by the party.

I obtained a map of the battle that showed the position of every body of combatants, and after spending a month in the immediate vicinity a certain spot impressed me as extremely likely – were the story of the scout true. The owner seemed surprised, after admitting that he cleared that land in 1851, when the description of its trees in a state of nature was given; but admitted its correctness, and when asked what was found there said: "The skeleton of a big Indian." There was no other near, or did he know or ever hear of another in the vicinity. From a probable misunderstanding as to the nature of the first wound, it was expected that a broken thigh would be the positive evidence, and the writer was disappointed when in reply to a question regarding any marks the farmer said, one thigh had been broken, and a ridge had grown around the bone.

Clarke, Proctor's interpreter, told Capt. Warfield of Gen. Harrison's force that afternoon of the battle that Tecumseh was killed and his body carried off by the Indians.

Lossing Blackhawk told Col. C.S. Todd, U.S.A., the same, except that he was carried off by his followers. (Ibid. War of 1812-1815.)

Shane, the star witness at the inquest held in the morning after the battle, refused to identify the body that had been skinned as that of Tecumseh, but told the Governor of Ohio that it was not, as the chief had a broken thigh, and the ridge around the fractured limb could be plainly felt.

Harrison's failure to report the death of the chief was not "extraordinary," as no positive evidence was received.

Eggleston says:– "The death of Tecumseh was not known in the American army for a long time," but he fails to say when it became known. Historians know little of the great Shawnee. They would not follow the trial of that white man, and without his story the life of Tecumseh will always be incomplete.

The Indians never intended that the tale should be told, and all they ever said had one of two objects in view, to gain by the story or to mislead the white. Notice the similarity between Johnson's tales and those of the Indians. The scout's description was given after the annual visit to Tecumseh's grave in the "ripe corn moon" of 1851, and the land was cleared the previous spring. In 1856 Tobias told a reporter when asked about the chief's grave: "White man, he know." But Johnson had been dead two years. Later he admitted, "Partridge, he know." But Partridge was also in the happy hunting ground. Tobias never, to a white man, admitted that he knew; nor so far as I can learn did he ever deny it. There is plenty in the traditions of the frontier yet untold to make an interesting "Story of Tecumseh."

Albert Greenwood
Hillsboro', N.H.

A New Battle Cry

Feb. 14, 1914

Yesterday a box of pills was brought to a house which had the directions written in both French and English! Where is this sort of thing to stop? First we have bilingual post cards and now we have bilingual pills! Down with the bilingual pills!

Yours for the public good.

Peter McArthur
Appin

Socceritis

December 1, 1914

Being a reader of your usually fair paper since first coming to Canada (seven years ago), I was surprised to see your editorial on "Socceritis." Is your space so plentiful that you can afford to waste it with such piffle? The Pall Mall and Westminster Gazettes have ever been enemies of soccer. If you take the trouble to inquire you will find that thousands of football players and "fans" are at the battlefront to-day. Aye, and Toronto has sent her quota. You say various forms of the disease are making their appearance in Canada. Your sports page has never been particularly kind to soccer. But the good old British game of football will live in Canada when Yankee baseball (diseased) is dead.

Soccerite

How to Win a War

June 11, 1915

In your issue of May 19 last Mr. M.R. Rowse, Bath, Ont., makes an excellent suggestion regarding getting inventors, or any other persons, for that matter, as to means or methods in battling at "the front" with the Germans. Their using of gases, barbed wire and other deadly obstructions and means ought surely to meet with similar schemes of offence and defence originating from the brains of the bright allies. There is nothing new in gas method of poisoning, the stink pots of old fighters and the "Greek fire" that preserved Constantinople from invasion for so many centuries were the same means as now obtain among our "friends" the enemy. "The stink pots" were vessels containing stifling gases, were hurled by catapults or other devices and were shattered to pieces when striking the ground, or other obstruction, which received the gases when they got in their work. The manufacture of "Greek fire" ceased after the use of gunpowder, and the secret of its make is now lost, as really there was no more use for it after Soleiman conquered the Greeks.

I do not know that the following suggestion contains much value, but it is just possible it may have been overlooked by military leaders. I would say, make use of "chain-shot" to remove barbed-wire entanglements. Wire, posts and all other obstructions can be removed by this method, and the debris would be driven across the enemies' trenches and play havoc with their unkempt hair when combing it as it crosses their trenches, and if there are any foolish

Germans in the way they will surely become objects of sympathy for the Tommies who send the "ball and chain." The old pirates of our boyhood days made good use of this method in cutting down the masts of their victims, and we are told the method was quite effective. The engineers in the army or navy can readily work out the details so as to make the chain-shot method of removing pestiferous obstacles out of our Tommies' way. There is some fellow who reads the papers, I am sure, who has the germ of an idea to stop this submarine game. He had better give it to the public who will nourish it to fruition. The submarine can be beaten. It is man's invention, and man can beat it. Dan O'Connell said "no law devised by man could ever be formed so perfect but some other man could be found who could drive a carriage and four clean through it."

In this war every British subject should do his bit to aid the German militarist to become extinct just as the "pirates" did.

Fred T. Hodgson
Collingwood, Ontario

◆

July 3, 1915

As the descendant of an Englishman, I would like to see England hold her own in this war. If the enemies are usually to outflank each other why not build an air fleet large enough to carry a large army to the rear of the enemy and then move forward to attack him in the rear. That is a piece of strategy I have not seen worked, but I believe it is practicable.

Clayton Murphy
Toledo, Ohio

Squaws
December 23, 1915

In your article entitled "The Path Of Fire," you refer to the wife of a Mohawk chief as his "squaw." Why? Is not "wife" good enough? I never heard an Indian use that term. Certainly the Indian women dislike it.

I've wondered how it originated. In looking over an old register of baptisms I think I discovered a clue, e.g., note the following: Baptized Dec. 27, 1842: Hannah dau. of Annikoonce and Waubagesshigqua, two months old; Julian, dau. of Bauwauraukee and Bushauquodrookwa, three moons old. In all cases "qua," "equa" or "orqua" were employed as a termination to a woman's name, consequently they were "quas," "equas" or "orquas" corrupted by whites into "squaws," as I am told those western rivers were altered from Beau and Belle to Bow and Belly.

Say Indian woman instead of squaw, or wife when required, and thus avoid unintentional offence to those kindly, long-suffering people we call Indians, with about as much justification as we use the word squaw.

As regards permitting them to fight our battles they ought to have the privilege they are certainly worthy of – our recognition as Canadian-born loyal subjects of our King. My own fear is that if sent to Europe they may suffer from homesickness, even more than our white soldiers. Indians have always fought by fits and starts. If they possess dogged tenacity it has to be proven.

It is singular the women have more of that quality of patient perseverance which many of the men lack.

Walter Rigsly

Bouquets from a Tangled Garden

James Edward Hervey MacDonald (1873-1932) created a sensation when he exhibited The Tangled Garden, a scene of the vegetation around his own home. Its brash oranges, rusts and golds were too much for Saturday Night art critic Hector Charlesworth, whose denunciation of it made The Tangled Garden the most controversial work of art ever painted in Canada. This letter, MacDonald's defence of his work, was so well received that he became the spokesman for the "Algonquin Group," as the artists who were to become the Group of Seven were then known.

March 27, 1916

I have read with interest the criticisms made recently in the local press on the present exhibition of the Ontario Society of Artists. It is probable that artists generally are glad of the publicity given them. Their work is made to be seen, and though they would prefer to note more frequently in their critics an intelligence at least equal to that expended by themselves on their painting, and would naturally rather become noted than notorious, they like to hear the big guns of criticism, whether directed against them or fired in their favor. It is evident that a drive of some kind is on. That is better than stagnation in the trenches.

But "drives" have a new feature these days – "the gas attack" – and though this is not an innovation in literary and art criticism, it has so fallen into disrepute that even the critics are rarely using it. One is therefore surprised to see this asphyxiating cloud emanating from the critics. Their remarks are literary, sententious, eloquent, and paternal. They are learned in the law, know something of John Ruskin, Whistler, Benjamin West and Oscar Wilde. But they seem to have derived little from study beyond their power to quote precedents for their action. The essential significance of these precedents, as they bear on the right relation of the artist and critic, has apparently escaped them. One would almost think them unaware of the fact that if the function of the artist is to see, the first duty of the critic is to understand what the artist saw. Yet they condemn apparently without understanding and without making an effort to understand, forgetful of Goethe's caution for doubtful cases, that "a genuine work of art usually displeases at first sight, as it suggests a deficiency in the spectator."

One makes no claim that "The Tangled Garden" and other pictures abusively condemned by the critics are genuine works of art merely because of their effect upon them, but they may be assured that they were honestly and sincerely produced. Their makers know when "vaudeville ideals" are in keeping. If they planned to "hit" anyone anywhere it was in the heart and understanding. They expect Canadian critics to know the distinctive character of their own country and to approve at least any effort made by an artist to communicate his own knowledge of that character. One is also justified in retorting that there are apparently "vaudeville ideals" in journalistic art criticism. The work of the critics is not without a suggestion of the slap-stick and the Charlie Chaplin kick. They affect to "hear" pictures, to "smell" them, and to taste them but it must be granted that they do not claim to have seen the pictures they criticize adversely, their sensibilities apparently being too shocked for proper action. And have they not overlooked the ethical consideration? One would not plead for the exemption of pictures from adverse criticism, but it seems only right that such criticism should be kept within limits that are now frequently unobserved. A ribald and slashing condemnation, without justifying analysis, of any picture approved and hung by a committee of artists is rarely, if ever, necessary in the public interest. The exhibiting of a picture does not force it on the critic. He is asked to share it. The artist is not paid to exhibit his picture. It is his stock in trade and certainly should not be flippantly lowered in the estimation of the public. Yet this is done regularly by critics. Men to whom a tangled garden is as foreign as an Indian jungle, who are better acquainted with the footlights than with sunlight, who may never have seen a bit of rocky Canadian shore in the bright sunshine of an October morning, who were perhaps "Dancing Around with Al Jolson" when the artist was experiencing the dramatic elementalism of Georgian Bay, will gaily bang the painter with their windy bladders and whoop about "the sincere passion for beauty," "crudity of color," "experimental," "comfortable" and "interpretative" pictures.

Space is lacking for a detailed consideration of the pictures ignored in these and other comments, but one may assure the critics that it can be demonstrated that every one of these pictures is sound in composition. Their color is good, in some instances superlatively good; not one of them is too large. Their nationality is unmistakable. Undoubtedly they are not what the artist would like them to be, but they are "truly interpretative," if one understands and is interested in Canadian language.

Another critic who buzzes angrily through the "Tangled Garden" is an artist who belongs to no Canadian art bodies, exhibits at no Canadian exhibitions. He poses picturesquely and pathetically in the lone furrow. In his interviews he considers it "illegitimate" for Canadian artists to experiment, but it would seem to be the fact that in a new country like ours, which is practically unexplored artistically, courageous experiment is not only "legitimate," but vital to the development of a living Canadian art.

"Tangled Gardens," "Elements," and a host more, are but items in a big idea, the spirit of our native land. The artists hope to keep on striving to enlarge their own conception of that spirit. And they remember, sometimes, "that the best in this kind are but shadows, and the worst are no worse, if imagination amend them."

J.E.H. MacDonald

The Imagist Poets

June 1, 1916

First it was the controversy in your columns regarding Mr. J.E.H. MacDonald's modernist pictures at the Ontario Society of Artists, his "Tangled Garden" and "The Elements." Now there is the Dollard / Phelps contest over Imagist poetry also staged in your arena. If only you could induce a duel between the disciples of Mozart and

Stravinsky we should have a fairly complete assortment of artistic disputes.

May I be permitted to add a stick or two to the healthy flames by continuing the argument in regard to Imagist poetry? I have read "The Imagist Anthology, 1916" and have found it stimulating. Dr. Dollard has cracked it on the head with a heavy, if not a discriminating, club, but fortunately Arthur Phelps has rushed to its aid and has resuscitated it, at least for a while, until its arch-enemy in these quarters gets breath for another attack.

"To be modern is to be color-intoxicated," some present-day philosopher has said, and it is this color-exaltation of the Imagists which makes them so attractive to those who are not fond of drabness, however "respectable" or conventionally proper.

Take, for example, John Gould Fletcher's poem, "Clouds Across the Canyon." Dr. Dollard in his review of the book quoted one or two examples, which he held up to ridicule – unjust ridicule, I think, in at least one of the instances. He did not quote the selection. It is simply ablaze with color, and illustrates a dominant characteristic of much of the Imagists' work, its similarity to the new color movement in painting.

Here is Mr. Fletcher's "Clouds Across the Canyon": –

Shadows of clouds
March across the canyon.
Shadows of blue hands passing
Over a curtain of flame.

Clutching, staggering, upstriking.
Darting in blue-black fury,
To where pinnacles, green and orange,
Await.

The winds are battling and striving to break them:
Thin lightnings spit and flicker.
The peaks seem a dance of scarlet demons
Flitting amid the shadows.

Grey rain-curtains wave afar off,
Wisps of vapor curl and vanish.
The sun throws soft shafts of golden light
Over rose-buttressed palisades.

Now the clouds are a lazy procession:
Lithe balloons bobbing solemnly
Over black-dappled walls,

Where rise sharp-fretted, golden-roofed cathedrals
Exultantly, and split the sky with light.

What a glorious piling up of color!

A controversy similar to the one in your columns is raging also in English and American reviews – the real position in literature of "vers libre." The nomenclature of the subject is so new that it does not seem to be clearly defined yet, but it seems that Imagism is simply a branch of "vers libre," although some critics, including Lewis Smith in The Atlantic Monthly, use both terms interchangeably. There is a wide difference, however, between what is called Imagist poetry and the work, for instance, of Edgar Lee Masters in "The Spoon River Anthology." There is a resemblance in form, the absence of rhyme and also of rhythm as we have been accustomed to recognize it, but the subject matter is not the same. The thought in Imagism is more poetical and colorful, although not more incisive or virile than in Masters' character sketches.

As to whether or not "vers libre" is easy to write – Dr. Dollard complains that it is too easy; Mr. Phelps, in this case at any rate, is more generous to his fellow-poets. As a matter of fact, if you examine such poems closely, or, better still, if you attempt to write "vers libre" yourself, you will find that it is not nearly as simple a matter as it looks. Pelham Grenville Wodehouse, in "Vanity Fair," moans that every youngster and every elevator man is scribbling poetry today, since they are no longer trammelled with the annoying necessity of finding a rhyme for "window" or "warmth." "Vers libre," however, demands a much more vigorous vocabulary and much greater incisiveness than conventional verse, and here lies the pitfall. Let anyone try for the first time to write what hostile critics claim is merely child's play and he will be flatly bored at the commonplaceness of the result.

Now, whatever faults may be charged against Imagism or "vers libre" in general, commonplaceness is not one of them, for if it were ordinary, no one would bother his head about it, and there would be no controversy. It is this very quality of the extraordinary that makes "vers libre" notable, and that quality does not come without care and its own special technique.

But even suppose Imagism were easy to write, surely this is no conclusive evidence against it. Inspiration, even in conventional systematized poetry, sometimes overleaps all difficulties, and pours out its soul without labor.

Canada is a new country, although strangely conservative, almost reactionary in its artistic standards. Would it not be encouraging if, for once, we joined a procession at least somewhere in the neighborhood of the beginning? Why don't our poets experiment with "vers libre"? Mr. Arthur Phelps did have some interesting specimens in your columns a short time ago, and there is a strange rumor afloat that Dr. Dollard himself is writing what appears to him to be the accursed stuff. A few younger men, privately as yet, are also making efforts along the same line.

Should not the movement in this country, slight as it is, be encouraged rather than laughed out of court by ultra-conservative opinions and tastes?

Main Johnson

Kaiser William's Number

February 8, 1917

"Here is wisdom. Let him that hath understanding count the number of the beast: for it is the number of a man; and his number is Six hundred threescore and six." Rev. xiii, 18.

On July 27th, 1914, the very day that the great war broke out – when Austria invaded Serbia – Emperor William of Germany was 55 years and six months old, which in months counts 666.

To those who believe that this prophecy has no bearing on the present war, this will pass as a remarkable coincidence. Bible prophecy, however, is past, present or future history.

The number of the man refers to something, and age in months is the most reasonable and simplest application. Simplicity is a significant feature of this revelation. "Let him that hath understanding count the number." This involves a calculation. The count of the Kaiser's age in months is so simple that a child who can count may understand.

W.D. Watson
Toronto

◆

February 23, 1917

I have just noticed in The Globe of the 8th inst. the communication of W.D. Watson re the Kaiser and the number 666. The subject is by no means exhausted by Mr. Watson's discovery. First, take the present conditions of the United States. The reason why Woodrow

Wilson is President of the United States today is because of the division of the Republican nominating convention of 1912. Because of that division both Taft and Roosevelt became candidates for the presidency. Had Mr. Roosevelt received the nomination and there had been no division within the party he would certainly had been president today, and American history for the last two years would have been very different from what it is, but whether better or worse it is not necessary that we decide. The interesting thing about it is that there were exactly 666 votes cast for Mr. Taft at that convention.

Now for the word "Kaiser": Place after each letter its number according to its place in the alphabet and you will get the following: K 116, A 16, I 96, S 196, E 56, R 186. Now there are six letters in the name; well, then place six after each of these numbers, add all together and you have 666, as well as a pair of 666s in the last column. What importance the people in Bible times attached to letters and their place in the alphabet and to certain numbers you must find out from some other source; or did the Apostle simply see a vision, and describe what he saw as best he could, himself not understanding the full meaning of what he wrote?

D.G. MacKay
Park River

Cats and the War

August 14, 1917

The milk that cats drink is a total loss, and a theft from deserving demands. Cats destroy our insect destroyers, the birds. The only thing a cat can do to help win the war is to die as quickly and quietly as possible. As a patriotic duty we ought to assist every milk and bird-consuming cat to do this.

H.C.
Brantford

Blasphemy in Smoking Cars

May 2, 1918

Travelling this morning between two stations on the Grand Trunk Railway I noticed a young man garnishing his conversation with some particularly rank blasphemy, and I (out of curiosity) counted seventy-one oaths.

Putting on one side the wickedness of this horrible blasphemy (all of which was uttered during a thirteen-minute run, at the end of which, I am thankful to say, I reached the end of my journey), why should a passenger either have to go without his smoke or be compelled to listen to it? For I observe that the human hogs who indulge in such talk as I have instanced seldom do so except in the smoking car. And why, if a decent man wishes to smoke on a journey, is he to be compelled to have his ears polluted in this way? It is no new experience to me, I am sorry to say, but there surely ought to be some remedy.

I might add that I have not included the gems of filth with which the party referred to interlarded his blasphemies.

George W. Harvey
Forest, Ontario

Ouija Boards

January 23, 1919

I dare to say that if the Ouija board devotees will take a trip out into the countryside into a locality that is for miles absolutely free of telegraph and any other kind of electrical wires, say at a farm house, where nothing but candles or oil lamps are used, those devotees would never get any semblance of a message, except during a thunderstorm. But on the return journey they might test the board at intervals as they approached telegraph, telephone, electric light and electric power wire systems and be surprised at the results.

The spirit of electricity is useful in its proper useful spheres, as we all know, but if monkeyed with is likely to cause confusion, particularly if invoked or "incanted" to attack the magnetism present in human frames (Ouija board users).

Further, what's the use of using this spirit of electricity to pump out the time-expired spirit spirit of knowledge left behind in dead bodies in the graveyards? Even African witch doctors know better than try that game.

Cyril Dallas
Toronto

Chapter 4

The Typical Canadian

April 1, 1978

During my travels last summer, I saw a definition of a Canadian, applicable to the condition in which we find ourselves today. It went something like this:

"A Canadian is a man who leaves a French movie, climbs into his German car, drives to an Italian restaurant, orders Dutch beer and Danish cheese. Then, when he arrives home, doffs his Korean shirt, Romanian trousers, and Polish shoes, dons his Taiwanese dressing gown, turns on his Japanese stereo, picks up an American ballpoint pen and writes a letter to his Member of Parliament, complaining about the unemployment situation."

Not a particularly scholarly bit of prose, but the message comes through loud and clear.

S.H. Grant
London, Ontario

◆

April 6, 1978

An April 1 letter to you from S.H. Grant inferred some concern about the "condition" of a typical Canadian.

What he neglected to point out was that the French movie probably starred Geneviève Bujold with subtitles by some bilingual Canadian, that his German car was loaded with Canadian nickel, lead, aluminum and synthetic rubber, that his Dutch beer arrived in a CP ship returning from dumping a load of paper in Amsterdam to print the Heineken labels, that the Danish cheese shipment was financed and insured by Canadian institutions, that the Asian and Central European clothing items were effectively specialization swaps for sophisticated and natural resource products of our country.

Japanese stereos and American ballpoints also have their share of Canadian components and trade offsets but, more important, they come from societies where people are more inclined to redress grievances by energetic entrepreneurial effort than by written supplications for media or government intervention.

R.H. Jones
Toronto

The Flag

August 17, 1901

In today's Globe you suggest that instead of abolishing the ridiculous device that transforms the English red ensign into the Canadian flag and substituting therefore the maple leaf, it would be better to keep the English flag undefiled, so to speak, from absurdities, and invent a new and distinctive Canadian flag to be flown in comparent with the parent bunting. Will you permit me to express the hope that the authorities will not follow The Globe's advice in this matter. On other occasions, yes, but not on this. We have too many flags already, and the idea of adding more seems to me to be a wrong one. At present there are five distinct British flags, and not five in a hundred, no not five in a thousand, of the population of England or Canada could tell the particular circumstances under which each of the five should be flown. Ask the man in the street to state the circumstances under which the Royal Standard should be hoisted, and what exactly the Royal Standard is; when the Union Jack is flown, and when one of the ensigns, instead of the Jack, and which colored ensign for which occasion. Then put him on the deck of a ship, figuratively speaking, and ask him to indicate the circumstances under which the several flags are flown. If he answers these questions correctly he ought to be made a Bishop or an editor, or some such dignitary, at once. I once saw the Royal Standard flying over a camp of Northwest Mounted Police, and asked a friend in command of a troop what they meant by that. He replied, "H'sh! Nobody knows any better and it's the only flag we have. Besides, the Governor says he likes it better than the red ensign, and has asked for it to be hoist over Government House."

The French have one flag, and find no need of another; the Americans have one flag, and no one has suggested a second – for the United States – though some years ago down south, but no matter, we won't talk about that. There is some duplication in some of the other continental countries, though none with a bouquet of flags as we have – and the consequence is that while every one knows what the French and American flags are, it is only a small percentage of people who could describe the Russian, Austrian,

German and other continental ensigns. By all means, remove that eyesore from the British flag – an indignant British Columbian once described the Canadian flag as being the British Ensign with the ringworm – and put in its place a maple leaf or a beaver; either of these, and one only, would answer the purpose. As for the proposal to have two flags, which must necessarily be flown together to complete the emblem, I feel sure, sir, that if you think that over you will see that it would not work satisfactorily. We are the greatest dependency that ever was, in postage stamp language, so for Heaven's sake let us abolish the heraldic ringworm and have a decent emblem.

M. St. J.
Toronto

The Peony and the Maple

Nov. 23, 1914

Shall the peony replace the maple? No. Never! I suppose some old fogy wants to make money selling peony roots, or draw a nice royalty on a new national anthem he has cooked up. Well, we won't sing "The Peony Forever," so there. Even a heathen Chinee would recognize a maple leaf, whereas a peony might be mistaken for a 'mum, a bunch of cotton, or a snowball – ten to one the latter, judging by the strange ideas some people have of this Canada of ours. It's the "Maple Leaf Forever" for us, and all the O.H.S.'s in the world can't change it.

Berlin Readers

> The loyalty of the citizens of Berlin, Ontario, was further proved in 1916 when, because of anti-German sentiment during the Great War, the town renamed itself Kitchener, in honor of Lord Kitchener who drowned at sea that year.

◆

June 6, 1964

The design for a national flag being apparently still open for discussion, and certainly for protest, it may not be too late to suggest the following:

A beaver rampant felling a maple tree vert, amid a shower of deciduous fleur de lis in a field of wheat or, in the distance, a range of foothills. That would take care of Ontario, Quebec, Manitoba, Saskatchewan and Alberta.

For the Maritimes, Newfoundland and British Columbia, a border of wavy lines azure along the staff and in the fly, with salmon argent, leaping from the waters. These representations faintly obscured by a delicate wash of pastel grey fog.

Although usually to be found in a coat of arms and not in a flag, a motto could be included: "Honi soit qui n'accord pas."

Space would preclude heraldic representations of the prime minister, the premiers of the various provinces and leaders of parties in the House; of the latter, one would certainly be rampant.

A. Murray Garden
Toronto

To Stand on Guard
November 2, 1949

The Honorable Russell Kelley has been quoted in The Globe and Mail as having taken exception to a song entitled O or Oh Canada, that is frequently heard, particularly in Quebec, where it is looked upon as something of an anthem.

Mr. Kelley thinks the song lacks reverence, and that it does not end properly. He might have added that it does not even begin properly. It begins with, and is full of Os, sometimes bellowed and sometimes moaned. O is zero. Oh indicates doubt, surprise, fear, contempt, apology, pity or pain. When it ends you can take your choice, regardless of how it ends. Moreover, the best way to "stand on guard" is very quietly.

C.F. Kendall
Chute à Blondeau

Red Leaves, Red Money
July 11, 1974

Has our pseudo-liberal republican Government been tampering on the sly with yet another of our national symbols?

I refer to the colorful representation of our Canadian coat of arms on the front of our currency. Look closely and you'll see that at the base of the shield there are three red maple leaves on a white background or field. Yet the original coat of arms bore three green maple leaves on the same field! Has some smart-alec in Ottawa put

77

one over on us? Are they trying to make a nineteenth-century heritage conform to a late twentieth-century red-leafed horror? Am I laboring the point too much by saying that a red leaf is a dead or dying organism, but a green leaf is a living, vibrant one, fulfilling its function of contributing energy to the whole plant?

Ross A. Short
Paris, Ontario

◆

July 22, 1974

Re the letter from Ross A. Short who drew attention to the color of the maple leaves in the lower third of the Canadian coat of arms on our paper currency. Mr. Short indicated that somehow the present federal Government was tampering with national symbols because those leaves really should be green and not red.

Ten years ago, I had something to do with preparing background information for the then Prime Minister on Canadian symbols, and there are one or two comments which might help Mr. Short, and be interesting to your readers.

The Canadian coat of arms had the three leaves in its shield colored green pretty generally until 1957, when the color changed to red. The original grant of Arms in 1921 by the late King George V proclaimed Canada's national colors as red and white; and in describing the symbols on the shield the proclamation was silent about the color of the three maple leaves.

The committee appointed by the late Sir Robert Borden to advise on the Canadian Arms prior to the proclamation issuing, seem finally to have come down in favor of red leaves, partly so as to distinguish the Canadian Shield from those of Ontario and Quebec. But the Royal proclamation failed to declare for red or for green leaves in the shield (though it identified Canada's colors as red and white), and in the end, green leaves were generally used in depicting the Arms until 1957.

It is in that year that certain refinements and revisions were considered, including one proposed by Her Majesty the Queen; the opportunity was taken to have the color of the leaves in the shield corrected, but not before there had been consultation with heraldic experts, including the College of Arms in London, which fully endorsed the change. So it was that in 1957 the then Diefenbaker Government officially designated the new Canadian Arms including red maple leaves on a white field, in accordance with Canada's national colors declared by the King in 1921.

It was that symbol of three red maple leaves which, in 1964, the late Prime Minister Lester Pearson proposed as the appropriate and distinguishing Canadian symbol for a national flag. The rest of the story is well known.

No, the present Government can neither accept the blame, nor claim the praise for the leaves in the shield of Canada's Arms on our paper money.

Alan R. Winship
Ottawa

♦

July 27, 1974

Perhaps it is significant that the maple leaves on the coat of arms on our paper currency "turned red" as officially designated by the Diefenbaker Government in 1957.

The green days are long gone. Our currency value is well past its fall. It's surprising that there should be any leaves left on our coat of arms in this the inflationary winter of our dollar.

Alfred E. Miggiani
Toronto

Chapter 5

The Age of Modernism

In June 1918, Arthur Lismer (1885-1969) received a commission from the Canadian War Records Office to paint the Canadian armed forces at their base in Halifax.

September 12, 1919

It is an excellent sign of growth when we see in the public press a lively argument going forward on the relative values of the qualities of modernism in art, as evidenced at the Canadian War Memorials Exhibition. It is a sign that modern art is compelling in its interest to arouse the sentimentally inclined to voice their protest. The people who demand from the artist paintings that present only an imitative, photographic reproduction of all the trivial incidents of color and form in nature – are getting a shaking these days. The artist is beginning to demand something from them in return. He is compelling the exercise of intelligent thought from the onlooker. The modern painter is not a charlatan as so many old-timers are willing to believe. He is emerging rapidly into the purer atmosphere of individual expression, and gradually dropping the props and crutches of dependence on other arts that have given his work, hitherto, a false value. A picture that could more easily have been expressed in language or music, or drama, had better not have been painted at all.

Such pictures in the Canadian War Memorials Exhibition as "The Gas Attack," by Roberts; "The Gun Pit," by Wyndham Lewis; and "Void," by Paul Nash, and a few others, apart from their graphic value, are presented in the unmistakable language of paint.

They are not beautiful; they are not sentimental; they are well drawn and vividly presented.

Let others paint the "heroics." These are men of thought and high intellectual capacity. They have seen service, and experienced these things, and their pictures will live as striking commentaries on the horror and foolishness of warfare, when the academic battle scenes will have passed into the same class as the weary leagues of the battle paintings of the Napoleonic wars.

Arthur Lismer
Toronto

Yukon

February 17, 1920

I have noticed an error which finds its way frequently into the columns of our press, more especially in the dispatches and correspondence. It is the words "the Yukon." Why should it be styled "the Yukon"? It is not correct to say "the Ontario" or "the Alberta" when speaking of the Provinces. But "the" is invariably stuck in before Yukon when referring to that territory. It is proper for Americans to say "the Yukon," because they mean the river. They never say "the Alaska." The word "the" before Yukon is superfluous, and should be deleted every time, except when it refers to the river.

A.G. Gowanlock
Scarboro' Junction

Defining a Gentleman

April 16, 1920

We who do not see The Times are indebted to The Globe editorial, "An Attack on Canada," for our knowledge of Mr. Stephen Leacock's overseas effort on our behalf, but we are even more indebted to The Globe for having defined so clearly a most important point which has been too long ignored by prohibition controversialists.

It would appear that now the keyword to the whole discussion is the word "gentleman," and that henceforth disputants on the question of prohibition will each conclude his attack by the declaration, "Anyway, you are no gentleman."

Time was when examples of Christian tradition, ranging from Noah to St. Paul, were used as arguments, pro or con, in the alcoholic dispute, much to the disgust of pious people who shrank from the sight of Bible stories being bandied about on posters and campaign literature. Let us pray this method of controversy is now over, and that hereafter caste, not conscience, will be discussed.

It will be amusing to witness the revival of that time-honored debate as to what a gentleman really is. Indeed, this democrative age has forgotten those subtle distinctions which were so important to our grandfathers. "He carries his wine like a gentleman," "A gentleman's drink," "Gentleman adventurers," "Gentlemen of the road," "Gentlemen ... the King," and a hundred other expressions redolent of spirits, old wine or bitter ale, will be flung in the teeth of earnest prohibitionists. And that fabulous monster, "Nature's gentleman," the terror of all blue-bloods, will haunt the dark corners of our clubs and drawing-rooms.

Finally, someone will discover that a gentleman is an animal far too delicate for preservation in anything weaker than alcohol, and it will be decided by a referendum vote that the species be allowed to become extinct. The reports of the vote will read something like this: – "A heavy vote was cast by 'ladies' of every description, fore-ladies, chair-ladies, char-ladies and 'perfect' ladies, who were especially well represented. Only a few 'women' voted, they looked poor but proud, and it is said they lost their votes."

But here I wake up to find still in my hand the book I was dozing over, in which G.K. Chesterton says of Charles II: "He was a gentleman, and a gentleman is a man who obeys strange statutes not to be found in any moral text-book, and practices strange virtues nameless from the beginning of the world."

Harry Baldwin
Toronto

Why Woodpeckers Peck

May 4, 1920

In your issue of April 28th Peter McArthur says the sapsuckers (I would call them woodpeckers) are puncturing his pine trees, and he would like to know why, and the result, and cure.

They are not looking for sap or insects, but instinct tells them to cut rows of holes around the trees and they will surely die, and then insects will breed in the rotten stump and provide the food they like. The best cure is the shotgun.

Alex. Gray
Niagara Falls, Ontario

Is the Globe a Globe?

For nine months in 1838, Samuel B. Rowbotham, who called himself "Parallax," camped out at the Old Bedford Canal in England and, standing up to his armpits in the water, peered through a tele-

scope down a long, straight stretch of the canal at ships six miles away. Because he could see them clearly and not obscured by the curvature of the earth between them, he reasoned in his book Zetetic Astronomy, the earth was therefore flat. He continued his experiments constantly until 1870, attracting a strong and devoted following. The battle between the "planists" and the "globularists" went on for many years thereafter.

December 25, 1920

When lights of lighthouses of comparatively low elevation are clearly seen very far out at sea, the explanation given by astronomers is, "because of the reflection of the lights on the clouds," etc.

For instance, the light on Cape Hatteras (which is 270 feet above sea level) is often seen by mariners 40 miles out at sea as a clearly-defined point of light.

The great searchlight on Mount Lowe, 3,420 feet above sea level, is seen on the Pacific 130 miles out.

The light at Port Said, 180 feet above sea level, I have personally more than once seen 25 miles out on the Mediterranean, a clearly-defined point of light.

But if water in seas and lakes is curved, in proportion to the radius of 4,000 miles of the globe, then Hatteras light should be 800 feet higher than it is; the Mount Lowe light should be 7,800 feet higher than it is; the Port Said light should be 230 feet higher than it is. These everyday facts, substantiated by mariners, are lightly dismissed with the word "reflection."

The above, as a preface, may help to a clear understanding of the rare phenomenon we witnessed this week. Port Dalhousie, 30 miles from Toronto on Lake Ontario, was clearly seen from the island and elsewhere by thousands of citizens, as reported by The Globe of the 9th. Houses and trees in the day and lights at night. The complacent explanation is not "reflection" this time, but a "mirage." A mirage is an "optical illusion of seeing things which do not exist at the locality." But Port Dalhousie is there, and has been there, when on that day of "good visibility" it was seen very distinctly.

Now, if the water in the lake is curved, as per globe theory (after allowing for height of eye and the arbitrary demand of a supposed refraction), that town should have been 500 feet higher than it is, to be visible 30 miles away!

The late Sir Richard Proctor, the latest godfather of modern astronomy, commenting on an experiment made by a gentleman in England, has this to say in his "Myths And Marvels Of Astronomy," p. 250: "Of course if he (Parallax) had, with his eye a few inches from the surface of the water of the Redford Canal, seen an object close to the surface six miles from him, there manifestly would have been something wrong in the accepted theory about the earth's rotundity."

This is a weighty confession! But Proctor had not the manliness nor the courage to test the truth of the assertion (which anyone with a good telescope may verify); instead, he pours contempt on the assertion, and holds the gentleman up to ridicule, of which Proctor was a master.

The fact, however, remains that a small boat, say a gasoline launch, can be traced going away from one who is up to his armpits in the water, for six miles and more, on a clear day, with the aid of a good telescope.

There is something wrong with the accepted theory (sic) about the earth's rotundity.

G.W. Winckler, C.E.
Toronto

◆

June 15, 1925

Your correspondent Mr. Winckler has several times written you expressing his opinion that the earth is flat – not round.

This is also my opinion for the following reasons:

1. Such expressions as "Get off the earth" are proof that the earth is flat like a pancake. If it were round, you could not get off the earth.

2. Such an expression as "on the level" would not have any point at all if the earth is not flat.

3. I have often heard my friends say they had almost reached "the jumping off place" or the "end of the world." How could the world have a "jumping off place" or an "end" if it is round, like the astronomers say?

4. Dear Mr. Editor, any one who has ever slipped on a banana skin will bear out me and Winckler that the earth is flat, like a pancake. Yet Sir Wm. Herschel, Sir Isaac Newton, Galileo, Kepler, Columbus and Copernicus say it is round like a ball. Some people never seem to use their brains.

It seems strange and almost like a dream that me and Winckler should have been among the first to find out that the earth is flat.

The absurd popular notion as to the earth's rotundity arose, I think, during periods of sun spot frequency which occur usually during the summer solstice or heated term; these, being acquainted with the obliquity of the ecliptic and the line of the equinoxes intersecting the nodes of the equator, are dominated by zodiacal constellations and possibly accentuated by the conjunction of the planet Saturn with the sun's left limb, or maybe with the moon's lower limbs, which, I may say in passing, are at times hidden, or should I say draped, by a cloud.

In further confirmation or proof that the earth is flat I would refer those interested to the following works of science: Gulliver's Travels, page 162; Baron Munchausen, page 163; Grimm's Fairy Tales, page 164; Little Red Riding Hood, page 165, and Saturday's Racing Tips, page 166, which stated that many left the race track feeling that the world was stale and "flat." This closes the controversy as far as I am concerned, as I do not intend to write any more letters.

Wm. E. Britt
Toronto

Calgary

January 27, 1921

Colonel George H. Ham, in his article entitled "Scarlet and Gold: Olden Times in the R.N.W.M.P.," in Maclean's Magazine, January 15th, says that "Colonel Macleod was deputed by Sir John A. Macdonald to confer a name on the post and he called it by the name of his paternal home in Scotland, 'Calgarry,' which is Gaelic for 'Clear Running Water.' The spelling reformer has since been busy, and so we now have the name with the single 'r.'"

There may be a Calgarry in Scotland, but I cannot find it on the map. Calgary Castle and Calgary Bay on the Island of Mull and Calgary Point on the Island of Coll (all three spelled with one "r") are in Argyllshire. When Calgary, Alberta, received its name, the Marquis of Lorne, son of the Duke of Argyll, was Governor-General of Canada, 1878-1883. Is it not probable that the name of Calgary, with one "r," was selected as a compliment to the Governor-General?

H.F. Gardiner
Hamilton, Ontario

◆

February 3, 1921

Regarding the letter from H.F. Gardiner on Jan. 27, I have not a map of Scotland handy, and a good one seems to be hard to get, as it appears to me our public schools are still using the same one that was used in Scotland 50 years ago.

I would say that Calgary is a small hamlet or clachan on the mainland part of Argyllshire. My recollection of it is of a few houses, one-story and thatched, on a gradual slope running down to fresh water – I think a river, or it may have been a small lake or pond.

More years ago than I care to remember I passed through it with three score of sheep in a drizzling Scotch mist, and one of my collies, a black with tan feet and muzzle, picked up a thorn in his foot. Rather than desert my dog I stayed on the side of the road all night. After my sheep had settled down for the night, as I was cold, wet and hungry, I slipped over to the clachan, and an old lady who was spinning in the middle of the kitchen floor gave me a twist of Bracksey. As this was the only time I remember eating this twist it has remained in my memory.

I have no doubt but that the spelling is Calgary. I am under the impression that Mr. Ham may be right in attributing the giving of the name to the city of Calgary to Col. Macleod, as in all likelihood he came from there. If not, some other poor wanderer whose home was the little clachan, and who looked back on it as the fairest spot on earth, has christened it. To my eyes when I saw it, it was far from being an Eden, but then a poor lad driving sheep in a heavy Scotch mist may not have seen all its beauties.

W. Carmichael

P.S. – The dog's name was Corbie – no doubt French for crow – but this was the name given to crows at that time in Scotland.

W.C.

♦

February 9, 1921

Regarding the controversy over the spelling of "Calgary," arising out of an article on the Mounted Police which appeared in Maclean's Magazine, let me say that while my authority is not Col. Macleod himself, the information was obtained from an old resident of Calgary, and from officers of the Mounted Police, from whom I had made inquiries. I have no doubt as to the accuracy of my statement, or at least in the bona fides of my informants.

Geo. H. Ham

February 10, 1921

The correspondence relative to this question must have left many of those who have been interested enough to follow it pretty badly bewildered. Even the very location of the original Calgary has now been brought in question, one writer placing it on an island, and another on the mainland of the county of Argyll.

Having stayed in the place during a stay in the Hebrides a few years ago, perhaps it may be possible for me to be of some assistance.

Calgary, Calgary Castle and Calgary Bay are situated in the northwestern part of the parish of Kilninian, on the island of Mull. Near by, at Sunipol, Thomas Campbell, who lies in the Poets' Corner of Westminster Abbey, as a youth of eighteen, in 1795, entered on his duties as a private tutor. At Littermore, in the same parish, David Livingstone's grandparents, Neil Livingstone and Mary Morrison, were married on Dec. 27, 1774. At Tobermory, the capital of the island, is the submerged Florida, one of the Armada's great vessels, sunk there in 1588, and the inspiration of one of Campbell's poems.

As to the spelling of the name, all the Scottish maps have "Calgary," while "Calgary Postoffice" was the legend affixed to the lonely cottage where I left my mail. The castle is owned by "The MacKenzie," as his Gaelic neighbors style him, and is beautifully situated at the head of the bay. The bay itself opens towards the Island of Coll, whose young laird entertained and ciceroned Johnson and Boswell so nobly in 1773. Though somewhat shielded by that low-lying island, the grim, black cliffs of the bay in question are nevertheless indescribably scored and weather-beaten, and witness to their age-long resistance to the raging Atlantic.

No Gael I met would venture on the etymology of Calgary with anything like confidence, beyond stating that "Cal" signified "harbor." That suffices, however, to lead us to conclude that it was sentiment and not science that conferred the name "Calgary" upon an inland town.

W.H. Adams
Methodist Parsonage
Thornton, Ontario

◆

February 21, 1921

Referring to recent correspondence in your columns, my good

friend Col. George Ham is correct in saying that the place was named by Colonel James Farquharson Macleod is honor of his birthplace in Scotland. The post had formerly been called "Fort Brisebois," after the inspector who first located there with the Mounted Police. The Scottish name was generally spelled with two r's, as in Glengarry.

R.J. MacBeth
Vancouver, British Columbia

Some Contradictions
December 6, 1921

The account of the meeting to promote the bridge between Windsor and Detroit reminds me of the old recipe for (alas!) punch:

A little sugar to make it sweet
A little water to make it weak
A little lemon to make it sour
A little whiskey to make it strong
A big high tariff to prevent trade
A big high bridge to foster trade.
"What fools these mortals be."

W.E. Barker
Toronto

Is This Fashion?
January 23, 1922

I notice that people are going crazy over fashion in Toronto. I saw two young girls yesterday going along Yonge Street with their overshoes flopping about loose. I asked a well-dressed lady if that was the style here. She said, "Some crazy people call it style." I should think it would be a good scheme to have the police stop any young girl appearing out with her overshoes not fastened up, and have her head examined, as it looks so degrading to see a young girl with not enough clothes on her to flag a train, and her overshoes flopping around her feet.

John Grant
Toronto

February 9, 1922

Mr. John Grant, in his brief letter in The Globe of Monday, is quite justified in his strong condemnation of the new "fad" of the pretty Toronto girls wearing unfastened "galoshes" or overshoes. It is a very untidy fashion and will soon wear itself out. No young lady wants to display big feet; and those "galoshes" must be frightful to look at. They will not last more than a month. Only young ladies with big feet – I mean with some good excuse – will persist in wearing 'em. This excuse does not occur once in a thousand cases.

But a very good case can be, and has been made out for short skirts as long as, of course, reasonably warm stockings are worn. It is all very fine and picturesque to quote Herrick's familiar lines:

And from beneath her petticoat,
Her feet like mice peeped in and out
As if they feared the light.

But the petticoat in Herrick's days, worn down to the ground, gathered all kinds of dust and "et ceteras," as an American humorist would say, and even on Toronto's clean pavements would gather rubbish untold.

"A Mere Man"

A Hunter's Experience

January 15, 1923

I have hunted and shot all the way from the Muskoka boundary to Port Arthur, and killed everything from moose to mice since I was a kid.

Having paddled and portaged on practically every river of any size in the territory, I have been sung to sleep by wolves and sung awake by them. I have heard them run down and kill red deer in broad daylight. I have seen wolves, both singly and in packs, at odd times – never more than five in a pack (no doubt this was a family) – and as many as fourteen in one season, and shot one. I got this fellow out of a pack of five. Why didn't I get the rest? They wouldn't wait. And they missed the opportunity of a lifetime to sample a highly-flavored peach-fed fruit grower from the Niagara Peninsula.

In October, 1912, on the Spanish River, I was standing on a moose trail, making a noise like a stump, while my guide was tracking a wounded bull moose a hundred yards away. A timber wolf ran up to within ten paces of me before he saw me. The surprise was mutual. The wolf recovered first. He was loping, but stopped, and turned in a length, tucked his tail between his legs, laid his ears back and evaporated.

I fired two shots and honestly I don't believe the bullets ever caught up. The fact that I read "Little Red Riding Hood" when a kid may have something to do with it. I have had wolves within fifty yards of me on three different occasions, but as soon as they discovered it, they lost no time at all in increasing the distance.

It will be hard for you to get accurate information from trappers and woodsmen, as these men as a rule are shy and not handy about putting their knowledge on paper.

Colin Phillips of Bisco, a guide and a trapper, told me about ten years ago that a few years before, when bringing a load of furs in by dog-train to the Hudson's Bay post of Biscatasing he was followed by wolves from away north of the Height of Land, to within ten miles of Bisco Lake. The trip lasted two days and two nights. In the daytime the wolves followed at from 200 to 400 yards, but at night they circled his fire so close that he could see their eyes. His dogs were so scared they slept mostly on top of him and so close to the fire that they singed their fur. But he made the trip, with no casualties on either side. This was about the first of March, and Mr. Phillips claimed that at about this time wolves often follow dog-trains long distances, especially if they contain female dogs. After all, a wolf is only a wild dog.

Mr. Phillips' estimate of the size of this pack was 15 or 20 wolves, judging by tracks. I opened the crank case of the wolf I shot and found that he had recently eaten two frogs, one mouse and a section of beaver (no man). To verify the truth of this call up Jack Miner, Knox College, Toronto. He is a friend of mine, and also knows Mr. Phillips.

W. Edwin Troup
Jordan Station, Ontario

The Slacker and the Hero

July 9, 1923

Re Dempsey-Gibbons fight in Shelby, Montana, your courtesy in regard to the publication of this letter is solicited. The efforts at this particular time of the Great War Veterans' Association, together with other associations representing Canadian and British veterans, to acquire by favorable legislation and Department of Soldiers' Civil Re-establishment routine just recompense for survivors of the great war for injuries and disabilities incurred through service in the trenches should, if appreciated, tend to create in their ranks feelings of aversion toward the past spectacle of a pugilist riding in his private railway car to the scene of his combat with an agile and plucky opponent six years his senior, and, with hardly a nickel in his jeans – and there, for an exposition of brawn and muscle squeezing financially dry every Montana pocket, whether within the greasy and odorous folds of an Indian's surtout, or beneath the chaps of whooping cowpunchers, while men and women of bloody trench, shell-plowed plain, and desperate salient, are beseeching means to support themselves and others dependent upon them through and by charity, labor and honest endeavor.

A lower disparagement of our vaunted "civilization" than the pugilistic ring at Shelby was never before afforded this continent; inasmuch, as by starvation, penury and disease its whole length and breadth, ever since Armistice Day, 1918, has received beneath its surface the emaciated and shrunken remains of heroes who are not and, apparently, never were accounted worthy of the triumphal acclaims accorded Mr. Dempsey, "slacker," and his brave but misled opponent, Mr. Gibbons, nor the rapturous thoughts their valor entertained. Dust, heat, curses, gibbering red man and squaw in a frenzy of wild and brutish excitement, kicking and squealing half-wild bronchos and cayuses, and a polyglot demoniacal medley of human types with perspectives of life narrowed down to the barest limits of human unregenerate vision, together with men bent on commercializing to the utmost the two bulks of human flesh feinting and clinching in their commercialized squared circle for mastery.

Such a scene, in part, formed the setting of an epochal drama created by means of wealth denied the defenders and sacrificial heroes of two countries, fair and lovely in aspect, but cruelly disappointing in point of right and proper thought and feeling, as exemplified by Shelby, Montana. Still, once again the "slacker" is promised an opportunity to add to his large bank-roll, this time by an American magnate, who has offered $300,000 in cold cash for a return match with Mr. Gibbons, though war orphans and war widows abound and suffer hunger and general want, war heroes wander hither and thither seeking employment, and the blind of them lift eyes heavenward in mute appeal for Divine succor and healing.

91

Where is a national sense of the fitness of things? Where its sense of honor? Echo answers, Where?

A.E. Vean
Imperial-Canadian Veteran
Ottawa

Shelby, Montana, did indeed lose in the fight, although it was through its own greed. A booming oil town, it desperately wanted a major boxing fight featuring Jack Dempsey. When it became obvious the town could not raise the $300,000 minimum Dempsey was promised, Dempsey tried to pull out, but Shelby insisted. The match was fought on July 4; a crowd of irate cowboys, enraged at the financial dealings, claimed Dempsey as a "slacker," and threw their lariats over the gates around the ring and tore them down. Dempsey escaped on foot with $260,000, running a mile to the railroad station. Years later, Dempsey was to tell a Globe and Mail sports writer that this had been the toughest fight of his career – not with Gibbons, but against the townsfolk of Shelby. Tom Gibbons, of course, lost; his benefit from the fight was a vaudeville contract with Arthur Pantages for the singular achievement of lasting the full 15 rounds with the great Manassa Mauler.

Capital Letters

February 7, 1923

In my letter published Jan. 30 I suggested that further delay in radically reforming English spelling is foolish, and that we should take the opportunity of dropping all our so-called "capital" letters. These letters did no great harm when writing was all done by hand, or even when all type was set by hand; but with writing machines, linotype and monotype machines, twenty-six unnecessary characters spell great waste.

It will be said that the capital letter is an aid to the eye in indicating the beginning of a sentence. If we must have a specially made letter to show that the sentence is finished, I suppose it ought to be the last letter of the sentence instead of the first. Consider the direction in which we are already moving, and remember the astonishment with which a citizen was first seen protecting himself from rain with an umbrella. We now write:

It followed her to school one day,
    Which was against the rule;

It made the girls all laugh and play
    To see a lamb in school.

Here we have four capitals. Only two or three generations ago
we should have thought we needed ten:

It followed her to School one Day,
    Which was against the Rule;
It made the Girls all laugh and play
    To see a Lamb at School.

The Germans still use capitals for their nouns, and their printed
alphabet is our ancient "black letter." We survived the loss of the
Gothic spurs and angles. If The Globe would run a single column,
of really good matter of general interest, without any capitals, for a
period of three months, I suggest that it would have many imita-
tors, and good seed would be sown.

J.N. Fish
Regina, Saskatchewan

The Message in the Bottle

July 24, 1924

As we were motoring between Brockville and Prescott July 20 we
stopped along the river edge to have our lunch, and there I found a
whiskey bottle sealed. I broke the seal and found a note with
Ambrose J. Small's name on it and the cause of his downfall written
on it and considerably more writing. Kindly publish this, and for
further information come to me.

Harry Prosser
Cardinal, Ontario

> *Ambrose J. Small, a wealthy playboy and impresario who built the
> Grand Theatre in London, Ontario, in 1901, disappeared in
> Toronto on December 2, 1919, just a few hours after he deposited $1
> million into his bank account from the sale of a chain of six theatres.
> A reward of $50,000 was offered, and for years all sorts of sightings
> were reported from as far away as Mexican gambling parlors. The
> case was in and out of the courts for years; his wife Theresa, after
> her death in 1935, was accused of murder and subsequently cleared,
> and his assistant was caught with stolen money. But it appears Mr.
> Prosser's bottle went with him to the grave, for no trace of Small was*

ever uncovered, except by actors who claim to have seen his ghost in the Grand. The ghost, alas, has been silent.

Radio Pictures
December 9, 1924

Kindly permit us to thank you for your cheering editorial of Dec. 3 regarding the the glories of the age when "Christ establishes His kingdom on earth."

Does not the latest achievement of science, the transmission by man of pictures of living men by radio from the eastern hemisphere even to the western hemisphere, which seeming miracle was obtained on Nov. 30, 1924, eliminate even the necessity of "faith" in order to accept the statement of "The Word of God" Himself (John I, i, 14; Rev., xix, 13) communicated to us per His disciples that "as the lightning cometh forth from the East, and is seen even unto the West, so shall be the coming (or presence) of the Son of Man."

Ought not the Churches of the Living "Word" to unite for a closer investigation or discernment of the "signs of the times" in which it is our privilege to be living?

A Unionist Presbyterian
Hamilton, Ontario

The Image in the Window
January 15, 1926

In today's issue of The Globe, on page 3, there is an article entitled "Mysterious Figure Appears on Glass." Now this is not the first time this strange thing has happened. I believe it has not infrequently taken place during thunderstorms, when there happened to be moisture on the window-glass. Whatever is most clearly mirrored in the glass, thus moist, is at once set, as on photographic films. The lightning in some way dries the image on the glass and it becomes a negative, etc.

I know personally of two such cases. One took place in Owen Sound and there are people there now who can testify as to this fact: A dear old grandma sat in her usual chair at the window during a thunderstorm, and next day an exact likeness was discovered on the window-pane. I am told this likeness is greatly treasured by members of the family. The other case happened at Oberammergau during the Passion Play. A large, smooth pebble retained after a thunderstorm a perfect likeness of the man acting the Christ. The late Miss O'Meara, sister to Dr. O'Meara of Wycliffe College, Toronto, saw it, and told me about it.

The late S.S. Robinson of Orillia had a little booklet containing and explaining the scientific phenomenon. I remember well Mr. Robinson telling me all about it, as he read it in his little booklet. I write these few lines as they may throw a little light on the subject. The old lady may have been in the attitude of prayer at the time, or she may have held a crucifix or picture, which became reflected or photographed, as it were.

Richard W.E. Green
Islington, Ontario

The Old-Time Ball Player

May 5, 1926

The baseball edition of The Globe, celebrating the opening of the new stadium, awakened memories which may interest fans among your readers.

When I was a student at the high school at Cambridge, Massachussetts, where I graduated in 1866, the new method of playing ball was introduced with its "diamond" and hard "pigskin" ball. I was pleased to be given a place on the high school nine. In 1869 and 1870 I played first base on the Harvard College nine. This nine was famous, not only because it held the college championship, but also because it had the unique experience of touring the States and winning games from professional clubs, including the Athletics at Philadelphia, the Haymakers at Troy, the Forest City's at Cleveland, and the White Stockings at Chicago. At Cincinnati we played the champion Red Stockings, and in the last half of the ninth inning with two men out the score was 17 to 12 in our favor! Weren't we excited! An unfortunate accident to our pitcher, who was struck on the knee by a hot liner from the bat, interrupted the game, and gave it to the Red Stockings. We were a sad lot. By common consent the college boys outplayed the champions and deserved to win.

Those were the days of straight "underhand" pitching, and of large scores. Some gentlemen of Lockport, New York, had organized a baseball club and gave us a pressing invitation to pay them a visit. They were ardent but inexperienced. Lack of time prevented a full game, but at the end of the fifth inning the score was 62 to 4 in our favor!

It is worthy of note that a majority of us on the Harvard team were total abstainers, and did not use tobacco in any form. After 55 years, according to my latest information, five of us are still living.

Pardon the enthusiasm of an old-timer.

Willard T. Perrin
Dentonia Park, Toronto

The Change in Alberta

November 24, 1926

The present liquor act in Alberta is satisfactory only to the people who wish to buy their liquor easily, to the people who are selling it; to another class who simply do not wish to be bothered and, generally speaking, to those who are entrusted with the enforcement.

There is no doubt it is an easier law to enforce than prohibition. Why shouldn't it be, when it gives the drinkers everything they want? And yet it is a significant fact (rarely mentioned by the liquor defenders) that a much larger body of men are employed – and apparently needed – to enforce it than we ever had to enforce prohibition. The part-time reformers who railed and howled against prohibition and were grieved to the heart when they saw any drunkenness during its regime, are loud in their praises of this law and can look upon scenes of drunkenness now without a murmur. The facts, that more people now are drinking than ever before; that young drinkers are taking the places of the old ones when they die or are interdicted; that men are losing their positions; that automobile accidents are becoming alarmingly frequent – these facts do not seem to have any weight with the defenders of the present system.

The worst feature of Government control is that it sets a certain stamp of approval on an iniquitous traffic. Of course, a bootlegger appears in a new role when the Government undertakes to sell liquor. He is not only a law-breaker – he is something much worse; he is a competitor. But a bootlegger has a better chance to carry on where liquor is legally sold for it is harder to detect his operations.

It should be the duty of any Government to protect the people. Moral and physical welfare is properly a Government's concern; but when a Government undertakes to sell liquor, it becomes not the guardian, but the enemy of the people. If the advocates of the present system could see some of the letters I receive, I wonder if they would still be able to report that Alberta's law is "satisfactory."

It is not even satisfactory to all of the drinkers. One man, a stranger to me, wrote asking me to leave him interdicted because he could not go to town now without getting drunk and so, for the sake of his wife and family, he wished to have this done and it was done. He evidently believed in prohibition. But all drinkers have not this man's courage and manliness. Another letter received a day or so ago has this paragraph: "There is ten times as much drinking here now as there was when we had prohibition."

Much is made of the interdiction clause by the advocates of Government control. But surely it is a poor system that manufactures drunkards at an increasing rate. Interdicting a man does not give him back what he has lost; nor does it insure peace in his home life, particularly if his wife has caused the interdiction to be made. It's a poor remedy, at best, and the lists of interdictions, mounting higher and higher, show what is happening. Drinking is increasing at an alarming rate.

It all comes down to this: is it all right for a country to produce drinkers and drunkards if it is done legally, and the Government receives a rake-off? The defenders of Government control say it is. We say, "No!"

All eyes are on Ontario. We hope she will stand firm.

Nellie L. McClung
Calgary

> *Defeated Liberal Member of the Legislative Assembly in Alberta in 1925, Nellie McClung had been a front-line campaigner in the Manitoba elections in 1914, and had led the fight to enfranchise women in that province in 1916. Later, she was named to the CBC's board of governors and was made Canadian delegate to the League of Nations in Geneva.*

Chapter 6

The National Bird

*On May 8, 1927, the year of Canada's Diamond Jubilee, poets
Bliss Carman, Sir Charles G.D. Roberts and George Frederick
Clarke decided that Canada needed a national bird, and that it
should be the white-throated warbler because its call sounds like
"Sweet sweet Canada Canada Canada." Jack Miner, the celebrated
naturalist and creator of the Jack Miner Migratory Bird Foundation
and Sanctuary, retorted that the Canada goose should have that
honor. Then the public entered the debate.*

May 13, 1927

In picking out a national bird why not select our most beautiful all-
the-year-round bird, namely the Canada Blue Jay? What a handsome picture he makes and we will remember that, like the beaver
or any other emblem, he will appear most often on paper. He takes
his own part and thrives with the crow and hawk as his neighbors –
a valorous, proud, gaudy watcher of the woods.

Nothing escapes his eye, for he is ever on guard, a desirable
national characteristic. His note compares favorably with the eagles
and he lives an interesting busy life gathering beech nuts and seeds
of the pine. In his conduct he may not always be perfect, but neither
is the lion nor bear. He is easily located and his shrill, exuberant
notes are soon known to all who love the great outdoors. Bluebirds
are a symbol for happiness, so we would expect him also to satisfy
our poets. Why need we go further?

Jubilee
Waterford

♦

May 14, 1927

... Surely the robin is the one. We all know him, even the writer,
whose bird knowledge is very limited indeed. Some of us had no
training along these lines in our school days, and we would like to
be sure that we could identify the bird selected as the Canadian
emblem. We all love the robin. He is a bright fellow, has a cheerful

song, is very friendly, stays with us most, if not all the year, and is met with everywhere. Surely he is the logical choice....

Novice
Orillia

◆

May 16, 1927

In regard to a national bird, if one is chosen, it should be the robin. Some suggest a vote of children; if such a vote is taken the robin will be the preference....

N. Gray
Toronto

◆

May 16, 1927

... May I cast my vote in favor of the Canada goose – that strong, beautiful, loyal creature whom we can claim as our own, as we can no other? Even our good neighbors to the south admit that he belongs to us. True, he is not a song bird, but to my mind he embodies more good qualities, and is a greater source of inspiration to those who know him, than the sweetest singer in the woods....

Fred L. Roy
Peterboro'

◆

May 16, 1927

I am submitting a suggestion for a National Bird. Why not name the swallow? And just now as we are approaching Government liquor control, don't you think the "swallow" would be appropriate?

Chester Carson
Barrie

◆

May 18, 1927

Now, Canada is a vast country, more than half of North America, so the sparrow is too small to represent its immense territories. In my humble opinion I think the owl the more appropriate bird. He is a big, rugged fellow, with lots of back-bone. The first snow doesn't drive him away. When everything is cracking with frost in the stillness of the woods we hear his hollow "Whoo! Whoo! Whoo!" "What's that?" we say. "It sounds as if we're going to have a thaw." He is the king of the forest, with his big, bass ventriloquist voice.

In the summer we have the smaller screech owl; in the winter the Arctic owl, with his woollen stockings. The cold blasts don't affect this staid man.

A wise old owl
Sat in an oak,
The more he saw
The less he spoke.
The less he spoke,
The more he heard –
Why can't we
Be more like that bird?

R.G. Wilkinson
Inglewood

◆

May 19, 1927

… I would unhesitatingly recommend the song sparrow. This little bird arrives in Collingwood about March 25, just when the snow is nearly gone, and to hear its beautiful song at this time of the year gives one a thrill of spring and summer coming, for which it well deserves to be our national bird….

F.E. Courtice
Collingwood

◆

May 19, 1927

I think a bird to be emblematic should be one common to all parts of Canada, and one that is universally known by residents of both town and country; also one that cheers us by its presence both summer and winter, and is, in addition to this, one of the most useful insect exterminators that are to be found. The chickadee's cheerful note is heard all through the coldest, most blustery weather, and his jolly, careless "Chick-a-dee-dee! Chick-a-dee-dee!" and his friendly way of coming for crumbs and bits of suet should be an inspiration to us all....

F.M.
Bancroft

◆

May 19, 1927

... The selection of the Canadian goose would show considerable taste, especially near Christmas time. It is admired and relished by the best of men, in spite of the fact that it is rather homely in appearance. It is excelled only by the turkey gobbler, which would make a striking national bird. Perhaps I am prejudiced against the goose because a gander grabbed me by the coat-tail in April as I passed a local poultry yard.

Why not choose the bat, which is the most popular among the baseball fans and players and is just as beautiful as the English bulldog?

If Canada chooses a national bird it will undoubtedly appear everywhere from the calendar to the moving-picture screen. Then it should be a bird which will add a touch of color and a thrill of joy to the observer. When a man seeks a wife he chooses the most beautiful girl in the world. Should Canadians not, therefore, choose the most beautiful bird in our woods as a national companion? ...

T. Stanley Jaques
Parry Sound

◆

May 19, 1927

We quite agree with the suggestion of Mr. F.L. Roy favoring the goose as the national bird of Canada. We have with us the wild and the domestic goose. The full-grown male bird of either the tame or the wild goose is a bird of a majestic appearance. It is known that the wild gander is the leader of the flock in migrating from south to north in the spring, and from north to south in the autumn. Who has not looked up in admiration of those noble creatures gracefully winging their way through space?

What military officer could marshall his troops with greater precision than is exemplified by those wonderful birds in their flight, sometimes in the exact form of an acute angle, other times an obtuse, or a right angle, and flying high to avoid the bullet of the sportsman, evincing an instinct almost equal to reason? ...

R.H. Knowles
Toronto

◆

May 19, 1927

... We know all too little about our song birds. Doubtless before this is ended we shall know more. But I still hold to the "white throat" as our national bird. If we were to pick a bird that stays in Canada all year round we would name the English sparrow or that slate colored bird with the gargantuan appetite, which flits about lumber camps all winter long – the "Junco." The goose, yes, a noble bird that I love, his habitat is not only Canada, and his grey wing feathered the shafts which won for the English archers victory on many a hard-fought field!

But the white-throat? Sentimental reasons for choosing him, if you will; sentimental reasons for choosing any!

George Frederick Clarke
Woodstock, N.B.

◆

May 19, 1927

It seems that the momentous question of selecting a bird to be the emblem of Canada cannot be settled. I have much pleasure in naming the stork as a fit bird to fill the august position, based on the following toast:

Here's to the stork, a valuable bird
    Who inhabits the resident districts.
He doesn't sing tunes or yield any plumes,
    But he helps out the vital statistics.

A. Sutherland
Fenelon Falls

◆

May 21, 1927

... Have we not shown ourselves geese enough by allowing whiskey (Government) control to control us for some time without choosing a goose as our national bird? ...

A Lover of the Robin
Arnprior

◆

May 24, 1927

If we need and must have a Canadian national bird I vote for the ruffed grouse, or partridge. This bird, in its variant forms, spends the year round with us from ocean to ocean. It is a beautiful bird, with very rich and varied color patterns. Though the tints are different, it is quite as beautiful as the "Whiskey Jack," which, of course, was not seriously proposed as the Canadian national bird....

M.M.
Kingston

◆

May 24, 1927

Your opening up the question of Canada's national bird and the apt suggestions made at the start by our beloved poet, Bliss Carman, and his associates, that the modest, retiring white-throat, "Sweet, Sweet, Canada, Canada, Canada!" be selected, thrilled me at the time with great pleasure. Since then I have been an interested reader of the claims put forward for other aspirants. Jack Miner's favorite intellectual goose has an unfortunate name. Likewise his voice, "Honk! Honk!" from above reminds us rather much of that other "Honk! Honk!" on our streets. Surely Jack Miner does not want to name Canada "Honk Honk Land." ...

G.T. Donaldson
Palmerston

◆

May 28, 1927

In choosing a bird as the Canadian emblem I do not think the dove has been mentioned. Would the dove – the symbol of peace – not be a most appropriate emblem at this time when peace is what we need at home and abroad more than anything else? ...

Jeanette Leader
Wheatley

May 28, 1927

Although Mr. Fred Roy of this city puts up a strong plea for the Canada goose as Canada's bird emblem, I fear our experience would be similar to that of our merchant marine when they displayed the beaver emblem on their flags. They became known as the "Rat Line" on the high seas, and were obliged, for obvious reasons, to supplant the beaver by the maple leaf.

A goose is a goose the world over and is, I believe a native of every country under the sun, and I am afraid that any country displaying the goose as an emblem would cause considerable amusement. The "Canada" goose would be just a goose to other people than ourselves....

A. McNab
Peterboro'

◆

May 28, 1927

If the whiskey jack or blue jay is the same bird that I knew in the North as the butcher bird, please kill any proposition that suggests using it as our national bird.

Its traits are as bad or worse than the crows' in the destruction of smaller birds, especially their eggs and young. This butcher bird kills more for pleasure than food....

William Smith
Stevensville

◆

June 2, 1927

... Travellers passing through Salt Lake City, Utah, must have seen and admired the sea gull monument in Temple Square. It is a marble shaft supporting a ball, upon which are two sea gulls, with half-spread wings. It was erected in commemoration of the deliverance of the Mormon pioneers from starvation, when a plague of crickets threatened the destruction of their crops in 1848 and 1849.

Flocks of sea gulls appeared and preyed upon the destroyers until the pests vanished. Since then the sea gulls have been protected in Utah by legislative enactment.

Is it unreasonable to believe that we, as a people, might take pride in the creation of a similar monument in our city parks, and other places, holding aloft the noble bird, the Canadian goose? A small bird would appear ridiculous, perched upon a shaft, while Jack Miner's favorite would do honor to him and to our country.

Charlotte Talcott-Cox
Bloomfield

◆

June 4, 1927

With very great interest I am following the suggestions of a national bird for Canada. In regard to the goose, I never hope to see one mounted on a pedestal as representing our country. A goose is all right on the dinner table menu or in the farmyard, but, oh, save us from degradation and give us something beautiful by name and nature to represent this Canada of ours, where beautiful scenery, green fields of grain, together with flowers and sunshine, give us a real paradise. I might suggest a white pigeon (dove). They are beautiful to look at, enduring like our "Parliamentarians," sweet and lovely like our "flappers." So what more could our people want? In discussing the goose with some friends across the border, one gentleman said, "Yes, we are just waiting to ask you Canadians, 'Goosie, goosie, gander, whither do you wander?'" And the fun will be all at our expense. And, again, will anyone tell me why the goose was ever suggested to be our national emblem? I have always looked upon a goose as a fowl, not as a bird. We would all feel rather amused to hear anyone say, "Come here, birdie," referring to a goose. Now, wake up, folks, and give us something to look at and beautiful to think of as a national bird.

L.T.D.
Toronto

◆

June 10, 1927

Personally, I do not think we need a national bird at all. We have the maple leaf and the beaver, and I think this is quite sufficient.

Milton C. MacLean
Toronto

June 14, 1927

In selecting the national bird, something more than mere popularity is desirable. Would we want our emblem to look like a juicy morsel when depicted in cartoons alongside those of other lands? It looks as if we may yet have to fall back on a member of the hawk tribe.

The snowy owl would apparently qualify, but, being a night flyer, and a rare visitor to southern parts, he would likely be little known.

Our hawks are plainly visible to all and within reach of every city. They are a bird of the ethereal blue, ever soaring, hour on hour, with matchless wing power. They exult in the freedom of the upper air and mere joy of living, while their ringing cries carry far and wide. They are the kings of bird creation, treating with disdain the Bolshevik crows which rush clumsily at them.

Being a bird of prey, man occasionally donates to their bill-of-fare, but usually it is his enemies who pay tribute. Each kind should stand on test.

As for migratory birds, another country might choose the same bird, and so it would cease to be a distinctive Canadian symbol. Again, another people might decide to slaughter a certain bird. What then could we do? Does this limit choice?

Blue jay, although he bears the colors of our flag and those of a famous university, has, like the goose, an objectionable name. Robin is popular, but falls from grace about cherry-time, leaves us as a rule, and lacks distinctive outline like the aristocratic crest of the jay, the dignified head of the owl, the wings of the hawk. Outline is important, for it appears in unexpected places, such as in art, on coins and so forth.

Emblem
Waterford

◆

July 4, 1927

> Sakes! Have you heard the latest word?
> Canadians would adopt a bird;
> A feathered emblem they would fain
> Have signify our great domain;
> That I'm some bird you will attest,
> From ample proof found in my nests,

If birds are valued by their fruits,
Then I should count for some cahoots.

I do not glide on graceful pinion,
Warbling joy o'er the Dominion;
The only music that I tackle
Is my old cacophonous cackle:
But, bid it welcome, for it tells
Of varied treats within the shells,
And if you know it, tell, I beg,
The equal of the new-laid egg.

Come sing ye poets, sing of me!
Overdue is my jubilee!
Publish the praises far and wide
Of eggs, boiled, scrambled, poached or fried,
Tell how I've helped with modest calm
To lift the debt off many a farm.
Should birds inspire your soulful pen,
Just what's the matter with the hen?

A. Spencer
Toronto

Chapter 7

Mongrels and Other Bitches

April 28, 1928

BRITISH AUSTRALIA; MONGREL CANADA

With a heading like that every good Canadian will want to roll up his sleeves and fight. And rightly so. But what are the facts?

Something over 113,000 immigrants entered Australia during the year 1927, and of those more than 93,000 were British. About 20,000 were foreigners, and they came from no fewer than 30 different countries, so that the number from each alien source was very small indeed. The majority of Australians are determined that their country shall be kept not only a "white man's land," but predominantly British at that.

Now, how do we stand in Canada? Yes, Canada – because the alien floods in the West will reach the rest of Canada before long. Let me give your readers only four recent facts:

1. The Saskatoon Star of March 16 reports: "In the Canadian National Railway program to date the approximate number of those who have arrived in Winnipeg, the disseminating point, is 2,095. Of these 300 have been British, 450 are Scandinavians, 50 Belgians, 100 were Dutch, some 200 were Germans, 550 Ruthenians, 200 Poles, 125 were Czechoslavics, and 120 were Hungarians. Total, 300 British and 1,795 aliens."

2. Of the total of 855 already settled in Saskatchewan since March 1, 100 were British, 175 Scandinavians, 20 Belgians, 25 Dutch, 125 Germans, 200 Ruthenians, 100 were Poles, 60 Hungarians, and 50 were Czechoslavics. One hundred British out of 855. So much for what the Nationals are doing to populate our country with aliens.

Now, what is the Canadian Pacific Railway doing?

3. Winnipeg, April 13 – "The coming week will see approximately 2,000 new settlers arrive in the West over Canadian Pacific lines. The first special train will arrive in Winnipeg on Monday, made up of well over 700 new settlers, almost entirely from Central European countries. The second train will arrive next day, having around 350 immigrants; 120 from Central Europe, 60 from Scandinavia, and the balance from Great Britain. On Thursday another

solid trainload of Central European immigrants will reach the West, numbering approximately 800." So that in three days the C.P.R. dumped into the West 170 British settlers to 1,680 aliens, mostly of Central European origin. It is not stated who made up the balance of the 2,000. It is nearly certain they were not British, because, had they been so, the railway companies would have told us of them three times over.

4. A few days ago a trustworthy friend went down to the Immigration Building in Prince Albert to ascertain what was happening. The register showed that between March 1 and April 21, inclusive, there were 225 arrivals, and of these only 18 were British, and there was also 1 Dane. All the others were non-preferred Europeans, chiefly Poles.

We have been warned already that the Germans, Hungarians, Poles, Ruthenians, Dukhobors, Russians and Mennonites are coming in floods. Will those Canadians who object to the heading of this letter, "Mongrel Canada," please ask the Premier why he gave these two railways the liberty to denationalize this country nearly three years ago? It will take another two years to stop the flood, even if this iniquitous agreement is abrogated immediately.

George Exton Lloyd
Bishop of Saskatchewan
Bishopsthorpe, Prince Albert, Saskatchewan

> *Chaplain, Queen's Own Rifles, during the Northwest Rebellion of 1885; Rector of Rothesay, N.B., 1890, and founder of Rothesay College; chaplain of the Barr colonists in Saskatchewan, 1903, and Anglican Bishop of Saskatchewan 1922-1931. The city of Lloydminster was named in his honor.*

The Law of Gravity

October 30, 1928

During the past few days several articles have appeared on the subject of gravity. As the present generation understands it, the law of gravitation is as follows: "Every particle in the universe attracts every other particle with a force which is in the direction of a straight line joining the two, and whose magnitude is proportional to the product of the masses and inversely proportional to the square of the distance between them." This law has held from the day Newton saw the apple fall, but now that we have entered the "wave age" and a recent discovery confirms the idea that the universal ether is in a perpetual state of motion, a new theory presents itself, namely, that gravitation is the result of wave pressure.

How are all objects kept upon the earth by the action of waves? The explanation appears simple. On all sides and stretching above us the sky has the aspect of a dome. Considering that universal waves come from all directions with the same intensity, then the centre of pressure must invariably lie directly above us, and the line of least resistance would be toward the centre of the earth. The earth on account of its huge mass would stop or greatly reduce the power of the waves striking the other side of the globe, therefore, there would be little or no under-pressure counteracting that from above. Naturally the further an object is moved from the earth the more under-pressure it receives and its weight is lessened in accordance.

Now let us consider objects as we see them on earth and the variation of weight in pieces of equal size and the cause of weight in connection with waves. Matter is made up of atoms, the elements containing various amounts of atoms per cubic inch. The element with the largest number of atoms has the greater density, the greater the density the more resistance it has to the waves, and consequently the heavier it appears. Hydrogen, for instance, has almost a free passage for the waves on account of the openness of its atoms, whilst lead is the reverse, and radium more so, as is show by their weights. The emanations of radium can be attributed to the action of the bombardment of ether waves, the surface presenting an impenetrable atomic barrier, the power of the waves breaking up the radium atoms, destroying matter and giving forth a luminous effect in doing so.

The tides, supposed to be caused by the pull of the moon, are the result of side and angular wave pressure on the easily movable surface of the oceans, the centre point of high tide being the point on the surface of the earth that lies directly in line with the centre of the earth and the centre of the moon. It has been claimed by scientists that the earth bulges at the equator and is flattened at the poles, the distance from the North Pole to the centre being 26½ miles less than the distance from the equator to the centre, also that a weight set at one pound at the equator would gain a trifle in weight at the pole. This point alone I imagine proves the wave pressure theory, the flatness at the pole causing less under-side angular wave pressure than at the equator, consequently less counteraction against the pressure from above. Here is a point in reference to the centre of the solar system, the sun. Naturally, the sun is the centre; it would be contraverse to nature to be otherwise, being the largest member. Now, how can the sun have such a powerful gravitational pull and at the same time exert a radiation pressure that repels matter and prevents the members of the solar system from piling up into one heap? It seems like trying to prove a horse pulls both ways at the one time. What seems more logical is that the planets are compelled toward the sun by wave pressure, a balance of motion being produced by the radiation pressure that the sun emits, coupled with the orbital motion that is a birthright of the planets.

If the sun had such a powerful gravitational pull, sufficient to hold the earth in its orbit, what would be the result if we were on the opposite side with the earth between us? If it has such a pull, then, during daytime it must exert a counteraction on terrestrial gravitation, and things would be heavier and terrestrial gravitation greater when the sun's pull was released and we entered the period of darkness. But it is not so and could not be under the theory that gravitation is the result of the pressure of waves. The same thing applies when we are in the path of a total eclipse, with that large mass matter, the moon, directly between us. Then we do not experience any change in weight or any additional heaviness to our own bodies.

The formation of worlds from the nebular state would appear more correct by wave action than by attraction, the luminous gaseous elements being pressed into a heap by continuous bombardment on the more unprotected sides of the atoms that constitute these elements. The nearest to the centre of the nebula would receive the least amount of pressure, and consequently the matter around would be compelled toward the centre. It could not be otherwise.

In closing, I consider that by a little careful analysis many mysteries that perplex us both terrestrial and celestial could be attributed to the pressure of waves and the effects that arise therefrom.

Arthur Canham
Galt, Ontario

Okanagan's Ogopogo

March 12, 1929

If the highly creditable Logie family had photographed the monster eel which they all saw, their snapshot would not have convinced those of us who glory in incredulity. I know the Okanagan thoroughly, but no such monster appeared to me; and I have wandered around Chicago without being molested – how, then, can I believe that there is a serpent in the fruity British Columbia lake or a criminal in the windy U.S. city?

Lots of trusty people around O.K. orchards have seen about "ten yards of mystery" swimming in the lake, but they hate to admit the evidence of their senses lest they be derided by us nincompoops who have had no similar observation. No one claims to have seen twin Ogopogos, so hard cider has not exaggerated the phenomena. Four years ago, in a Penticton newspaper, a naturalist suggested that a "school of fish," or effects of light, atmospheric hill-top reflections, had deluded unscientific observers; later he saw "something" and was man enough to apologize for having ridiculed the unlearned. But, if there is a monster with a sheep's head, it should have had brains enough to have shown itself to so important a person as

A.W. Rodway
Toronto

Where a Yankee Comes From
June 19, 1929

In Wednesday's issue of The Globe one read with much interest W.S. Downs's words: "Yankee is the name used by the Indians when referring to the early English settlers. The late Chief Justice White of the Supreme Court of the United States told a Canadian that every citizen of the United States should be proud to be called a Yankee."

When we know the origin and the meaning of the word "Yankee" we will exclaim, "True, very true." To those with a scientific knowledge of the Indian language the origin and meaning of the word is as clear and transparent as sunlight. Yankee is a variant of the Mohawk word On-Kwa, frequently written On-key. And the outstanding meaning of the word is "We, or They. The Real People" (written in capital letters and emphasized). A further knowledge of the origin and meaning of this word is illuminating. In all the languages of the world, if the numerals one and two are traced to their origin, it will be seen that they have their origin in dualism. God and Two-God, or in Pagan theology, Lord and War-Lord. It has been claimed that Egypt was the cradle of civilization, and that here language was invented. The earliest known inhabitants of Egypt were the Ah's and the On's. In primitive language On-ah is the root or concept for God or Sun-Man. "On" has been retained as the masculine, while "Ah" has been retained as the feminine. On-Ah has been slurred to our numeral One. The dual of

On-Ah is Teh-on, Teh-onah, Teh-ah, sometimes written Teh-wah. The dual of Teh-wa has been slurred to Two. In primitive languages "K" or "Ek" is a plural for God or Sun-Man, and Ek is One in Sanskrit and Dwee is Two.

The "Genus" or family plural of On-kwa and Ton-kwa and the dual is Ton-kwa. In Mohawk one and two is On-kwa and Ton-kwa. And on the tombs of Egypt the On-kwa and Ton-kwa were carved as emblems of Life and Two-Life. So that On-kwa means God, the Sun-Man, and when applied to people it means "We, or They. The Real People."

Note the "Y" at the beginning of the word. In Mohawk "Y" is sometimes used as a feminine, as in Hebrew. On-gweh is Man and Yon-gweh is Woman. But "Y" is more frequently used at the beginning of the word to call one's attentions to the supernatural. Where On-kwa would refer to Man, Yon-kwa would designate that the Indian looked upon the men as more than natural. In the writings of John Smith, the first English explorer in these parts, these words are to be found regarding the Mohawk. "Such great and well-proportioned men are seldom seen; they seemed like giants to the English; yet seemed of an honest and simple disposition and with much ado refrained from worshipping us as gods."

Yon-key, slurred to Yankee, was the name given by the Red Men to the English, who seemed to them to be gods.

Margaret A. Brown
Brantford

♦

June 28, 1929

Over the signature of Margaret A. Brown of Brantford, your correspondent writes upon the origin of a name – viz., "Yankee" – and discusses it from a Mohawk point of view. Being utterly incompetent in the aboriginal vernacular of this continent it would be impertinent on my part as well as a waste of my time and your space to join in the discussion. May I, however, quote the definition given by our most competent scientific etymologist upon the word?

In Professor Weekley's "Etymological Dictionary of Modern English," the following definition of Yankee will be found: "Orig. (18th. Cent.) of limited application and perh. first used of Du. inhabitants of New Amsterdam (New York). From a dim. of Du. Jan, John (Cf. Jenkins). It has also been suggested that it is a back formation like Chinee, Portugee, from Du, Jan Kee, lit. John Cornelius, both of which names are used as nicknames in Du."

Yankee Doodle was a pop song during the War of Independence (1775-1783).

"And some be Scot, but the worst God wot and the boldest thieves be Yank." Kipling, Three Sealers.

Feeling sure that the Professor of Modern Languages in University College, Nottingham, will be interested in reading this writer's contention it will afford me much pleasure to forward to him the two letters, and then act upon Mr. Asquith's favorite advice and "Wait and see."

J.H. Cameron
Toronto

◆

July 3, 1929

As to the origin of the word "Yankee" as a designation of the inhabitants of the New England States of the Union (to whom only it was originally applied), let me repeat what I heard from a postgraduate in English at Harvard University, Cambridge, Mass., nearly forty years ago.

The sporty students of Harvard in its early days hired saddle horses from a farmer. In describing a horse or saddle this farmer would say: "Yankee good horse," "Yankee good saddle." On almost all occasions "Yankee" was used. In a short time the students began to call the farmer "Yankee" or "The Yankee." Soon other farmers were called "Yankee" and in the course of time it was applied to all the inhabitants. Was the Harvard man correct?

Geo. E. Honey
Fort Erie

Preventing Cancer

December 7, 1929

I notice from your paper the medical profession is having conferences at present with the main object of fighting cancer.

Records have proved that where the population is about half French and half English speaking only about 10 per cent of cancer cases are in French people. What is protecting the French? French people in Canada eat and act the same as English-speaking people, except as follows: The French smoke leaf tobacco; do not drink much liquor, except high wine diluted in water, and eat the round pea, peasoup, cooked with salted pork. Would this be protecting them?

One thing sure, the doctors will have a hard job to find a case of cancer on a Frenchman who smokes leaf tobacco, takes a drink of high wine once in a while, and eats the round-pea peasoup (not shelled).

Jos. E. Brisebois
Toronto

An Application for Attorney-General

After a gruesome murder in a "roadhouse" between Toronto and Hamilton and, in another case, after the dropping of charges of drinking against the sons of prominent citizens, the public cried out for stiffer sentences. In an editorial headlined "Wanted: An Attorney-General," The Globe demanded that Ontario Premier G. Howard Ferguson fire the current man and find one who was tougher.

August 11, 1930

The Globe has an advertisement – a special one – under the heading: "Wanted: An Attorney-General." I have applied for nearly everything without results – federal, provincial and civic. They have all promised plausibly and lied most royally. By the way, I wish that they or one of them would ask me to dinner to celebrate the great Conservative victory, or say, give me a pair of boots.

I am not a Colonel – I am not thick-headed enough, but I have made battalions for them, so I think I am entitled to a dinner.

I am applying for this position of Attorney-General, as I have an idea I am the man "Fergie" wants. He has told me two or three funny stories before about a position I applied for, and, as usual, was not warp-heeled enough.

I am sure that I am the man. I really could not be much worse.

The province is eagerly looking for a man. Good people do not look any more! I am knocking at your door; open it and give me a position.

If you think I am too good for an Attorney-General's job make me a doorman.

Yours in case another war breaks out.

Sergt.-Major George Dinwiddie,
M.V.D., D.C.M., Etc.
Toronto

Snakes in Ireland

October 3, 1930

Nearly every time I have taken up a Toronto newspaper since I came to spend a holiday on the shores of Lake Simcoe, I have seen some reference to snakes in Ireland.

It is quite true that it would be almost as difficult to find a snake in Ireland as a whale in the Lakes of Killarney, or a beehive at the North Pole, but, strange as it may seem, I have seen snakes – four large, dead ones – in Ireland when I was a boy. They were killed on the banks of the Douglas River by the local schoolmaster, and exhibited for all to see and behold in one of the principal shop windows in the City of Cork, shortly after receiving the compliments of the sturdy pedagogue.

Needless to state, the unusual occurrence caused a great deal of commotion, and more than one Irishman was afraid that the good St. Patrick was going to lose his reputation. Tradition tells us that, at the dawn of Christianity, the shepherd-saint banished the unpopular reptiles, and so black was the curse he put on them, that they never would return, even if they could.

But how did the snakes get to the picturesque little village of Douglas in the County of Cork? All the world wondered. However, when the excitement over their appearance reached the point of absurdity, the confession of a foreign sailor, who had the misfortune, or good fortune, if you will, of sailing under an Irish sea captain, brought peace once more to many troubled minds. The sailor, a skeptic by nature, and anti-Celt by inclination, wondered if all the yarns he heard from his master were true, so he brought a bag of snakes from some country where saints, scholars and sea-captains were unknown, and let them loose at the mouth of the tributary of the River Lee, just to see what would happen.

Now that the snake question is settled, I hope, I would like to know how much the Irish of Toronto know or care about some other phases of their country's history; but will be content with asking one question: "Did the Irish ever produce a first-class highwayman, one like Dick Turpin, for instance?"

Seumas O'Brien
Allandale, Ontario

Culture by Radio

April 16, 1931

A movement has been started across the line to teach culture by radio. Just how culture is to be "taught" is not stated. Perhaps the problem is to be referred for solution to the research laboratories which produced predigested foods.

Anyway, on some future occasion when a Canadian tourist is stumbling and mumbling over an explanation to an American traffic cop of why he exceeded the speed limit, he will not be irritated by the colloquialism, "G'wan, I ain't no mind reader." No! He will soothed, or perhaps stunned, by some such classic phrase as that addressed by Agamemnon to the enslaved Hecuba, the captive Queen of Troy:

I am no seer, nor can I uninformed
Trace out the secret purpose of your soul.

The American eagle is an ambitious bird, and if it makes up its mind to go there nothing can stop its flight to the Pierian home of the ancient muses.

Alfred O. Tate
Toronto

Diamonds? And Why Not?

August 7, 1931

Wonders beyond the belief of the average man lie in the great northland of Ontario and Quebec. Wonders of wealth, wealth and great prosperity to those who have faith and the will to do and to dare to put their feet on land where no white man has ever trod.

When one reads in the magazines and the daily press of all the wonders that have happened in the short past of this glorious Canada of ours it causes the average thoughtful citizens to pause and think on the might be's that lie in the not-distant future. It is only a short time, a very short time ago, when to think of Northern

Ontario having the output of gold and silver that she now produces would have been called a "pipe dream," and it would have been a pipe dream had it not been for the men of faith and vision who dared to tread the land where the foot of white men never trod.

While I write these few notes the Hon. Charles McCrea is up in the land of many hopes, the land of wondrous possibilities to those who have faith and can see the gleam of a Northern Ontario and Quebec peopled with millions of prosperous, happy people of a breed which will take a back seat for no one. In that great land which will soon be a front door for the commerce of Europe and the British Isles through the Ungava Straits into the Hudson Bay, Fort Churchill and the new port of the T. & N.O. Railway on James Bay, there are possibilities beyond the dreams of the average man. "It's coming yet for a' that." It is not necessary to have the vision of a prophet to see on the shores of the James Bay the smelters belching forth and the molten metal of the Belcher iron deposits running out of the retorts like living streams of life.

When that time comes, and it won't be so long, I am hoping I'll be around to chuckle and say: "Well, what about it? Didn't I tell you so? And that's nothing to what it will be."

It's a fact today that the Hudson Bay Company, who have been in the Great North Land for so long, even they are cocking their heads to one side and wondering, "What next?" The Chairman and his associates of the Abitibi Power Company, who have been in the Great North recently, are men of vision, and it must be a great satisfaction for them to see the gleam of their dream of the Abitibi canyon being harnessed with power that will be carried over the height of land from the Arctic slope to run factories and light cities and homes, hundreds of miles south. Progress – can you vision the Indians towing their canoes up the rapids only a few years ago from Moose Factory to the crossing of the Transcontinental Railway, eight miles east of Cochrane on the Abitibi River, bringing their shipment of furs to Cochrane, and now one of the greatest power stations in the world on these rapids?

Travelling – sure we're travelling, and the wonderful beauty of it all is, we simply can't be stopped, and there are reasons. We have the goods. We have the men, and, by Jingo, we have the money, too. Bennett proved that when he asked for his loan.

It is reasonable to expect that the T. & N.O. Railway will be shipping coal to Southern Ontario in the future. It is reasonable because there are forty miles of coal lands west of Abitibi. A little vision, a little money, and the men who know the song of the pine and the spruce, and then all these things will be every day talk.

It is a land where the returns, to those who would toil intelligently in cultivation, will be repaid an hundred-fold. Clay land, clay like meal when the summer sun shines on it, where the sun sets one hour after he leaves us here in Southern Ontario. Clay lands, all kinds of clay; merrill clay for cement, pottery clay, millions of tons of it, and the sand that goes with the making of pottery.

Such a land! If half the money spent in the Great War by Canada was spent in developing this great northern heritage of ours the possibilities of that thought causes our vision to see millions of happy people in that land of a million possibilities.

Clay land! Who dares to say there are no diamonds in Northern Ontario and Quebec. Produce the fellow who knows enough about diamonds to say there are no diamonds in Northern Ontario and Quebec. Why, it's only a few years ago I was told that it was all rot about gold being in Porcupine. "Oh, well, there might be," they said, "but it is only a float." Same story about silver in Cobalt in the early days.

Why, there should be diamonds in Northern Ontario and Quebec; the clay where diamonds are found, is to be found in Northern Ontario and Quebec; the blue clay that you can cut like cheese, with all kinds of pebbles in it. All it requires is the fellow who knows the diamonds in the rough to come on up and get them; not the knocker, nor the wise guy who knows it all, but the fellow who has vision and faith and a knowledge of how to hunt for diamonds.

The Ontario Government had faith to put down a diamond drill at Coral Rapids and they got the black diamonds, coal. I wonder if the Honorable Mr. McCrea has a crew out looking for diamonds; you never can tell, and if he had, who can blame him? He is a Minister of Mines in a province which for mines and possibilities of mines, no man living can tell what may be in the future of this great northern country of ours.

Why not diamonds in the great clay belt of Ontario and Northern Quebec?

John M. Daly
Indian Superintendency
Parry Sound

A Plague on Radio Crooners

February 9, 1932

    I'd rather hear
    A lecture

On political economy
Or perhaps a little talk
About the wonders of astronomy.
And further down
Upon the list
I'd listen to an oculist
Or some well-known
Philanthropist.
In fact, I would
Much sooner
Do anything
Than listen
To a so-called
Radio crooner.

I'd rather hear
A jazz band
Accompanied by static,
Or perhaps a ghostly play
Enacted in an attic.
And then sometimes
A little jest
Or music
Put on by request.
And later on
I think I'd choose
To listen to the daily news.
But not eternal
Songs of spooners
As sung for us by
Radio crooners.

But some there are,
Or so I hear,
Who come from far,
And sometimes near,
Who listen
With attentive ear
To those same
Radio crooners.
And so I have
begun to fear
That perhaps I am
A trifle queer
That I can't bear

Upon the air
The voice
Of a radio crooner.

Helen H. Watson
Toronto

A Remote Prospect

July 5, 1932

Perhaps "Bridge" is not a subject for the "Voice of the People," as players are not supposed to use their voices while playing. However, I noticed an item quoted from the Beacon-Herald stating that Miss Jessie Scott, Stratford, was dealt a perfect "hand" of cards – thirteen hearts. According to Principal Spring of the S.C.I. this should happen, according to the law of averages, only once in 5,364,473,786,548,879,283,923,744 hands.

These are staggering figures for one not used to counting more than 13, or at most, 52. Nevertheless, let us do some higher mathematics. Let us suppose there are 100,000,000 bridge fans, playing 25 hands each day every day for a year. At this rate it will take all year to deal 879,283,932,744 hands, and about 5,364,473,000 years to come around to the perfect hand again. Thus we may conclude that about the year A.D. 5,364,001,932 some player will again be dealt a perfect hand. In that remote future age some one will set about figuring when, according to the law of averages, it last happened before.

It seems to me we should not let this occurrence pass without due recognition. We should set up a bronze tablet to the fortunate lady and a golden monument to the one who shuffled the cards. We might also associate the names of the Stratford people with other people and events well known now, but which probably will be forgotten in five billion years. For example, we might note in bronze or brass that about the same time as this rare phenomenon happened, Mrs. Putnam flew the Atlantic solo, the first woman to do so; an Imperial Conference was held at Ottawa; Gar Wood won a speedboat racing trophy; the Americans won the heavyweight championship from Max Schmeling; and Amos 'n' Andy started the O.K. Hotel.

Of course, the learned principal's pen may have slipped when he was figuring, and, at all events, we hope we may get a good hand of bridge before five billion years of continuous playing.

Bridget Bridgen
Comber, Ontario

An Old Legend

July 19, 1932

The celebration on Sunday at Niagara of the 140th anniversary of the institution of the Masonic order in the district brings to mind the gruesome tale of "Morgan, the kidnapped Mason."

While searching through a file of old Niagara Gleaners, dating from 1823 to 1832, many references were found to the story. Andrew Heron, the editor, was rabidly anti-Mason and lost no opportunity to give a dig at the order. He advertised on sale at his office Morgan's book and also an anti-Mason Calendar.

On several occasions he announced the finding of Morgan's body, followed a few days later by an item such as follows:

The Gleaner, Nov. 12, 1827: "After all the corroborating proof published in a late Gleaner that the body that was found lately near the Oak Orchard was that of the late Captain Morgan, it is said, notwithstanding, that there is stronger proof still that it is the body of one Timothy Moris drowned lately in the river."

But an item of June 23, 1827, caps the climax. "It is said that the old ladies in the neighborhood of Fort Niagara are in continual fear in consequence of Morgan's spook, and the young girls are actually afraid to be alone. Sometimes he is seen like a wizard, darting across the Niagara upon a broomstick; at others he presents himself in the heart of the great Israelitish city of Ararat with a pair of compasses as though he was planning a palace for the Grand Judge. But his most favorite advocation appears to be sailing up and down the cataract upon a Mason's trowel, using its handle for a rudder."

Isabel McComb Brighty
St. Catharines

How to Laugh

June 26, 1933

Cheerfulness is a tonic for the mind and body. It has a beneficial influence upon the blood, nerves, and physical organs. Cheerfulness is a valuable business asset. It attracts and keeps friends. Cheerfulness is the antidote to worry, fear, discouragement and depression.

Hence the art of laughing should be assiduously cultivated. A rippling, silvery, melodious laugh is seldom heard. Sounds are emitted supposed to represent a laugh, but usually are merely tittering cachinnations or loud guffaws.

A simple way to learn to laugh is as follows:

1. With closed lips sound the letter "M" in staccato style, slowly at first, then more rapidly. Thus: "M-m-m-m-m."

2. Purse the lips and say "Hoo" several times. Thus: "Hoo!-hoo!-hoo!-hoo!-hoo!"

3. Sound "Ho" several times. Thus: "Ho!-ho!-ho!-ho!-ho!"

4. Sound "Ha" several times. Thus: "Ha!-ha!-ha!-ha!-ha!"

Finally run the four elements together. Thus: "M- m- m- m- m-hoo- hoo- hoo- hoo- hoo- ho- ho- ho- ho- ho- ha- ha- ha- ha- ha!" Gradually increase in speed.

When you finish reading the foregoing aloud you will have already produced a very good laugh.

Grenville Kleiser
New York

A Monument for General Pike
September 22, 1933

I notice by the papers that "we Americans" are going to be allowed to erect a monument to General Pike, the man who, in the War of 1812, set fire to the then village of York. This is certainly a rather unusual friendly gesture on the part of a British community.

I notice in recent years a great tendency to gloss over many facts in past history. (E.g., I myself have Canadian cousins who belong to the fourth generation in Canada.) Now it has been told over and over again that, in the spring of 1813, when General Pike fired York, it was a cold April, especially at night; that all the younger men were away at the Niagara front. Now here is where the McCain family enters. It is reported in the family, and used to be so stated in some histories, that the General set fire to the village and turned into a frosty night 400 old men and women and children. At this time there lived there an old Irishman by the name of Mike McCain. He came out of his burning home, with several grandchildren, asking who set fire to the town. A soldier told him it was General Pike, who was then making an uneven track down the street. Mike picked up a brick and hit him in the head. Just then the British remnant of some forty to fifty soldiers, who had been left behind with the ammunition stores in the fort, blew it up. Debris fell all around. General Pike was carried into the ship Madison – but these fellows always maintained that it was the brick the Irishman threw (enraged at the turning out into the night of his small grandchildren) that killed Pike, and not the explosion, as was immediately reported.

Do any of the Canadian McCain family still living have this record? Let's build the monument. It shows the spirit of a new age, although I see no monument to General Robert E. Lee in Boston.

Thomas McCain
Fort Dodge, Iowa

Shaw's Midnight Frolic

October 6, 1933

The most amusing episode of the Canadian Authors' visit to England, our meeting with George Bernard Shaw, has started such a flock of varying and contradictory stories that I had better put on record at once what actually happened. The facts are at least as interesting as any of the fictions in circulation.

I have myself been prominently quoted as telling Mr. Shaw, "If you come to Canada, you will be left severely alone." As it was on my initiative that Mr. Shaw had come to meet us in London, such a prediction, very like a threat, would have been equally ridiculous and rude.

Mr. Shaw, too, has been charged with the rudeness of accepting an invitation to dinner and not turning up until 11 o'clock. Of that special crime he was not guilty. He had declined the Forum Club's invitation to the dinner preceding the reception, but had promised to attend the reception later, which he did. That it was very much "later" was unfortunate; but he did not break his promise.

It was a curious speech he made. Of course it was sparkling and startling, as his habit is. We expected that, and were not disappointed. But as it went on it became "curiouser and curiouser," as Alice remarked of another adventure in Wonderland.

Mr. Shaw confessed that he did not know Canada – he had "missed an opportunity" when he came round by Panama instead of crossing the Dominion from Vancouver. He has been reported as declaring that "he would not go to Canada, because if he did he would be lionized and his life made miserable." On the contrary – I was taking notes of his speech for our association's official magazine – he said: "I think I will go to Canada and make that trip to Vancouver." Meanwhile, ignorance of the country could not prevent him from describing it and even foretelling the reception he would get from the inhabitants.

"I suppose," he said, "that I shall be mobbed all over the place, or be blindly idolized." And even that was not the worst fate in store for him. "If I go to outlandish and savage places like Canada I shall become a victim of intellectual starvation," he said – and said all in the same genial tone, with the same benevolent smile, as if he were saying "when I go to a Garden of the Muses like Canada I shall enjoy the perfect feast of Reason and Flow of Soul. "

From anyone else in the world, his words, flung in the face of educated Canadians, could only have been taken as an insult. He, however, is the "chartered libertine of debate"; his charter, by general consent, allows and almost demands the most extravagant language. On this occasion, what probably happened is that he was in a peculiarly jocular mood; he was surrounded by a warmly appreciative audience ready for almost anything he chose to give them; and losing sight of the little "almost" he let his vocabulary run away with him. I doubt whether he knew the words he was using till he had used them.

Some of his English hearers, though not (so far as I could see) of our Canadians, showed plain disgust; they either believed Mr. Shaw meant what he said, or thought it an ill-mannered sort of joke to tell his Canadian fellow-craftsmen that they were savages from a savage land and he could not spend a few weeks in their company without intellectual starvation.

The lady presiding was clearly embarrassed by Mr. Shaw's provocative speech, and suggested a Canadian reply. I had been asked to act as spokesman for the oversea visitors that night, and had already returned thanks for the club's hospitality. As no one else now stepped forward, I had to. I did not as rumor has alleged express my anger or resentment at Mr. Shaw's speech. On behalf of the Canadians I thanked him very warmly; he had given us a most amusing and delightful speech; whatever parts of it some might question they all agreed with him when he admitted that he did not know either Canada or the Canadians. That was unfortunate; but the defect, of course, would be cured by Mr. Shaw's projected visit, which I most heartily pressed him to carry out as soon as possible. As to his reception in Canada, I assured him that he would be neither mobbed nor blindly idolized, but would be welcomed with all the respect due to so distinguished a citizen.

The demonstrations of approval that followed, and the thanks I continue to receive, show that I represented not unfairly the views of my fellow-Canadians.

Howard Angus Kennedy
National Secretary, Canadian Authors' Association

Former editor, 1891-1910, of The Times Weekly of London, and later Secretary-General of the Canadian Authors' Association.

Ominous Arithmetic

March 29, 1934

Permit me to offer the enclosed example of sibylline mathematics as a contribution to current disarmament discussions.

First Boer attack on the British in Natal	1881
Add years vertically as shown	1
	8
	8
	1
Which gives the date of the Boer War	1899
Which lasted three years	3
	1902
Add years as before	1
	9
	0
	2
Date of the Great War	1914
Which lasted four years	4
	1918
Add years as before	1
	9
	1
	8
Date of?	1937

Credit Mrs. Albert Slade, 980 Queen Street West, Toronto.

R.S.D.

Killer Sheep

June 8, 1934

Newspapers report many incidents of dogs worrying sheep. Why not train sheep (as we did in England many years ago) to defend themselves against dogs?

It is not difficult to a person that understands animal training. Rams are easy to teach. One killed a wolf last September. At the same time it teaches dogs not to worry lambs. Black-faced sheep are the most courageous.

John Bird
Toronto

Wanted: Game and Good Cooking

August 13, 1934

Jack Miner's article, "Ontario, The Great Playground," in the Aug. 6 issue of The Globe, affirms a fact that has long been known to all lovers of the Ontario wilderness country: that the economic welfare of the Province requires a far more vigorous and efficient policy of game and fish conservation than has been the case heretofore.

There is no question whatever that Ontario has the opportunity to become the greatest playground area on the continent, thanks to her strategic position in relation to the bulk of the American population, the extraordinary beauty of the granite backcountry and a multitude of the most glorious freshwater lakes to be found anywhere in the world.

Properly conserved, developed and merchandised, the backcountry can furnish the basis for a tourist traffic whose value may easily eclipse most other industries. But conservation, development and merchandising are essential. The backcountry must be made accessible, the forests considered as a scenic wealth rather than as potential timber wealth, fish and game preserved, and civilized accommodations at all price scales provided.

Peculiarly enough, or happily enough, perhaps, the backcountry, besides offering infinite tourist possibilities, presents a most serious marginal land problem. Since the decay of the lumbering industry social conditions in backwoods Ontario have been shocking. The problem of settlers on marginal lands, however, is one which the depression-quickened consciences of Governments everywhere are facing, and surely the same will be the case with the new and enlightened Government of Ontario. Mitchell Hepburn and his Minister of Lands and Forests have a ready-made solution to hand. Ontario is the one State or Province in which marginal land can be made to pay immediate dividends. Its future lies not in timber, but in tourists.

Most Ontarians are either indifferent to the value of the waste lands or take for granted that tourists will flock and keep on flocking with no greater incentive than sporadic advertising campaigns in United States magazines. There seems to be a strongly held belief that as water flows down hill so will tourists flow to Ontario. Observing the concerted efforts of a dozen States to attract the same business, one doubts the validity of this belief.

Another popular fantasy, widely held except by persons of Mr. Miner's experience and knowledge, concerns the abundance of Ontario's wild life. It would surprise many people to learn that one can find more wild life with an hour and a half's journey from New York City than in most parts of Ontario backcountry, except Algonquin Park. Last week I had better small-mouth black bass fishing in a New Jersey lake an hour from New York by train than I have had in my own lake in Frontenac County for the past ten years. I have watched with amazement men fishing for brook trout from the bridge where United States Highway No. 1 crosses the Raritan River, less than thirty miles from the Empire State Building. Unlike the famous fishers of the Loire, these men were catching trout.

An hour's journey further west across the Delaware in Pennsylvania one can find State game preserves where deer are so plentiful as to have become an actual nuisance. The same holds true of various parts of New York, New Jersey and Pennsylvania. Making every allowance for the greater wealth of those States, their progress in the preservation of the wilderness is nevertheless a generation ahead of Ontario, and if the Province seriously hopes to realize on the value of her "lakeland paradise" she must first learn that this tourist business is highly competitive and that the time has come for something to be done about it.

Another interesting and relative point:— a few years ago the New England Tourist Association — made up of Government bureaus in Vermont, New Hampshire, Massachusetts and Maine, made a survey to determine what actually attracted visitors within their borders. Every conceivable source of information was studied. Thousands of questionnaires were sent out. The results were compiled to serve as the basis for an extensive advertising campaign. What was the answer most often received? Scenery, golf, cool nights, sea bathing, good roads, mountain-climbing? None of them. A majority of the answers to the question "What brought you to New England?" ran something like this: "We had always heard that New England had a reputation for good food."

The answer is so simple and obvious that one blushes not to have guessed it, but it is nevertheless worth remembering during any preparations for better roads, bigger fish, wilder game, and greener golf courses. The most important thing about a hotel, winter or summer, is its kitchen, and most of those in Ontario, heaven help us, are terrible.

Merrill Denison
New York City

Playwright, raconteur, journalist, broadcaster, historian, summer resort owner (Bon Echo, Ontario), and conservationist, Merrill

Denison was the author of several plays, notably Brothers In Arms, a one-act play written on a Danish-pastry bag, which is believed to be the most produced play ever in North America. He also took credit for coining the phrase "the Canadian identity crisis."

Music in a Stove

November 26, 1934

I was greatly interested in an item about hearing a radio program on a stove. In Brantford a few years ago an open stove with a long pipe, in a cottage, caught music and voices. It was faint, but unmistakably a radio program. It faded when the fire grew hot, as in the Aylmer case.

I spoke to a local radio man, who came to connect my radio later. He thought it was just imagination, I guess. The house was a corner house; the pipe was long and against an outer wall. The stove was an open-faced coal stove, an old-fashioned type. The music was quite clear, but the voices indistinct. It seemed to disappear after the stove and pipe got sooty. I wondered then and I wonder still.

(Mrs.) R. Chandler
Woodstock

Radio Reception

January 8, 1935

My old radio failed to function for some reason, possibly worn out, so I at great sacrifice bought another, hoping to get some return for the $2 license.

Did I get it? Sure. My brand new Canadian-made radio got, I should think, everything but the splendid efforts the Canadian Radio Commission and Canadian stations were broadcasting.

On Saturday night I thought I would like to listen to the hockey game that the General Motors Corporation so generously pays to have broadcast. Did I get the same? As yet I am uncertain. Perhaps some radio fan will be able to tell me.

This is what came via CRCT (CFRB – nil):

Sixteen and one-half minutes; no score –
And her arms around me –
Thousands suffering from stomach trouble –
A lady sings –

Intercepted by Cook –
Cook and Jackson shoving each other's chins –
Look for message of relief; WWL –
Droning banjo. Dear old daddy –
Charley Conacher gets it –
Thirteen seconds to go –
When the violets bloom again –
Fost Hewitt shouts "No score!" –
Second period: Same or almost as crazy as first –
Third period: A grand battle between Foster Hewitt and
somebody yodelling –
Foster Hewitt a bad second.

Now, I am not criticizing the CRCT programs, as I have never
heard one complete – only snatches. They sound like a Canadian
Commission cocktail – a little of everything well shaken. If I buy a
Chevrolet car, I will certainly expect to get better results than the
G.M.C. are getting for their money. But that is their affair.

Say, who arranged those wavelengths and positions? Eddie
Cantor or Amos 'n' Andy? They must be failing as joke-makers.

A.C. Sawyer
Port Burwell

Was the Pied Piper "Pied"?

February 9, 1935

Your editorial on Thursday on the dissimilarity of English pronun-
ciations all around the world brings forward once more the necessity of reforming our spelling so that it may "look something like"
what we wish to say. You quote Dr. Edward Ford of Oxford
University on the little Cockney girl who thought the "Pied Piper"
was so called because he was "pied" (paid) to chase the rats out of
Hamelin. It is, of course, an old claim of Londoners that their
pronunciation is but a retention of what in Shakespeare's day was
the fashionable English, and a well-known passage in Act 3 of
"Romeo and Juliet" seems to support the claim.

We could easily reform our written signs for spoken sounds,
that is, our alphabetic letters, so that anyone might write down the
exact sounds. It stands to reason that the best models would soon be
copied in the writing and speech of all – accomplishing, probably,
what Dr. Ford desires.

Anyone can see that the words "pied piper" may today be properly written for their true sound just as well in the following ways as that which we call "correct":

Sound	Spelling
by	pyd pyper
buy	puyd puyper
guide	puid puiper
eye	peyed peyeper
I	pid piper
height	peid peiper
sign	pigd pigper
pine	pide piper
choir	poid poiper
island	pisd pisper
aisle	paisd paisper
aye(yes)	payd payper
aye(yes)	payed Payeper

The number of ways in which these spellings can be combined, as pide poiper or peid pyper, runs into several hundreds – giving hundreds of chances of misspelling. Yet this is only one instance of over 20,000 words difficult to spell in our present senseless system (which itself would be better written "sensles sistem"). By a simple reform of the alphabet, making only a net addition of three letters to the present 26, all English words without exception could be phonetically spelt and two years' waste of non-educative work at school for every boy and girl could be avoided. Multiply the saving by 150 million, the number of people who speak English, and you get its value in cash and moral.

Ernest B. Roberts
Toronto

P.S.: And I am not "pied" for this bit toward reform!

The Panhandler

July 18, 1935

Yesterday while I was out to lunch a young man of about 20 came to my office and asked for Mr. LePage, stating that he had a letter which he had to deliver to him personally and get an answer. My secretary told him that I would be back in about an hour. Shortly after I returned to the office my secretary brought in a letter, beautifully written, stating that the bearer had come from Sault Ste. Marie and had been trying to get work all the way from there to Toronto without success, and would I give him a job polishing windows, washing the car, etc., etc. The postscript stated that he had not had anything to eat for two days, as he had exhausted his time for eating at the welfare hostels.

I immediately went to the outer office, with the intention of helping the poor fellow along, but when I saw the man, a heavily built, muscular sort of chap, I was satisfied in my own mind that he had never written the letter, so I asked him if he was prepared to do farm work. He stated that he would be delighted to get a chance, and I therefore telephoned the Employment Service of Canada about it and told them that the man had had nothing to eat. They replied that if I would send him over with a letter they would feed him and have him on the way to a farm with steady employment.

I gave the man a letter and promised him a good meal on his arrival at the Employment Office. I was going to give him some money to speed him on his way, but the Employment Agency warned me not to do so, and he left, as I thought, to get his job.

A few minutes later my secretary happened to be passing one of the offices on our floor and noticed this man going in, and she immediately telephoned the switchboard operator of that office to warn her employer that this was another "racket." It was too late; the employer had already given the man money, but he was so incensed he made a tour of the building. He found him on the next floor down coming out of one of the other offices where he had made a "touch" and he had him escorted from the building.

This is a "new one" on me, and I am passing it along so that your readers may reserve their funds for worthy institutions which will look after deserving cases. The Employment Agency informed me that the man did not turn up for his meal and job.

A.E. LePage
Toronto

Canadian Cats

February 21, 1936

I, too, must voice my protest at the ignorance of a London newspaper, as displayed in the Halifax Herald's quotation from the London Daily Telegraph, regarding the custom of snowshoes for cats in Canada.

I thought that in this enlightened day everyone knew that while country cats are equipped with snowshoes, those in the city, where the streets are covered with ice, are provided with miniature skates.

It is such glaring inaccuracies as this that give offense to a high-spirited nation and weaken the bonds of Empire.

H.M.C.
Toronto

Blame It on Pluto

December 14, 1936

As a Frenchman, I want to make no comment on the British constitutional crisis; but, as an astrologer, I want to draw your attention to the mundane planetary aspects and influences at the time of the late King Edward's abdication from the British Throne, which took place at 10:42 a.m., Toronto time.

The moon was in direct opposition to Uranus twelve hours before the abdication, which indicates that exceedingly careful thought was necessary before any action or move. Three hours later, Venus was in direct opposition to Pluto, which indicates that no recourse or return could be expected if separations between him and his people were forced, also that the person and his possessions were in danger. Twelve hours later, or three hours after his abdication, the sun was parallel to Pluto, which indicates the gross removed, followed by purification and true worth, and this is an aspect through which falseness is defeated. Nine hours later the sun is square to Neptune, an aspect which can bring about criminal acts, dishonor, loss and extreme foolishness.

These very bad influences, coming as they did, all within twelve hours of his abdication, indicate the continuity of drama in the personal affairs of the late King.

It is your privilege to publish these horoscopic aspects and their indications if you so desire.

Fernand de Kuyper, Astrologist
Toronto

Cocktail Research

February 19, 1937

I notice in a recent news item in The Globe and Mail that a search is being made for the grave of the inventor of cocktails. The assumption is that this "invention" occurred during the American Revolution, but it dates as far back as Solomon.

This quotation, Proverbs 23:29-30, would make a very appropriate inscription for the proposed memorial: "Who hath woe? Who hath sorrow? Who hath contentions? Who hath babbling? Who hath wounds without cause? Who hath redness of eyes? They that tarry long at the wine; they that go to seek mixed wine."

Verses 31 to 35, included, if added, would make the effects of the invention quite clear, even to cocktail drinkers.

A.B.C.
Peterborough

Grasshoppers and Frogs

August 2, 1937

Several days ago Mr. John Armstrong, of Orono, Ont., wrote his friend, Mr. Albert Twiss, at Regina, Sask., saying that he understood that Saskatchewan had solved the grasshopper problem by starving them out, but that they still had bullfrogs seven years old that had never learned to swim.

A letter just received from Mr. Twiss of Regina, Sask., says: –

"You are right about the grasshoppers, but since receiving your letter we have had a two-hour rain and have taught the bullfrogs how to swim, but their throats are so full of dust they can't croak yet."

J.E. Armstrong
Orono, Ontario

A Cow Worth a Fortune

March 3, 1938

For over twenty years I have been a silent reader of your valuable paper, but a news item appearing on the fourth page of Monday's issue constrains me to voice my feelings. A young Brantford woman is quoted as saying: "Anybody ought to know that a cow gets up on its front feet first. I was on the farm for seven years, and it wasn't just for the view and the fresh air."

Now if this young lady's cows got up on their front feet first during those seven years, she has a fortune in them if she would only put them in a side show; every farmer in the country would give a good round sum to see them put on their act, as such a thing has never before been seen or heard of. As for the seven years which wasn't spent "for the view and the fresh air," one can't help wondering then just what it was for, unless, of course – well, there are some very handsome and romantic young swains on our back concessions.

Chas. A. Miller
Simcoe, Ontario

Mrs. 'Arris on Germs

May 27, 1938

I says to Mr. 'Arris, shame on that Mr. McInnes – the idea of him awritin to the paper acomplainin of havin no covers on the garbage wagons. This is a free country, I says, and I says I hopes they won't pass no silly laws preventin us busy housewifes shakin our dust mops outer winders or throwin our sweepins into the street, and I says I think it would be a blinkin shame if they stops the merchants from sweepin the muck and spit from the stores onto the sidewalk every mornin. Anyways, the white wings would lose their bloomin job if there warn't any dust and 'orses. It blows off the wagon again, says you. More work for the garbage man, I says – and there ye are.

Leastways, them Junior Leagers and sich are too busy buildin them sanatoriums for lungers and gettin campaigns to kill flies that feed on the dump to bother with a little filth and dust on the street, and them politicians has all their time taken up buildin airyplanes & bombs and all to fuss with a few germs. Never did believe in germs anyways – bosh, I says. Guess I know – me mother of nine children and buried six.

This leaves me well, Mr. McInnes, and I hopes you are the same.

Mrs. 'Arris

The Mighty Turtle

June 30, 1939

The article on Page 4 of today's Globe and Mail entitled "Turtle's Snap Survives Soup" is interesting and can well be true. I was in Florida in 1911, and witnessed a similar occurrence. Accompanied by a Mr. Stewart of Panama, Canal Zone, I was fishing near Old Fort Marion, Saint Augustine, and I caught a good-sized turtle. We pulled the boat over to the dock and Stewart chopped the head off the turtle with an axe and threw it on the dock. We then cut up the body of the turtle and filled a large pail with chunks of the meat. Two hours later Stewart took the large butcher knife with which we had cut the turtle and walked over to where the head was lying exposed to the hot sun. He tapped the severed head with the blade of the knife when the jaws opened and grabbed the knife from his hand. The knife-blade was broken in two near the handle as if it had been made of glass.

It is a fact that the head of a turtle after being severed from the body can control the working of the jaws for several hours. Your correspondent did not overstate the case.

John S. Marshall
Hamilton, Ont.

◆

July 5, 1939

There's more to this turtle business than you'd believe. When I had my farm at Cedar Springs I caught one of those Erleau snappers – in transit across my bean field. Old Pete Cramm, the village butcher, told me they were as good as terrapin, but explained they should be beheaded and hung up to bleed overnight. I beheaded him, by having my better-half poke his nose with a stick, on which he promptly clamped his jaws. This allowed the head to be pulled well out of the shell, so that when I brought down my trusty axe I not only took off the head but about three inches of neck. Then, with a piece of fence wire I hung my headless mossback up by the tail, where he bled overnight and left a small pool of dark-colored blood on the ground. The next morning I untied him and lowered him to the ground. To my surprise, he started walking away. In fact, there was still enough life in him to keep on walking, even when I stood on his back. When I placed him, inverted, in my lye-cauldron, I assumed that without a head and, ergo, without a brain, which is reputed to be the seat of sensation, there would be no cruelty in covering him with boiling water, to follow Pete's instructions about removing the meat from the shell. But that turtle, headless for fifteen hours, threshed and kicked like a party favorite put out of a political job. Even when I was cutting him up there were what looked like kicks of protest from his decimated members…. He made grand soup, which, when cold, jellied stiff. When I explained the circumstances to my scientific neighbor, Dr. George McKeough, he merely smiled sadly and said: "And I suppose, Arthur, as you boiled those pieces of turtle meat you had to stand by with a stick and knock them back in the pot as they clambered out!" In other words, no one would believe my turtle story. So it's a belated relief to me to find other voices attesting to the life-tenacity of this odd reptile.

Arthur Stringer
Mountain Lake, N.J.

> *Arthur John Stringer, born in Chatham, Ontario, wrote the Perils of Pauline melodramas, and was married to Jobyna Howland, the original Gibson Girl. The author of eleven novels of crime and spy fiction, he is believed to have come up with the longest title in the genre: "The Man Who Couldn't Sleep: Being a Relation of the Divers Strange Adventures Which Befell One Witter Kerfoot When, Sorely Troubled with Sleeplessness, He Ventured Forth at Midnight Along the Highways and Byways of Manhattan."*

Perhaps He's Bluffing

August 31, 1939

The sporting world would like to be informed as to where Adolf Hitler learned to play poker. He might, if he would, be able to give us some pointers on the technique of the game.

William T. James
Toronto

> *Meanwhile, that same day, on the border between Poland and Germany ...*

Chapter 8

The Cross on the Moon

October 25, 1939

On the night of Oct. 4, 1939, my sister, Mrs. W.A. Fell, who owns and operates Felpark Lodge at Long Beach, Sturgeon Lake, saw a cross on the moon about 11 p.m. quite distinctly. It was visible for several minutes. When she told me about it I thought it quite unusual, and decided to write to your paper about it. Others may have seen it also. I would be pleased to see an account of this in your very valuable paper, which I receive each morning.

W. Ellis
Omemee, Ontario

◆

November 6, 1939

I was somewhat amused to see a letter in your columns a short time ago from one of your correspondents mentioning having seen a cross on the moon. I fully expected someone else to reply to this but have not seen any comment on it.

Your correspondent can be of good cheer, the world is not coming to an end. Any time she wants to see a cross on the moon again, tell her to pick a nice moonlight night and look through an ordinary window screen and the cross will appear.

F. Kent Hamilton
Hamilton, Ontario

◆

November 10, 1939

I have just noticed a letter to your paper concerning a cross on the moon seen by Mrs. W.A. Fell, Long Beach, Sturgeon Lake, Ont.

For some time my husband has noticed the moon a peculiar shape at times. On Monday, Oct. 19, we were visiting in Trenton, Ont. My friend (Mrs. S. Woodward) and I also remarked on the queer shape of the moon. It was in the first quarter at that time. We are anxious to know if this is anything uncommon and will watch The Globe and Mail for reply.

Mrs. Thos. O'Neill
Ottawa

◆

November 10, 1939

In reply to W. Ellis of Omemee, Ontario, regarding the cross on the moon on Oct. 4 at 11 p.m., the cross can be seen any night when the moon is bright, provided you are looking at it through a screen door or window screen. Try looking first through the screen and then through the glass or open door, when the cross disappears.

Harry Windows
Toronto

◆

November 16, 1939

Reading about the cross on the moon in recent issues of your paper recalled to my mind that in the year 1917, while stationed at St. Peter's Mission, Lesser Slave Lake, Alberta, we saw for two nights in succession the moon on a cross. A reflection of light, probably about a foot wide to our eyes, in the form of a gigantic cross, with a full moon in the centre where the beams meet; and strangely enough the lower part or foot was as if broken unevenly at the extreme end. The mission staff all witnessed this phenomenon without window or screens between them, and the brilliant sky of a Northland winter's night.

M. Levason

◆

November 17, 1939

Regarding the interesting letters you have published about the recent distortion of the moon, may I be permitted to add a queer experience of my own?

Last week my girl friend and I were returning from a party and we distinctly saw a double moon; one seemed to slide rapidly toward the western horizon, while the other slid toward the east, though not as fast as the western refraction.

This phenomenon is undoubtedly due to refraction, though it gave us quite a turn at the time.

Laurence Hyde

◆

November 23, 1939

As your correspondent Mr. Hyde testifies, a friend and I also saw a double moon on Wednesday night last week and, as he says, the west one moved rapidly out of sight toward the horizon, while the other moved slowly toward the east. During all this time a peculiar ruddy glow seemed to light up the heavens until both moons disappeared.

My friend has been very unwell since that time and will not venture out after sundown.

Do any of your readers understand this phenomenon?

A. Graham
Toronto

◆

November 24, 1939

Noticing in your estimable paper the experiences that certain people have had with the moon, I should like to tell you of one of my own.

Three years ago coming home from a late New Year's Eve party I saw eight moons dancing in front of me. Some were full moons, and others at the last quarter. The peculiar thing about it all was the moons insisted on keeping in front of me.

Perhaps someone can offer an explanation for this peculiar phenomenon, but I do not believe it was due to light refraction.

Moonie

◆

November 29, 1939

I notice in your very interesting column a letter signed by one "Moonie." He (or she) says that he – or she – does not believe that the peculiar phenomenon observed last New Year's Eve by him (or her) was due to refracted light. Now, I have never had personal experience of such manifestations, but several friends have, very kindly, described to me in detail divers very interesting unnatural phenomena, which they separately have observed. Judging, then, by hearsay, I should indeed think that "Moonie's" eight dancing moons must have been in some manner due to refracted moonshine.

I wonder if I could take time to relate a most amazing disturbance on the face of the moon observed by a friend one beautiful moonlight night? He says he was lying on a hilltop, his mind in a sort of vacant state, you know, and he says he was just lying there looking at the moon and thinking how funny it looked. He says he could see the man in the moon very plainly. All of a sudden, he says, he saw a hand as well. He says he has never seen such a perfectly executed gesture. (Shanghai, isn't it?) He says he got up and went home immediately, and he has worn blinkers ever since!

Can anyone explain that?

Amateur Astrologist

♦

December 1, 1939

Reading the letters which have been appearing in your paper with regard to the moon brings to mind a phenomenon which was observed by the writer last summer. I am a surveyor and we were camping on the shores of Red Lake. One evening I noticed that the moon presented a strange appearance: it seemed to be square, and not round as it should be. I brought this to the attention of other members of the party, who were of the same opinion. I then set up the transit and observed the moon through the telescope. The round portion could now be seen, but what before had seemed to be the corners appeared as flames, which were shooting in and out. On the following evening we again noticed the same condition, except that this time only three corners were visible, the moon appearing like a triangle. Since the weather was cloudy for the week following I do not know if any further changes took place, and when it was again clear, the moon had assumed its normal appearance.

While this occurrence was probably due to some disturbance on the sun reflected upon the moon, I recount it at this time in case any of your readers should be interested in the event.

E.D. Sewell
Toronto

December 4, 1939

I have read with interest several letters in your columns on the subject of moon phenomena, and would like to make the suggestion to your correspondents that they should read a few paragraphs of the great French airman's book, "Wind, Sand And Stars," as conducive, perhaps, to a steadying effect if they at any time again feel inclined to muse cosmically, or comically, thus. The author, Antoine de Saint-Exupéry, tells us how once he had "slipped beyond the confines of this world" and was lost among the planets, but on this occasion he merely describes the moon as a "pallid ember" (and I suppose we may assume that he is a good enough authority, having been nearer to it than most people).

Apparently, too, when thus lost and setting their course with "dogged hope," as he says, for each step in turn (supposing them to be beacon lights), their tired eyes began seeing things, "errant signs, delusive fantasies, phantoms." However, not once does he mention getting a friendly smile, an encouraging nod or beckoning gesture from the Man in the Moon.

Edith Willock Smith
Toronto

◆

December 11, 1939

Several correspondents have recorded some curious physical appearances of the moon, and Mr. E.D. Sewell's contribution is noteworthy as regards its exact detail, as to the appearance of flames shooting in and out upon its surface.

This latest phenomenon has been previously noted and recorded by Charles Fort in his book "New Lands," with much other factual data that discounts the popular idea that the moon is only a reflector.

A moment's thought will surely show that a sphere would indeed be a curious shape for a reflector, and one I doubt any expert on illumination would choose, since it would only reflect from one small spot upon its surface.

The moon has been termed by theoretical astronomers as "the most troublesome body in the solar system" on account of its "erratic behavior," and its refusal "to strictly obey the Newtonian laws of gravitation." Now and again we find solemn columns in newspapers headed: "What is the Matter With the Moon?" "Moon

Off its Course," "Moon Ahead of Time," and so forth. There are many instances on record, one as recent as November, 1938, where the moon was fully eclipsed before the sun set, both orbs being above observers' horizon, disproving the "all three in a line" theory.

The moon is termed in the Scriptures as "a faithful witness in heaven," and if it witnesses to anything at all it is to the folly of the Copernican theory of the universe. For the Scriptures further testify that God made two great lights, the greater light to rule the day, and the lesser light to rule the night, and "it was so."

The moon is an independent luminary; its rays quite different from sunlight. Certain flowers only bloom in moonlight. In Deuteronomy 33:14 the distinction is clearly drawn: "And for the precious fruits brought forth by the sun. And for the precious things put forth by the moon."

What a commentary on our times it is to have this wholesale rejection of the cosmogony of Genesis, and in its place a theory whose roots lie in the speculations of a heathen philosopher named Pythagoras, who flourished around 500 B.C.

The fruit is seen in such Godless systems as fascism, nazism and communism; whether we realize it or not, these anti-God ideologies are the final outcome of men's rejection of God's truth.

A.S.C. Tebbit
Wellandport, Ontario

Chapter 9

Facing Life's Problems

November 8, 1939

Attention is being focused on the number of parents wheeling baby carriages with the occupants facing the back on the different streets in the city. When one considers that the child is born with an inferiority complex, necessitating the rigid attention of the parents to assist in natural development to overcome this factor, one cannot understand why the child should be handicapped through ignorance in receiving vital mental training necessary in building a strong member of the nation.

Observation discloses unceasing efforts of the child by constant squirming of the head to see beyond the body obstructing the view and absorb life through vision.

The most serious aspect is that the child is running away from actual contact, thus extending the power of inferiority, instead of, as nature intended, that it should meet life's battles bravely, with spirit and strength. The question arises: Why does the parent not walk backwards?" Yet this is simple logic on the part of the child, who also demands to know why the good Lord did not put eyes in the back of the head.

There is such a marked difference in the faces of children who are wheeled properly. They show intelligence, eagerness and activity to face the problems of life with courage, pride and fight to overcome fear in the battles of childhood, youth and citizen. It is pitiful to watch the kiddies, especially the boys, who rush crying to their mothers with their tales of woe when they should stand up and take their medicine or give the victor's blow.

Dad Gawain
Toronto

Lord Macmillan Explains
November 28, 1939

A Canadian friend of mine has sent me a cutting from your issue of, I think, 19th October, containing an article by Miss Judith

Robinson, in which some well-deserved animadversions are made on the captions of certain photographs which reached your office and which used the word "colonial" with reference to the Dominions. The animadversions were, as I say, well deserved, but they were not deserved by this Ministry! And with my many and intimate associations with Canada, I should be much distressed if they were.

I have made careful inquiry and I find, as I should have expected, that no such caption as Miss Robinson pillories was ever placed on a photograph in this Ministry. The responsibility must rest with the agency handling the photograph, over which we have no control.

It is quite possible that the attribution of the "gaffe" to this Ministry may be due to the fact that postal packets submitted to and passed by the Censorship Department, formerly, but no longer, under my charge, were stamped with the words "Ministry of Information." This of course did not mean approval of their contents by the Ministry, but merely that they did not contain matter offending against the Censorship Rules.

I am sure you will be glad to have this explanation and to accept my personal assurance that the Ministry of Information is sufficiently well informed not to refer to the Dominions as "colonial."

Macmillan
London

Lord Macmillan of Aberfeldy was chairman of the Royal Commission on Canadian Banking in 1933.

How the Red Man Was Born

April 30, 1940

According to Indian mythology, it seems that after Great Spirit had created the hills and mountains, the streams, rivers and lakes, flowers, herbs and trees, the animals and birds, and all other living and growing things, He sought to fashion human beings worthy to enjoy such peaceful grandeur.

So it came to pass that He shaped clay with His creative hands and baked it in His great campfire. When He drew it forth it was pale and covered with small brown spots. It had not baked enough. Thus came the first white man.

Then He modelled another form. This one He buried deep in the hot ashes. When He drew it out it was blackened and much too crisp, so He tossed it to one side. Thus came the first black man.

Once more the Great One modelled another form and placed it on the sacred fire, and he put sticks of poplar and wood around it. When He removed it from the fire it was shrivelled and tainted with yellow. Thus came the first yellow man.

The Great Manitou modelled yet another figure, even more carefully than before, packed red hot coals around it, and covered it with red cedar. Lo, when He lifted it from the fire it was of a reddish hue, and it was very sound and perfect in every way. Indeed, it was beautiful and good. He placed this new creation upon the shore of the most bountiful of all lands, and it lived and moved about in the mighty hunting grounds of the plains and forests. Rapidly it multiplied its kind, and it became the happy and care-free tenant of the Great Spirit's own beautiful garden ... Thus was born the child of nature – the Red man! I have spoken.

Big White Owl
Toronto

Big White Owl (Jasper Hill) was chief of the Six Nations of Brantford.

The Ways of a Censor

July 9, 1940

Wishing to send birthday greetings to our son (at school in England) my wife and I this morning addressed the following cable:

"All the best birthday wishes from us both. God bless you – Mum and Dad."

This was returned by the telegraph company which reported that the censor refused to pass a cable not signed with the sender's surname – which appeared, of course, on the telegraph form below the message.

Since a cable of this kind, signed as a business letter, would look simply silly to the recipient, I tried to get in touch by telephone with the local censorship officer – to see whether, in such an obviously personal message, involving no question of good faith, the rule was capable of relaxation.

Somewhat to my surprise I was informed that this official refused to speak to any member of the public.

Wishing to suggest to the proper authorities in Ottawa that this is an imperfectly correct attitude on the part of a civil servant (and because I did not remember at the moment under which Government department the censor functions), I then asked if I might at least be told the name of the ministry concerned. (It is, of course, the department of the Secretary of State.)

I was told that the censor refused not only to speak to me, but also to name the minister to whom he was responsible.

It is within the knowledge of your readers that several news items have recently been passed by the censorship, the publication of which might well have endangered Canadian troops. I do not particularize here, since even to name such stories might be to give "comfort to the enemy."

Thus, the censor's protection is not always adequate in matters of life and death. But in such a trivial affair as this, which I venture to bring now to your attention, his alertness is admirable – and equalled only by his arrogance.

The civil servant who refuses even to name the minister of the Crown under whom he holds his appointment is a biological specimen hitherto not known in Canada.

He blandly puts himself above the law.

We have watched for seven years past the process of gleichhaltung as applied (and with singular success) in another country by the Nazis. On the question whether gleichhaltung is similarly suited to Canadians, the censor may have his own opinion; I write in the hope that this kind of thing is still capable of correction by the responsible government authorities.

Gilbert E. Jackson
Toronto

Beer and Music

November 20, 1940

The Fourth Column chides Mr. Arnold Smith, Assistant Commissioner of the Liquor Control Board, over a regulation prohibiting singing in beverage rooms. This infringement of personal liberty is solely a musical protection found necessary because imbibers progressively sing off key. After four beers tuning forks are impotent and after six rounds each vocalist keeps time to a different drummer. When alcohol reaches the brain the auditory nerve is numbed and a metronome is inaudible. The optic nerve is also partially paralyzed, the eyes can no longer be focussed and a music score is as unsingable as a sticker fly pad. At 9 o'clock p.m. part singing may still be possible, but by 11 the early evening glee club is a "mixed chorus." When speech becomes thick, song is even thicker. No conservatory of music would select beverage rooms as first choice for the location of extension classes. Were beer a certain aid to choral skill the Mendelssohn Choir would be served schooners between numbers. Mr. Smith is radical but right; let the shoemakers stick to their lasts, the haymakers to their alfalfa.

George A. Little
Toronto

Why We Go to Church

February 1, 1941

We are having an interesting discussion on "Why We Don't Go To Church." I think it would be equally interesting to know why we do go to church. Perhaps some of your readers can enlarge upon the following reasons:

We have new clothes, or ones we keep for Sunday use, so we go to church to show them off.

Our parents and grandparents went to church, therefore we must go, too.

We stay in the house most of the week. It is nice to have somewhere to go, especially to see our friends and notice what they are wearing and whom they are with. It gives us something to talk about.

We are not afraid to go to church.

We like the minister.

The minister preaches a good sermon.

If the minister preaches from the Bible, and we concentrate hard, we can forget the troubled world.

It is a good place to sleep.

We take some active part in church work.

We love the music.

We have to drive the family to church, so we might as well go in.

The church in general is a good subject for criticism during the week.

We have to set a good example.

We belong to an organization that is attending church in a body.

We feel very religious for one hour every week.

We haven't a radio.

There is a church just around the corner.

The weather is bad. It will keep a good many people away. We must help to fill the pews.

It is a good idea from a business point of view.

We are deeply religious.

Churches are beautiful; therefore it makes us think beautiful thoughts.

We feel nearer to God.

We feel in need of spiritual advice.

We feel uplifted, we are given added strength and courage to go about our daily work.

The last four reasons are the better ones, but would you believe there could be so many? It is a revelation to the writer.

Dorothy Howard-Buckingham
Paris, Ontario

Gray's Elegy Dated

February 17, 1942

My reading informs me that Thomas Gray began his deathless poem, "Elegy Written in a Country Churchyard," in 1742, which means that it has its 200th birthday this year. On completion of the poem Gray gave it in manuscript to his friend, Horace Walpole, who showed it to many of his friends.

The poem as originally written was much revised by Gray in subsequent years. It is said that Gray wrote his "Elegy" in the precincts of the church of Granchester, about two miles from Cambridge. A contemporary poet said that Gray was probably the most learned man in Europe.

Because the "Elegy" is even today a widely memorized poem I have felt that many of your readers will be interested to learn that it was begun, if not completed, in 1742.

John C. Kirkwood
Toronto

◆

March 10, 1942

In regard to the recent interesting letter of Mr. Kirkwood appearing in your paper drawing attention to the 200th anniversary of the "Elegy" this year, I might mention that the poet revised it in 1750, a facsimile of which is in my possession headed "Elegy Written in a Country Churchyard, 1750." These changes, though slight, improved, if anything, the harmony, but the main change was the rejection by him of the three stanzas herewise:

Hark! How the sacred calm that breathes around
Bids every fierce, tumultuous passion cease;
In still, small accents whispering from the ground
A grateful earnest of eternal peace.

Him have we seen the greenwood side along,
While o'er the heath we hied, our labor done,
Oft as the woodlark piped her farewell song,
With wistful eyes pursue the setting sun.

There scattered oft, the earliest of the year,
By hands unseen, are showers of violets found;
The redbreast loves to build and warble there,
And little footsteps lightly print the ground.

The third, or "redbreast" stanza, as it is usually known, appears in the annex of some English editions, but I have never seen it in an American edition. The first two stanzas are becoming exceedingly rare.

I have a beautifully bound copy, folio size, original calf, of six poems by Mr T. Gray, and illustrated by Mr T. Bentley, dated 1753.

In regard to the first edition, note the following:

When Barton Currie, American editor and collector of rare books, paid $5,000 for a particularly fine copy of Gray's "Elegy," a first edition, published at six pence in 1751, his friends regarded him as a sort of amusing lunatic. Less than five years later he declined an offer of $10,000 for this same slim volume. "An Elegy Wrote in a Country Churchyard" is the way the title of the first edition reads. Very few of the original copies are known to exist.

Sigmund Samuel
Toronto

Though Sigmund Samuel (1867-1962) made his fortune in the sheet-metal business, he made his fame as a collector and philanthropist whose donations amounted to more than $2 million. Among his gifts were the Canadiana Gallery of the Royal Ontario Museum and the Sigmund Samuel Collection of the Group of Seven.

The Golden Mean

April 20, 1942

I have read with great interest and pleasure the article "Tobacco Deadly Foe, Says Gene Tunney," which appears in your issue of January 19.

Mr. Tunney, for whom we, in England, have the highest regard, is simply following the train of those who judge not fairly because they judge in haste. The fact, of course, is that with smoking and drinking and many other pleasant habits, vice lies in excess.

Nobody, for instance, defends the chain cigaret smoker. Perhaps, however, he might say, "Mind your own business," and as my business lies, among other things, in the selling of cigarets, I ask his forgiveness for citing him as a horrible, if profitable, example.

There is much to be said for Aristotle's maxim that virtue lies in the "Golden Mean."

Alfred H. Dunhill
London, England

Alfred H. Dunhill, chairman of Alfred Dunhill, Inc., was the son of the founder of the tobacco firm.

Go to the Barking Dog

April 21, 1942

Maybe it is no exaggeration to say that the resident of every town, hamlet and city in the country has at one time or another cursed the barking dogs that love to serenade mankind in the quiet watches of the night.

However, in our annoyance over the tortures inflicted by Fido and his friends, we should never forget that the bark of the dog is the finest example of pure tone that ever comes from a living body. It is the perfect model for mankind to imitate.

Great actors boast they can scream, shout or whisper after constant study of the dog's bark, and their voices will be distinctly heard by any one who hears the sound at all. This, they claim, is by forming their utterances in the mouth on the same plan used by dogs in barking, that is, by not allowing any breath to escape while speaking and dividing the words and phrases and sentences with sharp, clear enunciation in the mouth.

My old teacher in Toronto was Richard S. Lewis, author of the "Dominion Elocutionist," who taught us to read and recite by imitating the dog's barking in previous class exercises. Mr. Lewis himself was a splendid speaker and a great instructor.

I might add that husky voices, rasping and mumbling tones and voices that are cloudy and thick can be changed by practicing to imitate the clear tone of the dog's bark. Of course, there are many different tones in the voices of dogs, and it would be well to select the right breed.

When the radio was first introduced, the voices of announcers were at least slightly out of control, but now there is an army of announcers who have fine, clear enunciation. Maybe there are some still struggling for perfection who will not resent the aid of Fido.

R.A. Webster
Tucson, Arizona

Quebec and English Enterprise

May 29, 1942

Reading certain orations, one gets the impression that the enemies of Quebec are the English-Canadians. Not a word about the Nazis who are trying to put all free countries, including Quebec, under their brutal tyranny.

Speakers want Quebec to have a greater share of Government jobs; all except the dangerous ones of defending their jobs in wartime.

When it comes to minorities, how many English Protestants and Jews are there working for the City of Montreal, and how many for the Province of Quebec?

Just for a relief from all the grousing, how about an occasional tribute to English enterprise and ability which have contributed so much to the development of Quebec and given French-Canadians better jobs than any their own people had to offer? How many French companies give good jobs to the English-Canadians?

What Quebec needs is fewer agitators, less politics, and a vision of Canada which makes localities a mere speck on the map, a country where the genius and spiritual fervor of the French-Canadians will not be bottled up in one Province, but be a leavening force which will be an inspiration to the whole country.

A.Y. Jackson
Toronto

Alexander Young Jackson (1882-1974), a member of the Group of Seven, was born in Montreal. He served in the First World War as a private with the 60th Battalion, was wounded, and was then made a lieutenant with the Canadian War Records. After the war, he found himself with few personal resources. "All I got out of it," he said later, "was twenty tubes of white paint. It was probably this paint that was responsible for my becoming a snow painter as I had to find some use for it."

Major Murray

Gladstone Murray, a First World War hero, served at the BBC from 1923 to 1936, and was appointed first general manager of the CBC in 1936. In 1942, amid general criticism of lack of financial restraint, an outcry arose over his "exorbitant" monthly entertainment allowance, which averaged $205. During the inquiry by the House of Commons, his friends came to his defence, among them his old economics professor.

August 5, 1942

I want to congratulate you on your timely and admirable editorial on Major Gladstone Murray. I am sure that ever so many people will have read it with the same sympathy and agreement as I did.

I have known Major Murray for many years, over thirty years, ever since he was an undergraduate in my classes at McGill. I taught him economics, and if he has in any way fallen down in point of economics I must take part of the blame. But, with or without economics, Gladstone Murray made his mark at McGill as one of the most gifted and farsighted students we had in the forty years I had known the place. He made his mark and left it there, especially in the foundation of the McGill Daily, a famous journal now, but, as seen by most of us at its inception, a visionary impossibility. Nor has Gladstone Murray ever lost his connection with his university, remaining now an honored and helpful visitor to the college campus and the press room.

At McGill we all felt proud of his appointment to a Rhodes Scholarship, of his brilliant career at Oxford, and, still more, of his fine and patriotic service in the war. After the war I had special occasion to follow his rising fortune and to admire his singular ability in the world of journalism and radio. Our only regret – I speak for myself and for many others – was that it seemed as if Gladstone Murray's services were to be lost to Canada. Our satisfaction was therefore all the greater when circumstances changed and he came home, six years ago, to devote his talents to his own country.

I need not refer to the unfortunate difficulties of friction and jealousy, as between races and classes, that exist in Canada and against which all our public and patriotic men must struggle as best they can. Major Murray has had his share of them. If he has been too British in his sympathies I for one am all with him, but I am certain that at any rate he has never allowed such sympathy to lead him into unfair play.

But I have had very special opportunity to appreciate Gladstone

Murray's work here in one respect: that is, in the way in which he has been willing to seek out and encourage talent. His own bright intelligence invites a response from young people. When I was young, half a century ago, it was very hard for anyone without special political influence or money to break through and succeed on ability alone. Canadians were so absorbed in the question of the market for beef that they had little thought of the market for brains. As a result many young men of real talent spent weary years in routine occupations waiting and working.

Major Murray in his work here has been helping to change all that. Young people, beginners with something to give, Canadians with a talent to develop, have never knocked at his door in vain. Indeed they have found him on the threshold.

May I say that I think it would be a great loss to the intellectual development of Canada if any untoward circumstances discouraged Gladstone Murray from remaining in the service of the Canadian public.

Stephen Leacock
Orillia

Leacock's letter did little good. Gladstone Murray resigned as director-general of the CBC in November, 1942.

Stammering and Its Treatment

December 22, 1942

In an article on stammering which appeared in the press recently, I noticed that some misinformed person has again revived the fallacy that Demosthenes, the Greek orator, cured himself of stammering by placing a pebble under his tongue. Would I be given space in your valuable paper to correct this statement?

In the first place, Demosthenes did not stammer at all, but suffered from labored speech of a type known as bradyarthria. He corrected his defective breathing by pronouncing sentences while marching up hill, and he spent weeks reciting his orations within sound of the roaring of the sea, which he imagined as the roaring crowd in the Assembly. He even went so far as to shave his head, so that he would be forced to remain in his own cellar for months at a time, where he practiced before a tall mirror. He was not cured by putting a pebble under his tongue, but by so changing his mental attitude that he would not be disturbed by those situations which had caused him great fear in the past.

This man also stated that he could only remember having failed to cure three cases; and, of course, he blamed this failure on the pupils themselves. It is very regrettable that such statements are made. They tend to bring everyone connected with this work into disrepute. In the words of the President of the Society for the Study of Disorders of Speech, "it is only the quack who claims to have no failures." The practice of "the same treatment for all" simply means that all pupils are taught in class to drawl their voice or some other unnatural expedient.

It may be true that when the pupils leave the class of stammerers they "seldom fail" to use the drawl, but every year I come into contact with at least twenty boys and girls who find it impossible to put such methods into practice out in the world. Nevertheless, I don't wish to discourage any one who stammers; but in the interest of truth, I would like to state that no ethical school, medical doctor or speech clinic in the society claims to be able to correct over 85 per cent of those who are suffering from real stammering.

William Dennison
Toronto

William Dennison (1905-1981) was a Toronto alderman in 1942, and later mayor. His obituary in The Globe and Mail was headlined: "Stammering Farm Lad Became Mayor of Toronto."

Inside Fighting Canada

June 1, 1943

The Globe and Mail, in an editorial on "Objective Reporting," takes me to task for inaccuracy on "Inside Fighting Canada." It is a bright and interesting editorial. The charge with which the controversy started – that this was a motion picture of a "truly political character" – somehow got lost in the hullabaloo. It is all now, I am glad to note, a matter of accuracy in every particular.

This interest of Mr. Mitchell Hepburn and The Globe and Mail in accuracy will win wide and warm commendation. The first charge is that we are wrong in talking of the "hundreds of thousands of fliers" turned out by Canada. I might plead that our figure was intended to deceive the enemy, and that The Globe and Mail has spoiled a warlike manoeuvre by blurting out the truth. But my case is simpler. We made a mistake and will correct it.

Obviously we were thinking of the total number of air force personnel. In that case we would not have been so very far out; and even within these limitations a very fine record it is.

As for the second charge, there is supposed to be in the film some talk of Canadians as "people who make a national policy of voluntary service." The Globe and Mail can very properly take exception on the ground that this is a matter of controversy. It takes exception IN CAPS. I hope there are enough caps left, because I would like them for my reply, which is that this sentence is not in fact in the film. On accuracy the score is even.

So the shooting is over and the "take" consists of one flying pigeon that happened accidentally across the line of fire.

I shall make only this comment about accuracy in films. It is the same everlasting problem as in all newspapers. Where many hundreds of statements are made, errors will creep through. Newspapers will be the first to understand that, in the rush of production, it is bound to happen.

An errorless newspaper is a newsless newspaper, and I have never known the film that was not born with a couple of birthmarks. One newspaper, the old New York World, which was very proud of its scrupulous accuracy, ran a competition as to who could find the greatest number of errors in one particular edition. A friend of mine won hands down with 797. (Well, at any rate, it was hundreds.) To the great confusion of the New York World.

One day, when the war is over, I shall return The Globe and Mail's very great compliment to the National Film Board. I shall go through it with a fine-toothed comb.

John Grierson
Ottawa

John Grierson, founder of the National Film Board, coined the word "documentary" in 1926.

Unconditional Surrender

February 17, 1943

In an editorial of this morning's issue, The Globe and Mail refers to the expression "unconditional surrender," suggested, as the paper states, at the Casablanca Conference by President Roosevelt and fully concurred in by Prime Minister Churchill as the objective of the Allied offensive against the Axis powers. This phrase derives in American history from the period of the Civil War, 1861-65. It was employed by Gen. Grant, 81 years ago today (Feb. 16) at the siege by the Federal Army under his command, of Fort Donelson, a strong fortress of Southern defense on the Cumberland River. Following is the text of Grant's ultimatum to Gen. Buckner, the Confederate commander of the besieged garrison:

> Feb. 16, 1862
> Sir: Yours of this date proposing armistice and appointment of commissioners to settle terms of capitulation is just received. No terms except an unconditional and immediate surrender can be accepted. I propose to move immediately upon your works.
> U.S. Grant,
> Brig.-Gen.

The term "unconditional surrender" and the fall of the fortress, which immediately followed, electrified the North, dispirited as it had been by a long series of defeats and disappointments. In his memoirs, Gen. Grant narrates: "The news of the fall of Fort Donelson caused great delight all over the North. At the south, particularly in Richmond, the effect was correspondingly depressing."

The late Prof. Goldwin Smith, in his Political History of the United States, records that: "The capture by Grant of Fort Donelson on the Cumberland River, the great bastion of Confederate defense in the west, with a large garrison, was the first bright gleam of Federal victory; it, at the same time, revealed the commander whose tenacity had snatched success out of the jaws of defeat."

Harriet Beecher Stowe, in her sketch of Grant in her book Self-Made Men, states that the phrase ("unconditional surrender") has become "a permanent contribution to the proverbial part of the English language."

In view of the foregoing it is clear that the expression "unconditional surrender" has, as President Roosevelt well knows, a particularly strong traditional appeal to the American people. Gen U.S. Grant was often referred to colloquially, after his victory at Fort Donelson, as "Unconditional Surrender Grant."

W. T. White

> *The Rt. Hon. Sir Thomas White, G.C.M.G, C.B.E. (1866-1955), was Minister of Finance (1911-1919) and acting Prime Minister (1918-1919). It was under his ministry that Ottawa introduced income tax to Canada in July, 1917.*

Radio English

February 23, 1943

The fraternal relationship which has existed almost unbroken between the peoples of the north and south, respectively, of the 49th parallel since about 1814 is a matter of rejoicing to both sides of the line. But "I guess" (to borrow a phrase from the south) that each of our two countries wishes to retain forms of speech peculiar to itself.

The United States employs the good Biblical word "gotten" – long abandoned by the British peoples, who prefer the word "got"; a sort of verbal hammer-stroke. The word "diction" is used by our neighbors in a sense which I think threatens its continued employment by ourselves when we merely wish to signify the selection of words. In the United States it performs the additional functions of "enunciation" and "pronunciation."

Pronunciation south of the line shows a marked tendency to rob the letter "i" of its desirable force. For example, we hear on the radio the word "futile" pronounced "futle." If this is a growing menace it may bring about (through a regrettable standardization produced by the radio) a general pronunciation of the words ending in "ile" which would result in the construction of sentences in the literary output of the day having a quality of sound such as would occur in the following phrases:

Mungo Park, the explorer, on his travels through the host'le tribes of Africa, encountered monkeys having such remarkably prehens'le tails that juven'le members of the family were carried during the infant'le period of their existence wrapped to the body of their mother by this appendage. This rendered her less mob'le and more open to host'le attacks. In fact all effort to escape by flight were fut'le. The old or sen'le members of the tribe remained in their domic'les, took no part in the versat'le exercises of youth, and condemned themselves to a solitary life amounting to ex'le.

Sir Wyly Grier
Toronto

> *Sir Edmund Wyly Grier was past president of the Royal Canadian Academy, and a noted portrait painter; Sir John A. Macdonald once sat for him.*

Zoot Suiters

July 3, 1943

It is small wonder that there's so much rioting over the zoot-suiters. They are a clan of comic-page characters who are deliberately demoralizing our home-front efforts.

My dad and mother and sister and three brothers and I were walking down Colborne Street, Brantford, recently on our way home from a theatre when a car full of zoot-suiters made some sarcastic remarks about us.

They were boys whose ages ranged from 18 to about 25.

Dad is a returned soldier, and he was furious! He would have dragged them from the car one by one, only mother asked him not to make a scene.

Later, while we were waiting for the bus, we saw them driving around wasting gas, trying to pick up girls. When the girls ignored them they were called shameful names.

These young men of foreign ancestry are of army age – and yet they are not in it. And neither are they doing war-work like my dad and thousands of other loyal war-workers. But they are wasting material and gas for lack of which our boys are dying!

Eleanor Ann Rutledge
Brantford

Refugees and British Ideals

December 3, 1943

The Council of the Canadian Corps Association (in Ontario), through its secretary, Mr. O.T.G. Williamson, declared itself recently in The Globe and Mail columns as seeking "the preservation of British institutions" in this country by means of the exclusion from it of all European refugees, and specifically of those now in Portugal and Sweden.

There is here a slight confusion of terminology. The Corps Association may do something by this means to preserve in Canada the present proportion of persons of English, Scotch, Welsh, and Irish "racial origin," so far as that can be done without some increase in the birthrate among such persons. But it can do nothing by this means to preserve British institutions.

One of the greatest and most valuable of British institutions is that of the free admittance of refugees without regard to race or economic condition. It is an institution which used to exist in Canada, but has been abolished within the last generation or so by the efforts of those who share the views of the Corps Association, and who are by no means all of English, Scotch, or Irish "racial origin." It is an institution in virtue of which Great Britain has admitted since the Nazi tyranny began, and still shelters despite all the difficulties arising from proximity to the enemy, some 150,000 refugees.

The petition which the Corps Association opposes seeks the restoration of this ancient and valuable British institution in Canada, through the suspension, in favor of refugees only, of the regulations which prohibit entry because of racial or economic reasons.

The association desires to exclude from Canada "Central Europeans who have nothing to contribute to the support of British ideals." The present regulations, with which the association appears satisfied, operate chiefly to exclude those Central Europeans who have not a certain amount of money. The suggestion that people with little or no money must necessarily "have nothing to contribute to the support of British ideals" seems to put those ideals in an unattractive light. The truth is that it is extremely easy to assume that people whom we do not like "have nothing to contribute to the support of British ideals," especially if we ourselves are not wholly clear as to what those ideals are.

B.K. Sandwell
Toronto

> *Editor of Saturday Night magazine, and Rector of Queen's University.*

Speaking American

June 2, 1944

According to this morning's Globe and Mail, English children, on reaching home after being war guests of the United States for some years, startled their parents with their command of the American patois. This reminds me that on my meeting with Premier Clemenceau in Paris during the first Great War the old Tiger (he looked the part) greeted me with: "I do not speak English. I do not even speak American." This, of course, was only a pleasantry, as he had spent part of his early life as a working journalist in the United States.

F.D.L. Smith
Toronto

> *Frank D.L. Smith was the last editor of the Mail and Empire before it merged with The Globe in 1936.*

Good News

March 26, 1945

I guess the war must be going pretty well for our side. We have not been called on for a Day of Prayer for some time.

Beecher Parkhouse
Fergus

Wild Celebrations

May 4, 1945

When V-Day arrives, people who have lost dear ones during the years of human carnage in the first and second world wars generally speaking, do not want to listen to bombastic and spectacular speakers. Their greatest comfort will be quiet, with reverence and sympathetic understanding.

Sacred music, suitable old ballads, interwoven with dignified and sincere speakers – omitting commercials all through the day – would, I feel sure, be the wish of the majority, rather than "boogie-woogie" trash and the harsh, over-excited voices of commentators.

All beer rooms should be closed for 48 hours. For what is more degrading than to watch and listen to the objectionable behavior of drunken males and females? Such is not a feather in the cap of any Government with authority.

P.D. Robinson
Hamilton

Chapter 10

The Taste for Daily Papers

January 5, 1928

I have discussed the following phase of morning newspaper versus evening newspaper with a number of friends in an attempt to discover the psychology of newspaper reading. We all agreed that we place more confidence in the morning paper news and editorials than in those of the evening paper, and endeavored to find the reason.

My suggestions are as follows: (1) After a night's sleep and eight hours' cessation of the mental effort used in reading, we are keener for news and ideas in the morning, whereas by evening our reading desire has been more or less satisfied. This is analogous to a pipe-smoker who enjoys his morning after-breakfast smoke most because of his long abstention during his sleeping hours. (2) All proposed enterprises, as every one can vouch for, look more roseate in the evening than they do the next morning. The rosy hues of the night before give way to the more sombre and greyer hues of the morning after, and hence we take matters more seriously in the morning. Hence arises the common injunction: "You had better sleep on that before deciding." Are we more sober or less discriminating in the morning?

Accordingly some such explanation may account for the fact that we place more credence in what the morning paper gives in news and editorials. What we get from them resembles the soup, entree and meat courses of a dinner, while the dessert, raisins and nuts represent the news and editorials of the evening paper.

P.F. Munro
Toronto

◆

December 2, 1921

Just a few lines in regard to my father's wishes.

I was to write to you and tell you that he had read your paper for

41 years, and through his six months' sickness he enjoyed reading it as long as he could read, and then to have it read for him.

Likewise, I have read the paper for twenty years, ever since I was old enough to read. My father died on Nov. 17th, aged 77 years and 5 months.

Jacob Schwerdtfeger
Williamsburg, Ontario

◆

July 11, 1910

Your article this morning on objectionable city noises will be welcomed by many long-suffering citizens. Will you complete your good work by advocating for the suppression of the most objectionable noises of them all – viz., the unearthly and blood-curdling shrieks of the newsboys.

A Suffering Citizen
Toronto

◆

April 1, 1924

A good joke is going the rounds here today. Prohibitionists are being met with the remark that "The Globe has gone wet this morning." The mail sleigh coming from Spanish River to Gore Bay went through the ice and The Globes all got thoroughly soaked.

R.A. Smith
Gore Bay

◆

May 4, 1929

For your narrow, bigoted, religious opinions and editorials, and for your fanatical personal attacks on those you dislike, such as Mackenzie King and Sam McBride, I despise The Globe, and am frequently tempted to stop taking it, but for the sake of accurate news I enclose renewal cheque for six dollars.

S. Stuart Crouch
Toronto

February 11, 1930

Would you kindly tell me where this fellow William Randolph Hearst lives, who wants to buy goats. I have one for sale, and he can climb any mountain, no matter how rocky. He is white and pure; would do to lead the parade of Orangemen, or would be useful to any lodge that is without one for riding purposes. He chews up The Globe daily, but do not know what he would do to a yellow sheet. Price $50; but $5 cash would buy him.

Charles T. Palmer
Simcoe

◆

March 31, 1930

Recently there appeared a news item in your paper which stated that a new air mail service was about to be inaugurated, thus speeding delivery over our West. I presume only letter mail will be carried, and at a special rate. I wonder if the time will not come when The Globe will be borne speedily across the whole of Canada, thus impregnating its principles over a much wider horizon, and becoming in still greater degree a national paper. And I wonder if that wouldn't be a big factor in making for a more united Canada, and for a greater Empire.

Will Black
Grande Prairie, Alberta

◆

October 26, 1931

A few days after I cancelled my subscription a man purporting to be an agent of yours called on me and tried to bully me about it. I told him plainly why I would not pay for The Globe any further, and now I want to tell you why I plan to campaign against the Globe among the people of my churches.

It has long been obvious to me that you have a vicious animosity against the United Church. You are welcome to it, though I see no reason why I should help to pay to print it. My wife continued to take it for the Homemaker page, until she, too, complained that an unduly large amount of space there was taken up by letters slamming the United Church.

The egregious paragraph in yesterday's issue reporting the utterance of Some Regular Baptist half-wit is only an outstanding instance of the kind of thing you jump at and give a good place to. You don't really hurt the United Church, you know, by this kind of thing. You simply help these pitiable people to further demonstrate that Regular-Baptistism is an ebullition of religious ignorance and ill-breeding.

Your religious editorials cover with a thin veneer of self-approving pietism an astonishing degree of intellectual unreality and smugness.

I would say that you have the mind of an old woman but for the fact that I have known many old ladies of ten times your mental alertness and courage.

I can't stop any one from taking your paper, but I can, and I will, point out your bigotry and stupidity, and your very definite enmity toward the United Church.

Rev. R. Edis Fairbairn

With this letter, Reverend Fairbairn began a lengthy epistolary relationship with The Globe.

◆

March 31, 1939

Could some member of your very efficient staff spare a few minutes to ascertain with a stop-watch the amount of time wasted in turning pages while reading your front-page articles? I make it about five minutes, not counting the times one has to turn back again, because when one has found page 13 one has forgotten the context or the column number, but it would be interesting to see authoritative figures.

If I am right it amounts to some 28 hours a year, assuming each of these articles, on the average, to be read by one person.

I haven't your circulation figures, but if you will multiply by them I think you will find that it is in your power to effect a saving of some hundreds of years per annum in the working time of Canada, not to mention the saving in nervous energy and mental anguish caused by continually turning that invaluable journal inside out and outside in again, especially in a crowded street car.

Might these considerations not then be weighed against the loss of circulation that might be expected to follow from not having all the important headlines on the front page?

May I express the hope that the answer will be that The Globe and Mail has now a standing that would permit it to follow the great journals in arranging its news for the convenience of its readers rather than as a lure for reluctant coppers.

D.H.C. Mason
Georgetown

♦

March 5, 1955

Don Delaplante has written an interesting story in The Globe and Mail about his work in Northern Ontario. We are somewhat puzzled about the vacuum cleaner part of the article, wondering where he would "plug in" for current if he were stalled between Espanola and Little Current.

Our experience in damp weather is to spread a copy of The Globe and Mail "after careful reading" over the ignition system under the hood of the car when not in use. The paper will absorb most of the moisture and make starting the motor a delight.

Jim Boa
Toronto

♦

September 14, 1956

From the front page, "Signs and Portents" column of the Financial Post, we read, "Cheaper animal feeds are coming, made from old newspaper and wrapping paper" (ink and sizing apparently have no effect). "Flavored with molasses," the researcher reports, "cows really enjoy newspapers."

Granting Shakespeare's observation on nature's versatility and economy, "Imperial Caesar, dead and turned to clay," is not our speeded-up atomic-age researcher, with this witches' brew pushing our four-stomached, patient, ruminant servants altogether too far?

Besides, who of us would knowingly want milk or meat from these "literary survivors," along with his (or her) morning paper served at breakfast table? And Canada's present food supply (including dairy products – and "feeds") surely offers small warrant

166

for such cheapening substitution between the farm producer and his legitimate market.

A.J. Hamilton
Kingston, Ontario

◆

November 17, 1979

It is with great regret that I must give up my subscription to the Bible after nearly 100 years.

My father first subscribed to the newspaper about 1880. I came along in 1888 and really learned to read from the paper.

I can remember the shock to my father when the paper merged with The Globe, giving up the time-tried wisdom of The Mail and Empire for George Brown and Sir Wilfrid Laurier. It was almost too much for him. But, through two dreadful wars and the Depression, it was always the first thing to read in the morning.

This period (1880-1979) was claimed by my father to be the most revolutionary in the world's history.

He saw the invention of the telegraph, telephone and radio and the flight to the moon. The submarine. Movies and color TV, and so much else ...

We know The Globe and Mail to be the finest paper printed anywhere. My defection is due to the fact that at 91 my eyesight has reached the point that even with the best reading glass I can no longer see to read. Ours has been a long association and I bid you hail and farewell.

James D. Cumming
Havelock

◆

September 19, 1984

Congratulations. Your Sept. 10 edition deserves to be mentioned in the Guinness Book of Records.

In the story beginning on page 1, Pope Begins Canadian Visit, the turnover line ends with "to ritually ... " The second part of the infinitive, already split, appears on column 3 of page 5. Counting 35 words per news-column inch, I figure this represents roughly 7,750 words between the preposition and the verb which make up the infinitive "to kiss."

The Globe's impressive record for splitting infinitives probably could be equalled by a number of other newspapers, but this "longest split" should prove difficult to surpass in the Guinness annals.

Jean Guy Bigras
Ottawa

Chapter 11

The Atomic Age

August 9, 1945

The nations of the world stand aghast at President Truman's announcement concerning the atomic bomb attack on Hiroshima, and this is followed by a British announcement that Japan will be served with a new ultimatum: "We will withhold use of the atomic bomb for 48 hours in which time you can surrender. Otherwise you face the prospect of the entire obliteration of the Japanese nation."

In the name of humanity I protest with every fibre of my being against any ultimate aim in war such as is now indicated. We have execrated the German Nazi Party for their deliberate extermination of five million Jews. How can we possibly contemplate the massacre of over seventy million Japanese? What right have we, or any nation, to plan for or to threaten the destruction of a considerable portion of the human race?

This is not war at all. We have lost all sense of proportion in permitting such wholesale slaughter. It is absolutely outside the pale of human privilege for us to destroy 200,000 men, women and children at Hiroshima whatever may have been the crimes or errors of their leaders at Tokyo. Such wholesale indiscriminate destruction is not according to our traditions.

Do our Allied Governments contemplate in very truth the killing of Japan's entire population? I know, from long personal observation, how cruel and deceptive the Japanese can be; I am no pacifist or appeaser, but no misdeeds or enormities of theirs entitle them to be wiped out as a nation. The vast majority of her people are too ignorant to grasp the meaning of our threat; they know far more about earthquakes than about high explosives or the meaning of "absolute surrender," and doubtless they will be informed by their Government that the Hiroshima happenings were simply an unusually severe earthquake. No ultimatum of ours will reach or move the common people of Japan and in any case they have no machinery for making any response to it.

Then what about the Koreans? Included in that 72,000,000 population of Japan that we hear about there are no less than 24,000,000 Koreans – an enslaved people to whom the Allies have

promised independence once more at the conclusion of the war –
are they to be involved in the general massacre that is promised? In
Europe even a few hundred notorious war criminals are to be given
formal and exhaustive trials before they can be condemned to
death. How can our Allied nations presume to decree destruction to
many millions at 48 hours' notice, the vast majority of whom can
have no notion of their plight, and, in any case, no means of avoiding their fate?

Slaughter on such a scale as this would be a crime against
Heaven and humanity. Surrender must be obtained by some other
course than this. The mere threat of such wholesale murder casts a
stain upon the character of every nation that uses it.

Gerald Bonwick
Toronto

*Hiroshima was levelled on August 6; on August 9, Nagasaki
was destroyed. The Japanese signed a formal peace treaty on
September 2.*

Music for the Cows

September 24, 1945

Your editorial "Cows Have Feelings, Too" displays a shocking
disregard for science as compared with facetiousness.

Dr. Peterson's remarkable work with the dairy cow's nervous
and mammary system is well known to dairymen throughout
North America. Its practicability is unquestioned. Dairymen even
know that simply by changing milkers, or by washing the udder
with warm water prior to milking affects production.

Dr. Peterson's hormonic experiments in bringing virgin heifers
and sterile cows into production is one thing. But music such as you
suggest can only be a figment of the imagination.

I queried the Manitoba Agricultural College on this matter and
they assure me that they know nothing of such practice. They
doubt if any one can tell them whether a cow knows one note from
another.

When a cow deliberately puts her hind foot squarely into half a
pail of milk which a "decent farmer" intended to use on his breakfast cornflakes, what would you expect him to do? Turn on the juke
box, playing "Don't Fence Me In" or "Bringing In The Sheaves,"
or would you have him fetch old Bossy one squarely on the ribs
with the milk stool? Farmers have feelings, too. Or if a dirty tail

comes smack across his face is he to start singing "Let Me Call You Sweetheart," the while calmly picking his teeth with an alfalfa stem?

At any rate these songs seem more appropriate to the occasion than any pastoral symphony. And if the dairymaid and hired man in duet would sour the milk, would "The City Desk" and "Advice To The Lovelorn" editors do better? As a former hired man I doubt it.

J.D. Guild
Supt. of Agricultural Development, C.N.R.
Winnipeg

Splitting Up the Atom

November 14, 1945

An evening newspaper carries the headline, "Must Share Atom –" Well, what else could we do after splitting it?

I.D. Willis
Toronto

Traffic Violations

January 15, 1946

I see by your issue of Thursday that the Buffalo police have recently adopted the custom of stopping motorists whom they wish to congratulate for their good driving.

This announcement brought to my mind the account of a wedding attended many years ago by a waggish friend of mine. He had gone for a walk in the country and dropped in at a wedding in a small church out of pure curiosity, the parties concerned being quite unknown to him.

Having been shown to a fairly conspicuous seat, he sat quietly until the officiating clergyman came to the usual challenge as to whether anyone present knew "any just cause or impediment why these two should not be lawfully joined together," whereupon my friend rose slowly to his feet and waited until the eyes of the entire congregation were fixed on him. When the tension was at its height he remarked quietly: "I have no objection," and left the church before any comment could be made.

I imagine that being stopped by a traffic officer, only to be told that one's driving was unexceptionable, might give one much the same feeling. Even though the bride and groom at the wedding had perfectly clear consciences (as was doubtless the case) the little incident must have given them some uncomfortable moments. On the other hand, an uneasy conscience might have induced the guilty party to blurt out an unsolicited confession.

No one would appreciate compliments from our excellent traffic men more than I, yet I am willing to take them for granted and hope the Buffalo custom will not be adopted here.

(Sir) Ernest MacMillan
Toronto

Composer, conductor of the Toronto Symphony and the Toronto Mendelssohn Choir, and former dean of the Faculty of Music, University of Toronto. Sir Ernest's comprehension of gestures, social or physical, was exquisite; once, when his musicians complained that one of his scores was too difficult because part of the orchestra was to play in 4/4 and the other in 6/4 time, he soothed them by saying, "Well, those playing in 4/4 watch my right hand, and those in 6/4 watch my left."

Springtime in the Country

April 12, 1947

"Sap's runnin'." Yeah, but I'm the sap. I'm runnin' to the brooder house to see how many silly chicks have popped off in the last fifteen minutes. I'm runnin' to the chicken pen to shut up another half dozen broody hens. I'm runnin' to anchor the wood-pile against the spring freshet.

I'm runnin' to count the young apple trees the rabbits have girdled and the raspberry canes the mice have destroyed. I'm runnin' to finish odd jobs that should have been done in the long, peaceful, comfortable winter. Sap's still runnin'. It's springtime in the country.

Whoever warbled, Beautiful, Beautiful Spring tra-la, must have lived in a penthouse, far above and beyond the mud and slush and the exigencies of spring cleaning and chicken-raising. Sure the air in the country is balmy but so is everything else. The cows go balmy and break thro' the fences; the pigs get "tetched" and root their way to freedom; the hens loudly advertise a non-stop flight and take off for the chicken wire.

The dogs go balmy and commune soulfully with the moon at midnight; the cats shriek spring greetings from the barn roof all night, and the crows take up the shattering chorus in the pines at four in the morning. The children forget everything they ever knew and track mud all over the house. Friend husband decides we should go to town. The tractor pulls the car to the gate, teams pull us thro' mud-holes and wash-outs all the way to the highway and back, and we forget the tea and sugar. It's springtime in the country.

But, one cannot live in a penthouse and revert to the lure of rubber boots and keep drains and ditches running. One cannot rake leaves and grass and burn them in the long spring twilight. One cannot watch for the first shimmer of green on the willows, the curled heads of the bracken pushing thro' the soft earth and the carpet of trilliums in the ravine. One cannot wake one morning to find the wild cherry and plum "bursting with snow" and the blue of violets underfoot.

Come mud and mosquitoes, come baby chicks and housecleaning, come planting of peas and beans, perhaps we'll admit, "we're better here than there." Not so glamorous, mind you, in said rubber boots, faded jeans, muddy slicker and bandana, as the penthouse lassies, but happy with all and fairly useful – we hope.

Bess K. Wallace
Cobourg

The Days of Chewing Gum Cards
August 25, 1947

The first automatic vending machines to come within this writer's ken dispensed chewing gum in Toronto many years ago in much the same way as they do today. It is not, however, of chewing gum or slot machines that I write but of the wrappers that covered the gum. The first wrappers carried a picture of two hands each holding a hand of cards fanned out while underneath was the legend, "Spades trump, which wins?"

Presumably the game was whist for this was long before the days of contract or even of bridge. Why whist players of all people should have been singled out for this sales appeal is a question I shall pass over and merely state that very soon afterward there was a change. Formerly plain, the new wrapper appeared with a large, red letter on the inside. This letter was overprinted with text in fine type which set forth that a prize would be awarded to all and sundry who might send to the address given a complete alphabet. Here was something.

Collections were started by boys all over Toronto and it quickly appeared that some letters were in greater supply than others. The commonest of all were the Ms and Ns. Trading started in most of the schools with fluctuating bases of exchange values. For example an S or a P might be worth three or four Ms and a boy might possess fifty or more wrappers comprising not more than fifteen or eighteen letters. The owner of a collection of twenty different letters was envied.

This activity interfered with the orderly work of the classrooms and boys were forbidden to bring wrappers to school, even in their pockets, but trading went on unabated. At the highest point in our endeavor Jimmy Trounce and I found that our collections, if joined, would muster an optimum of twenty-four letters all different. There was no such collection in the school nor had any other two or more boys, so far as we knew, thought of joining forces. The letters we lacked were O and K. Time was running on and we became desperate.

We decided, naively enough, to go to the office of the company and frankly inquire if there were in reality any wrappers bearing the letters we lacked. One day after school we went. We opened the door without knocking to find ourselves in the presence of two men sitting opposite one another at a large, double, flat-topped desk which was covered with letters, envelopes and packages of the now-familiar wrappers.

Jimmy did the talking – "Mister," he said addressing one of the men without preliminary of any sort, "we have between us all the letters except O and K, would you please tell us if there are any Os and Ks?" This questions was put forward in a very natural and straightforward way; it was simple, honest and without guile. The man clearly was caught off balance and looked in amazement first at us and then at his partner. In the end the two of them burst out laughing and one of them said, "Sure, Sonny, there's lots of Os and Ks, just look at these." He reached for a package of wrappers and riffed the little papers through until he came to an O.

"There you are," he said with a cynicism we did not grasp at the time, "there's an O." We had closed in on him and were looking at the letter in astonishment. What we saw was a C clumsily filled in with red to simulate an O, a palpable fraud. All this happened a very long time ago and I must confess that while parts of the picture stand out with vivid clarity, other parts are missing or lost and from the point where the man showed us the fraudulent O there remains a total blank.

I lost track of Jimmy very soon after. In these days of doubt and uncertainty it would be a relief to solve at least one of life's lesser problems and it is possible that some old reader of The Globe or

The Mail did actually acquire a complete alphabet of wrappings with bona fide Os and Ks all complete. If there is such a boy will he kindly raise his hand?

George Wills
Coconut Grove, Florida

A Protest

October 19, 1948

My absence on vacation following the convention will explain my delay in writing you regarding your editorial on October 8, entitled "The One Sour Note."

My defeat I accepted with equanimity and with malice to none for my aim before, during and since the convention has been to do everything possible to maintain and preserve unity in the Progressive Conservative Party, without which the newly acclaimed leader, Colonel Drew, cannot discharge his great responsibility.

The derogatory references in that editorial to Mr. David Walker, KC, "and associates" are unfair, and compel me to write this, my first letter to any newspaper.

I know of nothing that Mr. Walker and "his associates" did that was not done in a spirit of fair and honorable competition and for that reason any suggestion that I at any time dissociated myself from him or them in what he or they did has no foundation.

Mr. Walker's devoted service to the Conservative Party since 1926 is evidenced by occupancy of such offices as President of the University of Toronto Conservative Club, President of the Osgoode Hall Conservative Club, and president of the Toronto Businessmen's Club. Furthermore, in every election since that year he has worked unstintingly without payment or reward. With such a record of service I am shocked that he should be singled out by you, for exile from his party. Your proposal that the "associates" of Mr. Walker be purged from the party is startling, for it places all who worked in my support under an unsupported suspicion of wrong-doing.

While fully realizing that unity above everything else is necessary if victory is to crown the magnificent work done by the convention, any unjustified criticism of my friends and supporters at any time and particularly when such criticism endangers that unity, will always bring me to their defence.

J.G. Diefenbaker
Prince Albert, Saskatchewan

Mr. Diefenbaker had just lost the leadership of the Conservative Party to George Drew, a position he finally won in December, 1956.

Love on the Airwaves

September 19, 1949

Some say that it is wrong ever to punch a man. Even if it is wrong, I can never resist that feeling when I hear some moron wailing, moaning and groaning over the air about love. Then, those hard-boiled girls screeching about the joys of philandering with a man, those I could dunk and choke under the water with joy.

Ottawa suggests raising radio permits to $5 a year. If it will clear and clean itself of soap, pop and drugs, and substitute high-class music, I would be strong for the double charge.

George Hebden Corsan
Islington, Ontario

Mr. Corsan was equally hard on tobacco, liquor, meat and milk, and grew many varieties of exotic fruit and nuts in Islington, on which he subsisted until he died, aged 95, in 1952, with the title of "Canada's Nut King".

City Hall's Pigeons

March 16, 1950

The Mayor and Corporation of Toronto once gave me a beautiful present. Today I am asking them, through the kindly medium of your paper, for a still more beautiful one. The gift I ask is the lives of the pigeons who make their home about the City Hall.

I read the other day that a discussion is going on as to whether it would be better to shoot, trap or poison the pigeons. The reason for this was not stated but I take it for granted that it is because the birds' droppings might deface the beauty of the City Hall.

Would anyone dare say that this building and its surroundings are more noble that Trafalgar Square or than St. Mark's of Venice? In both these places there are flocks of pigeons whose beauty is not only the delight of tourists but which are cherished by the authorities. I myself get a great deal of pleasure from feeding the pigeons of my neighborhood.

This morning I counted twenty-five eating the cracked wheat on a cleared space in my garden. They hop up and sit on the veranda. They perch on the roof but I cannot notice that their droppings have marred the looks of my house, which from its architecture I judge to have been designed by the same architect who designed the City Hall.

A curse might well fall on a city which killed its birds. So I ask this favor, probably the only one I shall ever ask, of our City Fathers.

Mazo de la Roche
Toronto

> *Mazo de la Roche (1885-1961) wrote the Jalna series, fifteen novels about the Whiteoaks family.*

No Cellars

October 15, 1951

How thoughtful of the Department of National Health and Welfare to issue booklets on personal protection under atomic warfare and how kind of you to illustrate it for us – but how especially nice for the people who have cellars in which to build shelters in case of atomic attack.

Have you ever considered the people who have no cellars, and no access to any – people living in apartments over stores, people sharing rooms on third floors, etc.? Perhaps this element is not worth saving, but being one of these lesser creatures, I think otherwise, and unless the Government starts working on street shelters where my brood and I can head for, I ask that you please refrain from publishing such disquieting information, or I, and others like me, may find ourselves safe and sound in some bomb-proof insane asylum.

(Mrs.) Ena Mitchell
Toronto

Showing the Socks

October 4, 1952

I read an advertisement in your paper the other morning which said there were over 300 lines of socks for men to choose from. Not fifty or 150, but 300! I thought: How amazing, and the pity of it is that the men don't even show them. Surely they should be worn over the trousers!

Can you not see how interesting this could become? We would

see stripes, checks, arrows, plaids, wools, silks, nylons, cottons, in about ten lovely shades. Think it over, men.

Dorothy Howard-Buckingham
Paris, Ontario

The Ukanaliens

January 2, 1953

Now that Canada's population is becoming more diversified with the influx of "new" Canadians, isn't it time we give them a "new" name? Something to embrace all the countries from which they came?

I suggest that they be called Ukanaliens. This word being derived from United Kingdom, Canada and Europe should cover them all.

I do not think that my Scots friends would object to the word – we have been called worse!

Jock M. Thomson
Toronto

Interplanetary Travel

December 12, 1953

It is amazing that many people are so discouraged with this world that they are seriously thinking of taking off for another planet, being under the impression that interplanetary travel will be a reality within a few years.

But even if it were, how do they think they are going to dig up the fare? They might find it rather costly at three cents a mile, especially if a 15 per cent transportation tax should be added. It would probably take them millions of light years to save the money for the trip!

Percy Maddux
Toronto

Telephone Solutions

May 7, 1954

Your timely editorial on the subject of the comprising system of telephone numbers with which we are now being beset and bewitched fails, alas, to strike at the heart of the matter. Five-figure numbers are not all that difficult to remember. The trouble arises when one is faced with the choice of a string of exchanges all bearing the same name but having different primary numbers.

The solution you offer, however, is probably the only one possible, and it could be brought into effect without in the slightest way upsetting the Telephone Company's plans. Let us adopt three-letter exchange names forthwith, with the exception of HUdson 1, RUssell 1 and WAlnut 1, which unfortunately have no letters to correspond with the primary figure, but which should present few difficulties so long as they bear their names in solitary splendor.

For the rest, there is an alluring variety of names which can be suggested, using the same holes in the dial; my own preferences come first in the line:

> EM 3: EMEtic, ENDeavour, FODder, FOE.
> EM 4: FOGbound, DOGhouse, ENIgma, ENHance.
> EM 6: FOMentation, DOMino, DOMinion, DONvalley,
>   EMManuel.
> EM 8: DOVetail, FOUrsquare, ENVious, EMU.
> HU 8: ITUrbi, GUTtersnipe, HUT.
> HU 9: GUY, IVY, HUXley.
> WA 2: XACtly, WABash.
> WA 3: WAFfle, WADsworth.
> WA 4: YAHoo, WAGtail, WAItress.

On with the good work!

T.P. King
Toronto

Ottawa's Compass

November 9, 1954

In your recent number I notice a pioneer compass, depicted under the helmet, on the "new, simplified coat of arms for the City of Ottawa."

May I call to the attention of the popular Mayor and the citizens of our storied capital that the magnetic needle of this compass is pointing to the northeast, whereas it should point northwest. In fact, Ottawa has more northwesterly magnetic variations than any other capital city in the world, because of its position southeast of the magnetic pole near Boothia Peninsula.

If the needle of this compass were changed to point northwest instead of northeast anyone could tell, even without the words below, that the coat of arms could only belong to Ottawa.

A.G.M. Bruyns
Georgetown

Canadian Culture
February 22, 1955

Why is Canada so desperately anxious to become cultured? In this world you cannot have everything; there is Nature's law of compensation. Culture needs time; long periods of time, and the right atmosphere, to create it. Canada has over 3,000,000 square miles of territory. But when Europeans left Europe and its disadvantages, they also left its advantages, such as culture, behind. I have been on the north shore of Lake Superior. When I came to Canada more than 50 years ago, you never heard of all this culture nonsense. I much prefer the Canadian in his natural, exuberant and boisterous nature. He is then amusing and original.

H. O'Brien
Bracebridge

Two Portraits
May 23, 1955

If you look carefully at the engraving of Her Majesty the Queen's portrait on our one, five and ten-dollar bills, you will see that the engraver has produced a portrait of his Satanic Majesty peering forth from the left side of Her Majesty's hair. Doubtless unintentional, but hardly an appropriate combination of two Majesties.

A. Murray Garden
Toronto

> *This shocking revelation reverberated for some time before the portrait was subtly altered. See the following.*

◆

April 5, 1956

It seems not to be a matter of the Queen's hair pictured on our

Canadian bills, but why does not the picture show her as a crowned head?

(Mrs.) Gertrude Nesbitt
Midland

♦

May 10, 1956

Members of the National Federation of Christian Laymen, right across Canada, requested the executive to ask members of Parliament to find out who it was that changed the original photograph of the Queen, taken by Karsh, so that the engraving used in the manufacture of our Canadian bank notes show the face of Satan carefully concealed in the hair immediately behind Her Majesty's left ear. John Blackmore (MP, Lethbridge) was the only member who acceded to our request, but he failed to obtain the information we electors asked for. Why? The electors interested in this matter realize that no artist or engraver would alter the original photo on his own. We still want to know "Who done it" and "Who ordered it done."

William Guy Carr
Willowdale

Chrome, Sweet Chrome

September 19, 1956

One day recently – at the age of twenty-eight – I came face to face with the frightening fact that we in the big city were a race destined to become extinct behind the steering wheels of our automobiles, if not violently, upon one of the trans-municipality bypasses that evacuate the nervous from their homes in the morning and from their factories in the evening, then quietly, at downtown intersections, waiting for red lights that never seem to turn green, or trying to outguess green lights that always seem to turn amber.

The world would not end with a whimper. On the contrary, it would end with a decided bang made doubly percussive by the furious engaging of fenders, bumpers and grilles. I saw our main arteries renamed after the clinical vices that accompanied such motoring: "Ulcer Boulevard," "Coronary Drive," "Concussion Crescent."

Thus, on that particular day, my thoughts turned to such questions as: Should I leave my address book to Charley? Will Walter and Nancy be really happy to get my Mackenzie King scrapbook? And then, suddenly, the word "commuter" flashed across my mind's eye like a test pattern. Commuter! That is what I would become. I would enter the ranch-style world of power lawn mowers, Bermuda shorts and portable barbecues – breathing the youthful air of a fresh new subdivision which some great developer had conceived while looking at life through beer-colored glasses. I would be the man in the grey nylon-orlon-dacron-acetate suit – catching the morning bus, hobnobbing with Bay Street-bound executives, alighting from the evening bus to be chauffeured home to a dry martini. My insurance agent's face would learn the mechanics of smiling again as I faced the prospect of beginning life someday at forty instead of ending it at thirty.

Came the first morning in my new world. I donned my finest synthetics and rushed to join my fellow commuters at the bus stop several blocks from my home. I was the first to arrive, and I remained alone quite some time, all the while reasoning that my colleagues must have been delayed over an extra cup of coffee, or the financial page, or perhaps a sophisticated chuckle provided by Pogo.

Then a stray cat joined me, snuggling against my trouser leg and bringing to my attention the fact that it was darned cold outside. And there we remained, the cat and I, neglected seemingly by all but the elements of time and the weather. Bay Street might as well have been Wall Street, now, for I would probably never live to jay-walk it again.

One half-hour later a passing motorist stopped, hailed me, and bade me enter. As I did so, the mobile Samaritan grinned. "New in Don Mills, eh?" he asked gently. My answer was concealed in a deep-frozen sob.

Now here I sit. My trusty auto is poised in the attitude of a thoroughbred behind a starting gate. The low gear of its Enigmatic drive waits for the touch of my foot. On my right a cab driver snarls at me for edging ahead of him. On my left a tubercular bus coughs and exhales its fumes at me. A transport truck, behind me, hisses through its brakes, its ten impatient tons itching to plow through me. Across my path flow dozens of fenders and bumpers and grilles and I hum softly the strains of "Chrome, Sweet Chrome." The lights turn green. With a cry of "Hail to thee, oh, mighty TTC, we who are about to drive salute thee!" I'm off. And I love it.

Some day when my children tell me they've learned that a

straight line is the shortest distance between two points, I will tell them that it is only true in the heart of the city. In the suburbs, it is the longest distance between two points. That is the mathematics of a commuter.

M. Torgov
Don Mills

> *Morley Torgov won the Leacock Medal for Humor in 1975 for A Good Place to Come From, and in 1983 for The Outside Chance of Maximilian Glick.*

Made in USA

February 23, 1957

I have read some of your papers and do not like your editorials or letters. If it wasn't for the United States your country would be more backward and illiterate than now. We practically own Canada through our investments and after all we stepped in to save Europe and Canada from defeat in two wars. Britain and France always have been cowards – fond of speeches but never good fighters. They left Canada with their sloppy traditions, poverty and broken English. The U.S.A. tries to help underprivileged countries and we will take you under our wing like so many other colonies.

Maria Trabolli
New York City

The Earth and the Moon

October 14, 1957

On the front page of The Globe and Mail there appeared an article entitled Shoot A-Bombs At Moon, U.S. Scientist's Test Idea. The scientist proposed a bombardment of the moon to be made with hydrogen bombs, in which the Russian scientists present at the meeting "seemed interested."

Well, it will be a very sorry day for the earth and its inhabitants if and when the moon is bombarded with hydrogen bombs – the ones that release an explosive energy of 10,000,000 tons of TNT each. Here is why. Although the moon is just a little over one-fourth the size of the earth, the latter depends for its very life upon the former, for the sole and vital role of the moon is to act as a brake upon the earth. Without this brake the earth would go to pieces. Here is how.

Suppose that through some frightful catastrophe the moon had been destroyed. The earth would then be freed from the braking power of the moon. As a consequence the earth would immediately start to increase its rotational velocity, resulting in an accelerating momentum of its centrifugal force, and a diminished gravitational pull of the earth. This would change the form of the earth from a sphere to the shape of a pancake. The earth would then explode, just as a fast-rotating flywheel would do.

And should the earth ever explode, all men, women and children, all the mountains, and all the waters of the oceans, seas, lakes and rivers would be hurled into space.

Well then. Could the moon ever be separated from the earth? Could such a catastrophe ever befall the earth? Yes, such a catastrophe could befall the earth; and it would be man-made.

For, given enough hydrogen bombs, released by United States and Soviet scientists, and were such hydrogen bombs exploded on the surface of the moon, the latter would either disintegrate into nothingness or it would be pushed off its orbit and hurled into the depths of space. The earth then, thus freed, would be able to start on its merry-go-round of utter annihilation.

So leave the moon alone!

Leonard W. Hartman
Toronto

The Dog in the Sputnik

A dog named Curly was launched by the Russians in Sputnik II.

November 8, 1957

I was surprised that you gave so much importance to the protest of British societies for the protection of animals against the cruelty done to a Russian dog put in the satellite for the purpose of testing the ability of living creatures to survive in outer space.

I believe that the human beings are at least as important and deserving of compassion as the dogs, but I have never heard of a single Briton or any British society protesting against their Government for betraying the Allied countries of Eastern Europe when the latter were coldly given to the murderous experiments of the Communist butchers.

Besides, thousands of different animals are sacrificed daily for the purpose of testing various drugs, medicines and so on. Nobody cries over them!

I think the dogs of all the races must feel proud that one of their kind was given the honor of exploring outer space in preference to human beings. So why all the fuss?

Steven Jackson
Toronto

◆

November 8, 1957

The fiery denunciations of Russia by the British National Canine Defence League certainly show that the Russians are not all clever. It seems obvious that the Soviet scientists should have sent up one of their Hungarian prisoners, thus incurring only mild and passing criticism.

V. Newman
Toronto

◆

November 8, 1957

I wonder if there is any truth in the rumor that Britain and the United States are to launch a satellite containing an elephant?

> Good-by little Sputnik,
> Farewell little dog in the moon.
> Be patient little Sputnik,
> We'll have an elephant in you soon.

And will they call it an Elephantnik?

F. Gorman
Ottawa

Trapdoors for Tellers
February 21, 1958

It was with some fascination that I read your published letter, entitled "A Scientific Cure for Bank Holdups," in which the writer describes a theoretical method of apprehending would-be bank holdup men.

Very briefly, the writer outlines an idea of a type of trapdoor placed in the floor immediately confronting the teller's wicket which could be sprung by a small knob operated by the teller, thereby precipitating the criminal into a chamber below. At this point, according to the plan, a small dose of chloroform would be automatically administered, thereby rendering the person unconscious.

Now this is a fine plan and shows some ingenuity on the part of the originator. However, I think some further protection could be afforded the teller by a minor change in which the position of the trapdoor would be changed to a spot on the floor immediately beneath the teller so that on the command "Hand over those notes" the bank employee could activate the mechanism as already described and he or she, not the bandit, would disappear into the chamber below accompanied by the money. This would also have some economical value as it would not entail the expense of the automatic administration of chloroform.

John L. Duffy
Toronto

Our Savage Country

The following letter was written to The Globe in Russian, and translated.

April 15, 1958

How long is Canada going to remain savage and uncultured?

(1) It is undemocratic that pensions are not being given to old people over sixty-five, but only over seventy, when they are ready to die, anyway. Only poor people should receive pensions. People who have an income from $33,000 up to millions should not receive any pensions. Family allowances should also be given only to poor people. Wealthy people with an income over $33,000 should not be getting anything.

(2) If pensions were given only to poor people, then they would be getting approximately $100 per month instead of $55. For $55 a month a person can buy only a piece of bread and a glass of water. What savagery!

(3) What barbarism that children fool around in big crowds on the streets and make it impossible to get by. Children should play in their own yard, or in parks. Children scream like savages – like Indians.

(4) Nowhere in the world are the streets as messed up as here in Toronto. Scraps of paper and garbage practically fall on top of your head.

(5) On the sidewalks teenagers scream and push, blocking the passage. They scream and push in such an uncivilized manner that you don't know whether you are in the city or somewhere in the woods.

(6) The same savagery prevails in the street cars. Boys scream, whistle and push around. You don't know whether you are among savage Africans or Indians.

Trofim Ivanow
Toronto

Lawyers and Literature

July 15, 1958

A correspondent asks whether any great works of literature have been produced by lawyers. It is interesting to speculate on how a lawyer would describe some heart-shaking romantic incident, such as a proposal of marriage. It might read like this:

"The aforesaid Henry Perkins, having consulted the father of the aforesaid Liza Luvelly, resolved to propose marriage and accordingly on the evening of Wednesday the fifth day of July in the year 1925 AD did present himself at the residence of Joseph Luvelly, being the domicile of Joseph Luvelly and Liza Luvelly, and at seven minutes after seven o'clock or thereabouts did seize the hand of the aforementioned Liza Luvelly and did ask her whether she loved him, whereupon she answered yes, and he took her in his arms with tenderness as defined in Exhibit A attached hereto and asked her whether she would marry him, provided certain conditions which he would specify forthwith were discovered by them jointly to be acceptable to the parties concerned, such parties being named in Exhibit B attached hereto and whereupon and notwithstanding the entry into the room of the maternal parent of Liza Luvelly, whom he had at some time previously addressed as 'you old battleaxe,' the aforesaid Henry Perkins, as the party of the first part, made a contract with Liza Luvelly, as the party of the second part, to marry her...."

Martin C. Fernie
Toronto

Bluebloods of Canada

October 21, 1958

So Canada, which many believed had a classless society, is now to have a privileged class set above its fellows; their names carefully hand-picked by a board of arbiters and appearing in a bluebook for and about bluebloods. And the name of the blue-bound, gold-embossed tome containing a list of the hallowed great: The Social Register of Canada.

Amid soft lights and scintillating music and in the presence of a select body of the press, later provided with silent typewriters with blue ribbons to record the historic event, Canada's best-seller was unveiled in a Montreal hotel in an atmosphere somewhere between an Irish wake and an Egyptian entombment.

As one of the 16,950,000-odd whose names do not appear in the Social Register, I claim one distinction for its Montreal publishers. They could not have chosen a more appropriate time to launch their distinguished barque. For, with Halloween around the corner, this is the time when many false faces and false fronts appear anyway.

Admission of Canadians to the counterpart of Burke's Peerage poses a number of problems; among them, how are we going to recognize the social elite? How dreadful to bump into someone, not knowing one had literally touched history at some vital point.

Another problem is, how is the blood bank going to determine the new blood type that has suddenly been discovered, unseen and unknown, coursing through the veins of Canadians? How will blueblood appear on the medical chart? RH Positive or RH Negative; or is blueblood what the label says: BB?

On second thoughts, for Canada to have such an august body always on tap, so to speak, may not be such a bad thing after all. Where else, for instance, would the United Nations, faced with dispatching an emergency force of 50,000 persons overseas, look than in the Social Register of Canada, where men and women selected for their good manners and social graces wouldn't dare haggle over the loss of a few drops of blue blood?

R. de R. Brett
Toronto

Defending Toronto

January 24, 1959

Your correspondents who criticize the inaccessibility of Metropolitan Toronto from the North do injustice to our city's military planners. Every foreign general who has ever planned a theoretical attack on this city knows that it would be suicidal to attempt an invasion from the North.

Inhabitants of North York, Toronto's northern bastion, know full well that even in peacetime the city's northern limits are almost impassable at the best of times. Let a drop of rain or a flake of snow fall and the whole city is hermetically sealed at its northern limits, without a cent of defence expenditure. No invading general worth his salt would risk his columns to the three sole routes from the North, narrow and encumbered as they are.

North Yorkers accept their role as perimeter defenders philosophically and patriotically. In the total absence of adequate public transportation to within the city fortress, they will sit for hours in their cars and admire the city's natural defences. However, as the population of North York grows even larger, imaginative forward planners already foresee the day when North Yorkers will commute to town by horse, tethering their steeds at a nominal charge, at the city's parking meters.

A.F. Lowell
Willowdale

Censorship

May 30, 1959

The latest batch of Canadian press notices of my book Canada Made Me brings with it a charge that – because the book has become difficult to obtain in Canada – a censorship exists. And the culprit is named as the publisher, McClelland & Stewart.

That a "hidden" censorship operates is undoubtedly true – a fact I had gathered from readers' letters, especially from those who live in the less-populated areas of the country. But the fault lies not with the publisher – though I can understand how such a charge could be levelled against him. For considerable publicity has been made of his public dismissal of the book; his refusal to have his name on it; and the fact that he is acting as a distributor for the British publisher "only to honor a commitment."

The censor has been the Canadian bookseller, who has (in cases known to me, and in such un-Provincial places like Montreal and Vancouver) refused to have the book in his store after selling the only copy sent by the distributor, and, in certain instances, refused even to order the book from the publisher at the request of a customer.

This kind of "patriotism," I find not only misguided but – considering what the book is about – ironic. That this should be the prevalent published opinion in Canada belongs mainly to the Canadian reviewers. The majority seem to be baffled as to what the book is about. And rather than admit their incompetence, they have done harm, by misleading their readers.

In England – where the question of defending the name of Canada does not arise in the literary parts of the periodicals and papers – the book has had a different reception.

Norman Levine
St. Ives, Cornwall, England

Canada Made Me was finally published in Canada, to critical acclaim, in 1979.

Explorer from Space

February 17, 1960

With all the guessing going on about the mysterious object circling the globe at the moment, I wonder why no one has suggested that it might be an explorer from another planet. If we keep on shooting things into orbit we must, in all fairness, expect the inhabitants of other planets to retaliate in kind, to find out what we are up to. If everybody would stick to his own planet, the universe might be a less fearful place to live in.

L.W. Oppenheim
Toronto

Chapter 12

Is This Toronto?

July 23, 1959

Darlene Anderson is to be congratulated on her election as Miss Toronto. However, I always feel that such youth and beauty is hardly representative of our city. Surely a much more appropriate personification of Toronto would be a middle-aged spinster suffering from a pharisiac religious mania and a secret addiction to the bottle.

Anthony C. Smith
Toronto

◆

February 12, 1926

Here's a query: Has the origin of our city's name ever been definitely established? Looking through my copy of Dewart's "Selections From the Canadian Poets" last night I came across a poem entitled "Ontario," by the late Dr. John George Hodgins, for many years Deputy Minister of Education in this Province. In the poem occurs the following stanza:

But where are now thy dusky Chiefs,
    That haughty warrior band,
Who long a mighty sceptre swayed
    O'er all this forestland?
Where are those dauntless spirits now,
    Those heroes of the past,
And where is proud Toronto gone –
    Thy bravest and thy best?

A footnote to the poem states that tradition had handed down the name Toronto as that of a famous Indian Chief.

E.S. Caswell
Toronto

March 31, 1932

In an editorial in Saturday's issue of your paper you refer to a disagreement as to the origin of the name Toronto. There would seem also to be a very good reason to doubt that the date, 1749, which has usually been accepted as the date of the founding of Fort Rouille, is correct. The Archivist of Quebec, Pierre-Georges Roy, has recently published six volumes of miscellaneous historical information under the title "Les Petites Choses de Notre Histoire." In Volume 3 occurs a section headed "La Fondateur de Toronto," in which it is stated that on October 9, 1749, the Marquis de la Jonquière, a Governor of New France, wrote to Antoine Louis Rouille, Colonial Minister of France, that it would be very valuable to establish a fur-trading post at the Toronto end of the well-known portage route, by which so much of the Indian trade was passing across Lake Ontario to the English post, Chouaguen (Oswego).

On the 15th of April, 1750, Rouille wrote from France approving of the project, but owing to the slow means of transportation the reply did not reach Canada until the early summer. Governor de la Jonquière, however, assuming that Rouille would agree, sent Chevalier de Portneuf, who was in charge of Fort Frontenac (Kingston), to establish the post, and he reached Toronto on May 20, 1750, with a sergeant and four soldiers, at the same time Intendant Bigot sent a party from Montreal with the necessary supplies for the post.

A small stockade and a storehouse for the supplies were erected during the ensuing weeks, and on July 17, 1750, less than two months later, so lucrative was the trade that 79 packages of pelts, valued at 18,000 livres, were sent eastward to Montreal.

It was considered, however, that the trading post was too small, and Jonquière ordered a new one built. Portneuf was again placed in charge of the work, and during the winter of 1750-51 a larger stockade, a house for the officer in charge, a guardhouse or barracks, a storehouse and a bakery were constructed, the work being well advanced on April 23, when Portneuf went up from Frontenac. The buildings were constructed chiefly of oak logs, but were not entirely complete, because some of the men had been unable to work owing to sickness. Stone had been gathered for a powder magazine, and Portneuf wrote that there was an advantageous site for a sawmill, for a stream (presumably the Humber) furnished water all the year round. Portneuf added that great economy had been exercised in the construction of the buildings, and that the trade would soon return the amount expended by the King's treasury.

It has previously been considered, by Dr. Scadding and other historians, that Portneuf began the construction of Fort Rouille on Sept. 1, 1749. Scadding quotes what appears to be the same letter of Oct. 9, 1749 (see above), but states that was sent by Count de la Galissonière, Governor of New France just previous to Jonquière. Monsieur Roy quotes directly from the letter in the Archives of Canada (Correspondence Générale, Vol. 93), and it would therefore appear that Dr. Scadding has led us into error in stating that Fort Rouille was established in 1749, when it was merely the recommendation that it be established, which was made in that year. If there are any documents to prove the contrary, they should be brought to light at once. If not, the date on the memorial cairn in Exhibition Park should be altered to 1750.

Edwin C. Guillet
Toronto

> *Edwin C. Guillet (1898-1975) was called "Ontario's most indefatigable independent historian," and taught school for thirty-three years before he was named Research Historian of the Ontario Public Archives. He was the author of twenty-five books, including Early Life in Upper Canada.*

Toronto Airport

August 16, 1973

It is, I suppose, a tribute to the eternal optimism of the PR man that Air Canada's public relations department should be holding a cocktail party this week for the press to celebrate the coming of age of Terminal 2. A letter accompanying my invitation (swiftly rejected) manages to suggest that everything at good old Terminal 2 is now hotsy-totsy. Unfortunately, the PR people have blundered; the party is being held at Terminal 2. I urge you to send only your youngest and toughest reporters – men skilled in long-distance hiking – to cover this pseudo-event. After struggling across that gargantuan parking lot and down those gloomy and apparently endless corridors, they are going to need a couple of stiff ones.

If I sound more than slightly testy, it is because I have just emerged from my umpteenth experience at Terminal 2 – one which has again reduced me to a stage of helpless rage. I have already suffered from baggage losses – turning up in sports clothes at a black-tie dinner because of "computer problems." My chilblains, from the Miles for Millions hike down those windy hallways, are improving. I have managed to combat the psychological depression brought on by the ghastly environs. But on Sunday night I reached the end of my rope.

I came back from my holidays with my family and 15 heavy pieces of baggage. Sky caps at Terminal 2 seem to be non-existent. I was told I could call one, but even a moose-horn produced no results. Worse, Air Canada has no facilities for calling a sky cap. Never mind, I didn't want a sky cap anyway. What I wanted was one of those little wheeled carts which airports from Prague to Hong Kong supply to their customers. I asked for one and was told that they don't exist in Toronto. Why? Because the Ministry of Transport has banned them from the airport.

I find this incomprehensible but the fact remains there isn't a cart to be seen. I then asked the Air Canada girl what to do. I tried to be gentle since it wasn't her fault and, like most Air Canada personnel at Terminal 2, she seemed to be on the very edge of a nervous breakdown. She suggested I trundle the baggage out, bit by bit. It was at this point that I reached a stage of impotent fury – feeling more than a little kinship with Kafka's poor Mr. K. Because once you take half your bags out of Terminal 2, you aren't allowed to go back for the other half. The doors work only one way. More to the point, two Mounted Policemen, fresh from their anniversary celebrations, are stationed at the doorways to prevent anybody entering.

Finally, my little children, my wife and I with the help of a harried Air Canada supervisor lugged, pushed and heaved the 15 pieces out the door in one great rush.

Outside, the unwashed waited, pleading to be allowed in so that they could find the people they were sent to meet. Because this is another of the several horrors connected with Terminal 2: There is no way you can be sure of meeting anybody debarking from an incoming plane. If they travel with only hand luggage they leave by one entrance. If they have bags they go to the baggage room and leave by another. Nobody is allowed to go to either the gate or the baggage room. This explains why the lobbies are full of people drifting about crying for their friends.

I suggest to you that the present situation at Terminal 2 constitutes a major scandal. Your paper has an enviable record of investigative reporting. But I have yet to learn from your pages or elsewhere exactly who is responsible for this scandal and why. Who built the thing? Who planned it? Who tampered with those plans? Are the architects anonymous or can they be named? Have they been given any further Government contracts? If so, why? Is the imbecile who banned handcarts from the baggage room still functioning in Ottawa? If so, who is he and why? Why isn't there parking space above the terminal? Who is responsible for making that decision? Who designed the color scheme? Who carries the can for the Don Jail atmosphere?

Don't send your young men to the cocktail party. Send them out ferreting. Because, though we can't do much about Terminal 2, short of blowing it up, we may just be able to avoid another disaster and another scandal in the future. What bothers me is that the same idiots who planned and built this horror are likely to be in charge of the next one at Pickering.

Pierre Berton
Toronto

> *Pierre Berton won the Governor-General's Award for Non-Fiction for* The Mysterious North *(1956),* Klondike *(1958) and* The Last Spike *(1971).*

◆

April 16, 1974

May I explain a fundamental truism to your writer Scott Young? In his column he takes me to task for calling him a Hogtowner, when in fact he was raised in Glenboro, Man.

Mr. Young should realize that being a Hogtowner is not a matter of geographical origin, but rather of mental attitude. Many other good Westerners have been corrupted also. This is why the selective breeding occasioned by an influx of westerners has not got rid of Hogtownism. There may even be a few Torontonians who are not Hogtowners, but they will be the enlightened few, and very rare.

I would like to suggest to Mr. Young that if he once was a westerner, he needs a refresher course. He has all of the symptoms of the Hogtown syndrome and is living proof that if the West is ever to rise again, we will have to ensure that our fifth column does not get brainwashed.

D.M. Street
Ottawa

May 1, 1974

I wonder if anyone really knows the derivation of the appellation Hogtown. I have only the glimmer of an idea, and it's a cinch D.M. Street of Ottawa has no idea at all.

I remember once hearing the name arose because Toronto, back in the days when its sports teams competed regularly with teams from smaller Ontario centres, would lure all the best players with money. We hogged the best players, hence the name. Marc Lalonde no doubt will see to it that we are not permitted to do this in the future.

J. David Gorrell
Toronto

When minister of fitness and sport, Marc Lalonde was instrumental in banning the fledgling World Football League from entering Canada in order to protect the Canadian Football League from undue competition. The team most affected by this was the Toronto Northmen, whose franchise was held by Toronto sports entrepreneur John F. Bassett

◆

May 7, 1974

J. David Gorrell wonders "if anyone really knows the derivation of the appellation Hogtown." The answer is yes, and the derivation is older and more innocent of metaphor than most of your correspondents, including Mr. Gorrell, would suspect.

Toronto was a name which was commonly applied as early as 1726, but was changed, by a royal proclamation of Aug. 27, 1793, to York, because Simcoe wished to honor the military success of the Duke of York. After some 41 years (long enough for the tradition to become fixed), the name Toronto was restored in 1834 when York was incorporated as a city.

The name York, of course, is English and it is the name of the capital of Yorkshire. Both the name and the capital are ancient. The Romans called the town Eboracum, which was translated into Old English as Eoforwic. By a series of phonological changes this became, after nine centuries, the modern English York. The Old English Eoforwic has two elements: wic means village or town, and eofor is the boar word. Since the boar is the male of the swine, the name can be translated simply and correctly as Hogtown.

Those who, like Mr. Gorrell, oppose Marc Lalonde's endeavor to remove the Northmen from Hogtown should remember that there is an ancient precedent for this sort of action. Just before the Battle of Hastings in 1066 (according to the Anglo-Saxon Chronicle), King Harold of England found it necessary to run an earlier team of Northmen (and their leader Harald Hardrada) out of the original Hogtown.

Reginald Berry
Islington

◆

July 20, 1974

Here I am all shook up again.

It's about Nancy Cooper's informative article on Cabbagetown (Cabbagetown's Changing Flavor Bodes Ill for the Renting Poor – July 16).

Why does she give no northern boundary? Queen, Parliament and River streets are all very well but for 40 years I've yearned for some surveyor, writer, assessor, tax collector, electoral bureaucrat or seeing-eye dog to label the northern boundary.

Like, I was born on the south side of Carlton Street near Sumach right behind what was then Toronto General Hospital. About 40 years ago I said, or wrote, that I was born in Cabbagetown.

You'd be surprised how many people called me a liar. They get riled up about it. So I keep reading things about the place and I get lists of who ran what grocery store and how many bars sold whisky at a nickel a nip and who had the best free lunch. I get told when Gerrard Street had cedar blocks as a road base and when some students in medicine hung a cadaver outside the Parliament Street butcher shop as a Halloween prank. But I don't get told where the northern boundary sat.

From Nancy Cooper I seek a recount.

Gordon Sinclair
Bala

Chapter 13

The Canadian Accent

January 23, 1961

In his very interesting letter on the Canadian accent, Mr. Robert C. Dick states that he was puzzled by being taken for French in the United States.

I have a suggestion that may help to explain it. Did you ever notice that Americans or, more properly, citizens of the United States, stress the first syllable where Canadians of U.K. ancestry stress the second syllable, particularly in words of French extraction? Examples are cigaret, ice cream, detail, garage, undertake, address, resource, research.

Now, perhaps you have also noticed that Canadians of French ancestry usually stress the second or last syllable, when speaking English. It is possible that a U.S. citizen might jump to the conclusion that a Canadian was French, if he heard only a few words so spoken.

I would also like to suggest to Mr. Dick that a possible reason for our accent being "unknown" is because it is extremely subtle, but it is there. All one needs to do is to board a bus at the Canadian border after having spent a few weeks in the United States. If you close your eyes and lean your head back you will find yourself surrounded by a sibilant "swish-swish" sound that sounds like the rustle of the wings of many birds, whirring, rising, falling, fading, rising often to a muted crescendo, then falling away.

Consonants are much in evidence, vowels rapidly passed over. I am not prepared to state what roots it reveals, but I do know that it does not sound like the State of New York.

The last time I had this experience I found myself thinking that it sounded like music in a minor key. Could that be the reason for its retiring quality?

Margaret Walters
Manilla

Canadian Cuisine

March 23, 1961

"There's no way to put the flavor of Canadian cuisine on celluloid," says an advertisement of the Canadian Government Travel Bureau.

I would consider this the least of the film service's difficulties, bearing in mind that the predominant flavor of Canadian cuisine is precisely that of celluloid.

Janet Underwood
Toronto

Advances of the West
April 29, 1961

In all the praise of the Russian cosmonaut we seem to be in danger of forgetting the scientific marvels produced by the West in the last decade.

Do the Russians have striped toothpaste, roll-on deodorants, colored tissue and mint-flavored cigarets?

R. Cooper
Toronto

The Russians Salute Bliss Carman
June 16, 1961

After reading your editorial Poetry Evening In Moscow, I was greatly astonished that the news published in the Soviet News Bulletin in the May 23 issue, about an evening in Moscow dedicated to the birth centenary of Bliss Carman, well-known Canadian poet, caused such a strange reaction of your paper. You called this news "puzzling and intriguing" and the reasons for the celebration "mystifying."

What is so mystifying in the fact that some public circles in Moscow (the USSR-Canada Society in particular) decided to celebrate the birth centenary of the famous Canadian poet? Is it bad that our people want to know better Canadian literature? It is an open secret that we highly value and pay tribute to the best masters of literature and the arts from different countries. We love and appreciate them for their genius, but not because of political considerations, as you try to show in your comments.

Nobody will believe that books by Mark Twain and Longfellow, Shakespeare and Byron, Molière and Maupassant, Goethe and Schiller, were published in the Soviet Union in millions of copies in Russian, Ukrainian, Lettish, Armenian, Uzbek, and many other languages of the peoples of our country, as a "propaganda move designed to win friends abroad."

You write that Bliss Carman's centenary received more attention in the Soviet Union than in Canada. It might be true, but I hope it is not our country that is to be blamed for it. It is a good tradition of ours to commemorate distinguished foreigners – the best representatives of different nations, whose skill and talent give enjoyment to the peoples of the whole world.

You probably know that in 1959 we solemnly celebrated the birth centenary of the great Scottish poet Robert Burns. Why? Because he became also our beloved poet. Last month our people celebrated the birth centenary of Rabindranath Tagore, famous writer of India, and I do not think that the Indian people met the news about it with suspicion.

That is why your editorial so surprised me. How could such an article be published about a good event? This is really "puzzling" and "mystifying." I don't believe that the Canadians are against cultural events that help our peoples to know each other better. As far as our people are concerned, you may be sure that every Soviet citizen would welcome "propaganda moves" in Canada such as poetry evenings dedicated to Pushkin, Lermontov, or Shevchenko. We would also welcome a Globe and Mail series of articles on Russian classical or contemporary literature.

I am sure that Bliss Carman, were he alive, would support friendship, not hostility. He sang of beauty of nature and man and strongly believed that goodness and truth in the end would win. Let us remember his words:

> There are no hurts that beauty cannot ease,
> No ills that love cannot at last repair.

I. Mironov
Editor, Soviet News Bulletin
Ottawa

The Queen's Stockings

August 15, 1961

Lucinda Crozier, in a report on a garden party at Buckingham Palace, reported that Her Majesty's stocking seams were painfully straight. One would hardly expect Her Majesty to leave the hands of her personal maid with stocking seams askew. But this raises an interesting question. A stocking seam can be downright crooked, slightly crooked, almost straight or completely and utterly straight – the ultimate desire of all careful stocking wearers – but at what point does the humble stocking become painfully straight?

To take my mind off nuclear weapons and their dire results I have approached this world-shaking question from all angles but I seem unable to come up with an answer. To my simple mind a stocking seam is either straight or not straight. However, when we are all crouching in our fallout shelters attempting to survive the atomic blast we shall if we're wise be wearing thick woollen socks in an endeavor to keep our feet warm, so stocking seams won't really matter.

V.M. Clark
Stouffville

The Fish Is a Shark

October 23, 1961

The question has been raised whether the fish depicted on the Resources for Tomorrow postage stamp is a shark or "just a fish." There are two quite different groups of fish – selachians and bony fishes. The first group includes the sharks and rays, the second contains practically all of the commercial and game fish of Canada.

The most obvious difference in appearance between the two groups is the possession of an unsymmetrical (heterocercal) tail fin with the upper lobe longer than the lower by the selachians. The only kind of bony fish with this kind of tail fin are the sturgeons. It is therefore impossible to draw "just a fish." It must have either an unsymmetrical or symmetrical tail fin. If it has an unsymmetrical tail fin it is a shark or sturgeon and the one on the stamp is not a sturgeon.

A similar problem arises in the matter of trees. Here again there are two main types – conifers and broad-leaved trees. The tree represented on the Resources for Tomorrow stamp is undoubtedly a conifer.

The fish on the new stamp is a shark.

J.R. Dymond
Emeritus Professor of Zoology
University of Toronto

Laura Secord's Cow

May 12, 1962

As this year is the 100th anniversary of the invention of Laura Secord's cow (a former sheriff of Montreal, a man named William Coffin, invented it in 1862), a bit of literary detective work done on the subject of Laura seems timely.

The last surviving descendant of James FitzGibbon to bear the family name is Miss Marjorie FitzGibbon of Toronto, and it is to her and to the Lundy's Lane Historical Society of Niagara Falls that I am indebted for the information which enabled me to figure out what happened to the original certificate which shows that Laura delivered her message to Fitz a day and a half before the battle.

In early 1845 there was a lively discussion going on in the Upper Canada House of Assembly as to the propriety of granting FitzGibbon $1,000 for his services, and a certain Mr. Aylwin strongly opposed it, saying that Fitz had wrongly taken credit for the battle of Beaver Dam.

On April 11, 1845, Mr. Charles B. Secord of Queenston, Laura's son, wrote a letter to the editor of the Cobourg Church refuting Aylwin's remarks and enclosing FitzGibbon's original certificate to Mrs. Secord as a piece of proof.

It eventually found its way into the hands of Sir Charles Tupper, and, in early 1934, was obtained by the Archives of Canada.

The late Dr. Henry Cartwright Secord, Laura's great-nephew, had photostatic copies made, one of which he presented to FitzGibbon's grandson in Toronto, and another to Fred Williams of the old Mail and Empire. Mr. Williams ran the story on the editorial page of his paper on June 23, 1934, on the eve of the 121st anniversary of the battle.

There never was a shred of proof that the message reached FitzGibbon after or during the battle.

Graeme Barque
Toronto

War and Peace

May 16, 1962

What does Controller William Dennison mean when he talks about celebrating, this year, 150 years of peace with the United States?

This year we celebrate the 150th anniversary of the outbreak of the War of 1812. Next year we celebrate the burning of York (now Toronto) by the Americans in 1813. Roughly 23 years from now we celebrate the 150th anniversary of the invasion of Canada by the American Hunters Lodges and the Battle of the Windmill. Fifty-four years from now we celebrate the 150th anniversary of the Battle of Ridgeway, in which Fenian invaders from the United States were repelled by the Canadian Militia in the Niagara area.

Fifty-eight years from now we can celebrate 150 years of peace with the United States, as 1870 was the date on which the last Fenian invaders were repulsed from Quebec. It is a fine thing to celebrate our history, but if we want to celebrate 150 years of peace, let's wait until we have actually had it.

True Davidson
East York

Reeve, and later Mayor, of East York.

The Hungry Lawyer

November 2, 1962

Mr. Ralph Hyman's article, The Problem Of The Dishonest Lawyer, says, "Many years ago in Toronto a lawyer bit his secretary where no nice girl expects to be bitten." The question immediately arises: "Where does a nice girl expect to be bitten?" My secretary was of no help with this problem. When I asked my wife, "Where would you like to be bitten?" she replied, "In Paris, of course." Clearly, the question is broader than that of anatomical selection as I had at first thought, but has geographical connotations as well.

Robert D. McCulloch
Belleville

Natural Rulers

February 27, 1963

I am surprised that Canadians have not yet realized why the country is in such deep trouble. Canadians in 1957 committed the major sin of any nation: We turfed out of office our natural rulers. By ejecting the patriarchal figures of the Liberal Party, Canadians showed themselves to be misguided, weak and rebellious adolescents. Thus trouble was inevitable.

To add to our troubles, we have been plagued by guilt feelings. Deep within ourselves we realized that we ought not to have turned on our true rulers. The tragic sight of the Liberal nobility sitting in Opposition, reminding the electorate that we were responsible for their plight, sharpened our guilt complexes.

Even the Conservative Party became infected with feelings of guilt. Mr. Diefenbaker, in 1957, convinced his party that they were as good as the Liberal Supermen, and could run the country just as well. But faced with the tacit hostility of the civil service, the armed forces and the Centre of the Toronto Maple Leafs, the Cabinet weakened and grew angry. Their anger was directed not at the Liberal Party, which was only claiming its own, but against Mr. Diefenbaker, who had deceived them. The Conservative Cabinet knew they were usurpers, and ought to return to the Opposition benches.

Therefore, let us, too, return to the natural order of things. Under the Liberal Government, and the strong father figure of Lester B. Pearson, we Canadian children will cease to worry about free speech, defence, and United States economic domination. Everything will be taken care of. Even the Conservatives will be allowed to criticize the Government in between closure motions. The New Democrats will be graciously permitted to provide ideas, and the Social Crediters will be tolerated. Our rebellion against our natural rulers will be over. It will be nice.

A.S. McGregor
Burlington

The general election was held on April 8, 1963. The Liberals did, indeed, return to power.

The Indians' Example

August 14, 1963

Some centuries ago, the Oneidas, Cayugas, Senecas, Tuscaroras, Onondagas and Mohawks faced a serious situation. Being good Indians, believing in the triumph of good, in the equality of men, respect for the individual and word of honor, they formed the Six Nations Confederacy and became known as the Iroquois.

However, perhaps they were even more wise than the Fathers of Canada's Confederation, because they recognized that the six different nations, being courageous, manly, confident warriors, might some day dispute, quarrel and shatter the Confederacy.

So they then formed a cross-alliance which bound the Six Nations closely together. They formed eight clans within each nation. There were the Wolf, Bear, Beaver, Turtle, Deer, Snipe, Hare and Hawk. They made each member of one of these groups a blood brother to every other man who was a member of this group.

As a result, a Bear of the Mohawks was a blood brother to every Bear in the Oneidas, Cayugas, Senecas, Tuscaroras, Onondagas and Mohawks, and this meant they shared the same fathers, the same sisters, and the same families. It worked wonderfully and the

Six Nations never did break apart. It stands just as strongly today.

Maybe Canada's many, many races – perhaps not six but 60 nations – should take a lesson from the Iroquois Confederacy and divide into eight or 18 groups so that right through the "warp and woof" of the tapestry of Canadian life there should be a brotherhood that binds. Then the Canadian "bear" would be brother to every other bear even if he spoke a different tongue, worshipped in a different faith, and lived in a different Province.

Kahn-Tineta Horn
Montreal

> *Miss Horn, a model and later an Indian rights activist, had been named "Miss Canadian History" in June, 1963.*

Invitation to a Union

January 2, 1964

"You haven't been invited," was how one American businessman last year retorted to my suggestion that Canada unite with the United States. I confusedly picked up the pieces of my national pride and fled.

(Mrs.) Marie-Therese McGuinness
Burlington

Chapter 14

Beard (Rhymes with Weird)

May 17, 1980

The news item concerning the dismissal of a taxi driver in Toronto for refusing to shave off his beard deserves comment.

As a long-time beard (rhymes with weird) wearer, I am well aware of the apprehension I engender – not from elderly ladies, for whom a smile, however hairy, is reassuring enough – but from other, more authoritarian types for whom a slightly unkempt appearance seems to be an affront, even a threat. Luckily, I live a sheltered existence, which means that my employers are tolerant enough not to ask me to come clean-shaven to work. So far I have been able to persuade them that hairiness is a natural human condition and that a personal preference for a beard is irrelevant to job performance.

In return, I exercise extreme forbearance; I don't ask people, even those under my control, to remove (figuratively) their three-piece suits and broad ties, even though they remind me of lascivious capitalism, and I have never told anyone to let their crewcut grow out, even though I dislike a militaristic look.

It seemed as though tolerance was paying off. But now I read that dictatorship with respect to appearance is allowable, that in a society that prides itself on personal freedom and tolerance an employee can be dismissed for wearing a beard! If it were not discriminatory, one might suggest a boycott of the Diamond and Co-Op cab companies until they back off and admit that they have no right acting as the lice of the nation by getting into people's hair.

Michael Troughton
London, Ontario

◆

May 24, 1980

The true objection to the wearing of beards has never been put better than by André Gide. The French writer had a full beard until middle age. One day he noted in his diary: "I have shaved my beard. I no longer wish to mask the emotions of the human face." Seeing the hordes of beardies today with their deadpan expressions, one recognizes the merit of Gide's sentiment. No beard is a good beard.

Paul M. Pfalzner
Ottawa

◆

May 28, 1980

The tenacity of nonsense! Now André Gide's sanctimonious twaddle, "I have shaved my beard. I no longer wish to mask the emotions of the human face," is aired by one of your readers who dislikes beards.

Paul Claudel and Paul Valéry were among other distinguished Frenchmen who thought Gide insincere when trotting out this sort of windy nonsense. With or without beard, Gide was always a dissembler. Madame Gide's anguished cry to her philandering husband, "Don't say anything. I prefer your silence to your dissimulation," is not easily forgotten. This in June, 1918, when the beardless Gide was off for a little romp in England with a 15-year-old boy.

Shaven chins and jowls are not always indicative of mental and moral qualities. Those who show prejudice toward the bearded have succumbed to the termite-ideal of pestilential uniformity. Such witlessness is absurd!

John Sanderson
Niagara-on-the-Lake, Ontario

◆

May 31, 1980

The comments of André Gide, that critic of beards, are in my respectful view far out-classed by William Shakespeare, who said: "He that hath a beard is more than a youth, and he that hath none is less than a man."

Harold J. Levy
Toronto

◆

May 31, 1980

Has your letter-writer not considered the waste of time caused by the unnatural desire to remove the normal growth that appears on the adult male face? If a shave is timed at taking five minutes per day, with approximately five million Canadians indulging in this ritual, then over 400,000 work-hours are lost per diem; hours that could be put to better use, such as improving Canadian industrial output!

Consider also that a beard may hide a large number of faults. Your writer may complain of the "deadpan appearance" on the "beardies" but what of the defects that a beard can mask? Spots, scars or a receding chin are but a few. I suggest that Joe Clark would have improved his image and, hence, his chances of winning the 1980 election had he grown a beard to disguise his lack of chin.

Clean living is not synonymous with clean-shaven. Growing a beard produces a saving of time, money and, in many cases, face.

Shaun Hobbs
Saskatoon

◆

May 31, 1980

I am not defending the unkempt, but I urge Paul M. Pfalzner not to make such sweeping observations.

Ottawa can be a cold place. It may be that this causes an excessive hirsuteness in its denizens. Your correspondent might be interested to know that here in Toronto hairs appear on the jaw, upper lip, lower cheeks and (sometimes) the front of the neck of a bearded man. Seldom, if ever, do they cover the eyes, forehead or teeth. These are important parts of the face and are able to transmit expression quite adequately on their own. If a gentleman has a million-dollar smile, no beard will detract from it.

Sometimes it happens that a striking beard covers up a handsome face, but one should not be troubled by this, as the face, after all, is still there. I would like to suggest to Mr. Pfalzner that any visage that is expressionless with a beard on it is probably just as boring without.

The beard has great advantages from the point of view of a young lady. I am a young lady and am a connoisseur of beards: I have had the pleasure of backing up my observations with research, thanks to the co-operation of some of the very charming men who wear hair on their faces. In my experience, it is much more pleasant to be on close terms with a man who never shaves than with one who does, particularly if he doesn't do it often enough. The texture of rough sandpaper has its place in furniture refinishing, but its application to sensitive skin is inappropriate.

The following relevant advice has been passed on for generations by the distaff side of my family: "A kiss without a mustache is like roast beef without horseradish." (We can, in this instance, include the noble beard; Those not partial to horseradish may substitute mustard.)

Alison White
Toronto

◆

June 7, 1980

It has been suggested in your recent correspondence that Conservative leader Joe Clark might have improved his appearance and his election chances had he grown a beard to disguise his chin. That is, of course, debatable, but it is a certainty that if more politicians wore beards, there would be fewer barefaced liars on the hustings.

Trevor S. Raymond
Cochenour, Ontario

Chapter 15

Coming Home

April 21, 1964

Your editorial Who Goes Where?, concerning the loss of population to the United States, has prompted me to add yet another consideration to this question, as well as to give vent to a personal
grievance. The point I wish to make is that in all the gnashing of
teeth and wringing of hands over the drain of talented people across
the border, Canadians have ignored or forgotten those who want to
come back, but can't.

I have no array of statistics to cite to reinforce this assertion. I
base it solely on my own sad experience, but one which I venture to
say is not unique. I am a graduate of a Canadian university, and was
fortunate enough to gain entry (through a generous American
foundation scholarship) to a highly regarded Ivy League university.
During my three-year stay, my intention of returning to Canada
remained steadfast, and I looked forward to the prospect. I foresaw
no problem in this regard, and was doubly assured by the numerous
outcries from Canadian educators, journalists and government
officials on the need for trained, professional people to fill the bur-
geoning demands of this growing nation.

Well, the day finally arrived. I received my advanced degrees in
political science, and prepared to return home, giving little regard
to the many attractive offers from American institutions. However, I soon received the rebuffs that only a spurned suitor can
experience. After several months of sending a host of applications,
inquiries, and entreaties to a multitude of academic and non-
academic employers, only to be greeted with polite (and sometimes
not so polite) solicitude, disinterest or complete silence, I am now
compelled to accept a position, albeit an attractive one, in the
United States.

Thus, my conclusion is that while Canada bleats out its anguish
over the desertion of many of its talented citizens, it might pause to
consider the cases of unrequited love, of which I am sure mine is not
alone. It is basically a case of making the opportunities that exist
known and available, not only to the home-based Canadians with
their close-at-hand contacts and accessible avenues of information,

but also to the foreign-based Canadians who seek to return.

In the meantime I, and I am sure others like me, must be content with scanning the back pages of American newspapers for Canadian news, eating Canadian bacon, and gazing wistfully homeward when the TV weatherman draws on his map the cold Arctic front coming down from the North.

Lloyd Axworthy
Princeton, New Jersey

> *Mr. Axworthy finally won his position in Canada, as a lecturer in political science at the University of Winnipeg, in 1965. He was elected MP for Winnipeg-Fort Garry in 1979, and appointed to the Cabinet as Minister of Employment and Immigration in 1980.*

Arrogant Voices

When the University of Toronto decided to give Adlai Stevenson an honorary law degree, students and faculty, outraged by U.S. actions in Southeast Asia, reacted angrily, and demanded that the university rescind its decision. The Globe and Mail denounced the protest, saying that "their position betrays an intellectual arrogance."

May 18, 1965

The only act of arrogance so far perpetrated in the debate over Mr. Adlai Stevenson's honorary degree is the insolent editorial which appeared in The Globe and Mail of May 15 and the offensively vulgar cartoon which was its appropriate accompaniment.

Such exhibitions of bad-mannered, self-satisfied impertinence are a normal feature of the columns of this newspaper. Its editorial writers are always ready, at a moment's notice, to lecture, dogmatize and pontificate about any subject in Earth or Heaven. With a minimum of investigation or reflection they are invariably quite prepared to pass judgments and issue pronouncements on the most complicated issues, and to rebuke and deride persons infinitely wiser and more gifted than themselves.

Like all bumptious dogmatists, they are extremely intolerant of opinions which differ in the slightest from their own. They have a natural and obsequious inclination toward conformity. Their minds are little better than rag-bags of the commonplace, shop-soiled orthodoxies of the day. They are only comfortable with "received" ideas, and ever eager to crook the knee to "established" reputations, particularly American reputations.

In short, The Globe and Mail editorial writers occupy a conspicuous place among the group of dedicated "yes-men" who form such a large minority of Canadian journalists. They have proved this often enough in the recent past: the editorial of May 15, Arrogant Voices, supplies a final and convincing demonstration. If a prize were offered for the worst exhibition of petty and pompous conformity in Canadian journalism – and Heavens! what a huge competition that would inspire – the award certainly ought to go to the little group of serious thinkers in the editorial offices of The Globe and Mail.

D.G. Creighton
Toronto

> *Donald Grant Creighton (1902-1979), chairman of the history department of the University of Toronto, won the Governor-General's Award for his two-volume biography, John A. Macdonald: The Young Politician (1952) and The Old Chieftain (1955).*

Blackout

November 18, 1965

As an admirer of the United States, I've been worrying about its increasing economic domination by Canada. The recent blackout – whereby immense areas of U.S. territory were plunged in darkness because of the irregular behavior of Canadian electricity on Canadian soil – has underlined my fears that American integrity is threatened by our control of their resources.

That the United States should be at the mercy of a neighbor, however friendly, is incompatible with its national sovereignty. Nor is this the first time we've put the United States in danger. During the Cuban crisis we were far from standing firmly behind them. And this, even though they allowed a Canadian air marshal to remain in charge of their air defences.

If I were the President I'd close the border and halt the pernicious drift toward continentalism.

Kildare Dobbs
Toronto

> *Kildare Dobbs won the Governor-General's Award for his book Running to Paradise.*

Death of a Nation

November 23, 1965

Richard J. Needham's article Death Of A Nation? scared me: not because of what Mr. Needham said about Canadian political irresponsibility, but because of his conclusion that Canada is going to be absorbed politically into the United States. What worries me is a possible fate far less desirable than that.

The illusion that Canada can join the States for the asking has enervated us for years. In the back of many an Anglo-Canadian mind slumbers the idea that if things get too rough here, there is always that way out. There isn't – at least not for most of us.

What American president would give statehood today to the Atlantic Provinces? Or to Quebec? Or to Ontario without Quebec to which she is economically and geographically joined like a Siamese twin? American interests already have in Ontario all they want – a market and a labor force for their branch plants. Why admit into statehood a province with a long tradition of independence politically, and enough population to affect the balance in the Electoral College?

But an American President might look with benign eyes on a proposal that everything in Canada west of the Lakehead be absorbed – a small population at present disgruntled with Eastern Canada, uncounted (and undeveloped) resources, water galore in British Columbia.

Thank God few westerners have yet reached the open desire of offering themselves to some union party which would make such a deal look glamorous, but unless our present infantile obsession with party politics abates, quite a number of them might. The result would be an Esau deal in comparison to the bargains they could make as part of a Canada that knew its worth and its own mind, but let nobody be astonished if, a few years hence, people will be talking about this.

As matters now stand, Canada has come to the verge of accepting herself as a nation of dual culture, and it has been noted in French Canada with gratitude and respect that Ontario, by and large, has stood for the nation. So, for that matter, did Quebec in the last election. It gave no rubber-stamp vote to the Liberals in return for favors received.

Before the next Parliament convenes, we may at least pray for some realism among our politicians. As Mr. Needham so rightly said, all the most of them talked of this past fall was scandals and handouts. Nor is there any need, in Frank Underhill's words, to "save ourselves from the States," but rather to save ourselves from ourselves. One of the best ways to fortify ourselves in this direction is to accept that Americans at best would never accept any part of us politically east of the plains.

Hugh MacLennan
Montreal

Hugh MacLennan won the Governor-General's Award for Two Solitudes (1945), The Precipice (1948), Cross Country (1949), Thirty and Three (1954), and The Watch That Ends the Night (1959), a record five times.

Newfoundland

January 5, 1966

I really think these Newfoundlanders are being awfully thin-skinned about their bogland and moose pasture and their Kick and Push, or whatever they call it. Don't they realize that they are being "discovered" and that vast wads of money will follow from the free-spending tourists who are bound to come in the wake of such publicity?

We here in Ontario have grown rich and fat on the American journalists who told their U.S. readers what funny-looking people we Ontarians are with our quaint toques and toboggans and how we say "hoose" instead of "house" and have to go to the Government to buy a bottle of liquor. It's so good down here (or up here, whichever it is) that it now takes the Premier and all the Cabinet to look after the tourists in addition to hundreds of thousands of civil servants working for the department of Tourism and Publicity.

Really, you Newfoundlanders, how backward can you get? Come on, now, get with it – spend some of that family allowance on a wood-carving course, ask Ottawa for a squad of Mounties to prop up beside the pulpwood, put on the tea-kettle, belt out some folk songs and get ready for the deluge.

You people are about the last of the North American stand-outs down there (or up there, whichever it is) and if you play this thing right you'll soon be unable to pay your income tax – you might even make such a success of it that you'll become a national problem and have to learn French and be promised a bridge to Port-aux-Basques every 50 years.

F.L. Pratt
Napanee

The Cruel Sea

August 15, 1966

While I appreciate very much your suggestion that Defence Minister Paul Hellyer should read The Cruel Sea while on his holidays, I have written two other books which might be even more appropriate. One is The Ship That Died of Shame, and the other is The Boy's Book of the Sea.

Nicholas Monsarrat
Ottawa

The Face of God

December 16, 1966

With regard to the statement in the article Who Was Jesus? that "What Jesus looked like is utterly unknown," the following notes taken from The Nazarene Gospel Restored, by Robert Graves and Joshua Podro, may be of some interest to those who have not read this absorbing if controversial book.

The physical aspect of Jesus: "A small man and uncomely" (Mid-Second Century Acts of John, 89). According to the earliest Christian tradition, He was red-haired, like David. St. Ephraim the Syrian, in his Gospel Commentaries, wrote that "God took human form and appeared in the form of three human ells. He came down to us in small stature." Tertullian mentions Jesus' "corpusculum" – His insignificant body. He adds, "nec humanae honestatis corpus" but does not describe His deformity. (Against Marcion 3:17) "If He did not have a heavenly look in His face and eyes the apostles would never have hastened to follow Him," (Jerome, Epistle 65). In several Talmudic passages Jesus appears under the pseudonym "Balaam the Lame." It is probable that "Physician heal thyself" referred to an injury visible to the whole congregation and that He had acquired this since His acclamation because, according to Samuel 14:25, candidates for the kingship had to be of unblemished body.

P. Lockwood Sr.
Rexdale

Mr. de Gaulle Speaks

On July 24, 1967, French president Charles de Gaulle stood on the balcony of Montreal City Hall and addressed a throng celebrating

July 27, 1967

General de Gaulle and Quebec Premier Daniel Johnson appear to believe that Quebec is Canada's Sudetenland.

Eugene Forsey
Ottawa

◆

February 26, 1968

It occurs to me that you might be entertained by the enclosed, a copy of a letter I, as president of La Ligue des Fils de la France Perdue, have written to General Charles de Gaulle requesting aid in liberating the state of Iowa, a part of the Louisiana Purchase, from Anglo-Saxon tyranny.

"We the undersigned, as founding members of the League of the Sons of Lost France, greet the Head of the French Republic and respectfully present to him our patriotic homage, the loyal wishes of the true children of a forgotten France, torn from the homeland 150 years ago. We are the sons and the inheritors, stripped of our rights, of the explorers who came on a civilizing mission to build a new world for France, to build the beautiful French province of Louisiana. Since the time of the shameful sale of our little country – a phony deal, because one cannot sell one's nationality – our fathers, like ourselves, have been subject to the harsh tyranny of a cold, hard and foreign race.

"Victims of Anglo-Saxon power, we are obliged to see the barbarian and nefarious hordes crush the magnificent plains of our Iowa, a French country scattered with rivers and old cities of which often nothing today reminds us of their native and heroic past except their names: Dubuque, Des Moines, Prairie du Chien, Belle Plaine; and near us, in another martyred country, the great city which still bears the name, a symbol and a hope, of St. Louis. We see our children bogged down in a vulgar culture, obliged to go to schools where French is not taught. We are deprived of everything which makes life tolerable for true Frenchmen, and that in a country which really belongs to us. We can only keep our memories and, after so many years, our hopes. We may lack strength, but we do not lack courage. We beg you to hear our cry. Help us. If you come to visit us, we shall be here: in spite of everything we remain erect and proud, conscious of our duty and our destiny. General, sir: we are at your orders. We stand in the service of France.

"Vive l'Iowa libre!

"Vive la Louisiane française!

"VIVE LA FRANCE!"

Laurence Lafore
Visiting Professor of History
University of Iowa, Iowa City, Iowa

O Canada

September 20, 1967

I have had exactly two rather unpleasant letters apropos a "shot," apparently carried in The Globe and Mail, showing me seated while O Canada was being sung in English at the Progressive Conservative Convention on Saturday, Sept. 9. These letters ask, "Why?"

I did not rise because the *words* of O Canada, either in English or in French, are not yet adopted, or proposed, as our national anthem. Only the music has, so far, been reported out by the Parliamentary Committee as a national anthem. I stand always when the music – the national anthem – is played.

I think you will find that, in speaking to the subject in the Commons, the Rt. Hon. the Prime Minister (Rt. Hon. Lester B. Pearson) stated that, were the words of O Canada to be adopted as the national anthem "some of the words of the French version might have to be modified." (More "deux nations" but not "two nations," I take it.)

I agreed, heartily, with Mr. Pearson. And I imagine most of your readers would have, including one of the two who wrote me, had they in belting out their English version of O Canada lustily, had before their eyes the translation of the français version I hear constantly in The Gatineau.

Les Anglais sing:

O Canada, our home, our native land
True patriot love, in all thy sons command.
We see thee rising fair dear land
The true North, strong and free,
And stand on guard, O Canada,
We stand on guard for thee.

Les Français and les Québécois sing in French (which in English runs):

Under the eye of God, by this mighty river

The Canadien advances, strong in hope.
Sprung of a proud race,
Blest shall be his cradle.
Heaven has cast his people's course
Here in this new world.
Guided always by that light
He shall keep well the honor of his flag.

Then comes the magnificent climax verse, of *rededication* to the battle cry of Louis, the Crusader King of France:

Sanctified love of throne and of altar
Fill our hearts again with thy immortal breath
Here among these *stranger* races
May faith direct our way.
May we learn to dwell as brothers
Beneath the law's clear sway
And raise again, as did our fathers,
The conquering cry, "For Christ and the king."

No, for that I do not stand. I stand for Canada. I am a *Canadian*, not a Québécois or "Canadien."

Charlotte Whitton
Ottawa

Alderman and former Mayor of Ottawa for five terms, from 1951 to 1964, and remembered for her feistiness. Once, during a reception which both she and the Lord Mayor of London, England, attended in their formal robes of office, the Lord Mayor leaned over and, indicating the rose she had pinned to her bosom, asked, "If I smell your rose, will you blush?" Miss Whitton seized the Lord Mayor's chain of office and snapped back: "If I pull your chain, will you flush?"

Why Women Wiggle
September 21, 1967

Please tell your Professor Scott Young that the wiggle he so entrancingly described in The Pelvic Bone and Miniskirts is not due to the shape of the female pelvis but to another related cause.

I was a medical student before I entered my present non-scientific profession, and the swing and sway of women's hips is caused by their shorter ischiofemoral ligaments, the blessed ties which bind the pelvis to the thigh in both sexes.

Donald Flock
Windsor

Trudeaumania

*Pierre Elliott Trudeau replaced Lester B. Pearson as Prime Minister
on April 6, 1968, and won the election on June 25.*

April 17, 1968

A deeply sincere thank you to Bruce West for his column Enough!
Enough!, begging the news media to give us a rest from Pierre Trudeau.

I could not agree more. Unfortunately, my wife (a highly intelligent woman and under ordinary circumstances a creature of
monumental common sense), as well as my 18-year-old daughter
and 15-year-old son, would willingly watch and listen to Mr. Trudeau for two hours a night, seven days a week, in prime viewing
time.

What the blazes can a man do, outnumbered three to one in his
own home?

Peter Brownrigg
Peterborough

◆

June 25, 1968

Sorry, fellas; the Liberals probably will win, but as a loyal Prairie
girl who wore fleece-lined dropseats all through grade school, I'm
voting for staid, "propeller-planc" Stanfield. We long-john types
just don't trust a swinging slickeroo.

Pauline Dix
Highland Creek

Direct Action

December 13, 1968

As your sports pages have already indicated, the Montreal–Toronto
hockey game played Wednesday night at Maple Leaf Gardens was a
stirring one. It must have made exciting television fare. I wonder,
though, if the people who saw it on television realized how much of
the game's edge was taken off by the catering of the men who
presumably run hockey to the commercial sponsors of the telecast.

I'm talking about the pauses in the flow of play imposed for the
sake of commercials. There were several occasions on Wednesday
when a faceoff was delayed for no reason at all, other than to permit
the ramming in of 60 full seconds of advertising. These pauses may

be tolerable if you're watching the game at home, free, and want to go to the john or something. But at the Gardens they're a pain in what Scott Young would probably call one's a–dash–s.

The worst case, on Wednesday, occurred late in the third period. Until then, many of the highlights of the evening had been provided by the Leaf line of Keon, Ellis and Oliver, whose forechecking and artistic passing (artistic by Leaf standards, anyway) had gone a long way toward making up for the defence's habit of getting out of position. Now, with the score tied 4-4 and time running out, the line skated out for what appeared to be one last chance to beat the best hockey team in the world.

And what happened? We got a *pause*. The players skated around; the referees scratched their heads and the balloon of excitement that had been expanding all evening began to shrink in a chorus of impatient boos. Commercial.

It could be argued, I suppose, that the Keon line, after working so hard all night, would have benefited from the breather. But that, surely, wasn't the point. The point was that before the pause the evening had had a marvellous shape of its own, a dramatic construction of goal against goal, rush against rush, the kind of pace that puts a classic Leaf-Canadien game high on the list of Toronto's theatrical attractions. And what the fans wanted at that time was a final confrontation, to see whether the gallant Keon and Ellis and Oliver could draw one last effort from their energy and pop in the winning goal.

But all that is theoretical, and my purpose is to offer a concrete solution. Instead of booing, let's hit those sponsors and the collaborative owners where they live: in the wallet. Were the offending sponsors Molson's? (There are ways – tiny portable TVs or even FM radios – of finding this out.) Then let's have the fans set up a chant during the pause of "We love Carling's Red Cap." Or any other beer. And keep it going. Meteor? Then how about something like "Wide track, Eddie Shack, we love Pontiac"? Anything at all. Just yell. Knock the product. Or sing the praises of a competitor. Are you listening, university students? For the fun alone it would be worth it. But there could be practical effects, too.

Just imagine the guys in the control booth. What are they going to do? If they turn the Gardens sound back on, the switchboard will burst into flames with calls from the paying sponsors. If they don't, and thereby eliminate the commentary (as they would) ... well, hmmm, that's a whole other thought.

But, either way, the advertisers will learn that they have no right to interrupt – and help to spoil – a game that 16,000 people have paid to see. Or, for that matter, to dampen the climax of an event they are sponsoring, presumably entertaining the fans at home.

In any case, I think even The Globe and Mail would agree that this is an unparalleled opportunity for free enterprise.

Peter Gzowski
Toronto

Oh, Oh

December 19, 1969

I would appreciate clarification of a point that has troubled me when reading your Parliament excerpts column.

Namely this: is it a journalistic rendering of general murmur or do "some hon. members" actually say "oh, oh" so frequently during House of Commons proceedings? If, in fact, exactly two ohs are emitted with such regularity, are they in unison? Do they indicate dismay, disgust or physical comfort?

It would be helpful if it were known whether they are expressed as: (a) oh (groan and/or sigh), oh; or (b) high-note oh followed by low-note oh (Depressionese); or (c) two single-note Toody-the-cop-style ohs.

Indeed, it would be reassuring to learn that the pattern may vary from day to thrilling day.

Mrs. Margaret Sorensen
Port Colborne

◆

December 19, 1969

The line in Hansard, "some hon. members: 'oh, oh!'" (with an exclamation mark) is intended to indicate the sort of background noise that caused the explorer, white hunter, or whatever, in 100 movies to declare: "The natives are restless tonight."

It isn't necessarily the case that the members actually have said "oh, oh!" although they may have done, indicating that the gent into whose speech it has been interjected has just got off something which is simply too much to swallow.

It may signify only a gabble of voices – "Why don't you sit down?" "That's a lot of nonsense," "Go soak your head," "Must we suffer through this?" – out of which the Hansard reporter cannot pick anything intelligible.

It also covers groans, hoots of laughter, sighs, snarls, guttural sounds in the back of the throat, sounds of encouragement, razzberries, cries of anguish – in fact, all that your correspondent mentions and more, with the possible exception of physical discomfort. It would be hard to say at any time whether an MP was motivated by physical discomfort.

George Bain
Ottawa

Back to the Cave

January 27, 1970

Eons of time elapsed during man's crawl from the cave to the castle. It's interesting to speculate, if one has time, on how long it took to accomplish the different episodes of his evolution.

How many millions of years ago could it have been that he became aware of the stench exuded by his body, and began to bathe? It could have been a thousand years, for instance, between his accidental discovery of how to create fire, and his accidental discovery one day, while barbecuing a fat piece of dinosaur, that the grease, falling on the wood ash, produced soap.

The point at which he began to clip and control his hirsute growth probably came when he found his colony of body lice and fleas no longer bearable. In millions of years his increasing ingenuity and searching spirit enlarged and beautified his speech, and each race, with its own language, produced eventually at different times a poet and genius like Shakespeare. The "visual arts" and music were understood by all his contemporary world.

I predict that the slide back to the cave from the castle could conceivably occur in 100 years. Already a percentage of the young are opting for the unwashed stage, and the stench. The hirsute appendages are increasingly in evidence. Frequently, particularly on TV, an interview with a serious young man contains a preponderance of "it's like," "uh," "y'know," "uh," "like I said," etc.

Many people believe that some modern art and sculpture would be more at home on the cave walls of Neanderthal man than in the castle art gallery. The entertainment sections of our daily papers often assume the character of the illustrations for a new book on pornography.

My nephew recently told us of an interesting friend of his who has made a large profit out of supplying hotel rooms with a free packet of Alka-Seltzer and Aspirin. I remarked that this was a wonderful commentary on the change which had taken place in recent years – it used to be a Gideon Bible.

It's an interesting topic. One hundred years? Perhaps only 10! Away we go, discarding our clothes, our civilization, even our speech, so that, eventually, back in the cave, man has reverted to his primordial vocal accomplishments – the scream of ecstasy or rage, and the groan of pain, with, in between, his original repertoire of the grunt, the hiccup and the belch.

Like I said, man, wow!

Mabel Drew-Brook
Toronto

Paradise Enow

June 19, 1970

In your issue of June 16 you reported our marriage in the death column.

To quote Mark Twain, may I say the report is "greatly exaggerated," and that my wife and I are living proof that one can be in heaven without dying.

J.L. Pigott
Thornhill

The FLQ Crisis

October 24, 1970

It's not because I question the integrity of New Democrats Tommy Douglas and David Lewis. They have plenty of that. It's their common sense I question, their political realism. They've learned nothing from the debacle of the Social Democrats in the Weimar Republic when a gifted thug whipped them to their knees, and nothing either from the defeat of the Mensheviks whose bones Lenin broke and tossed contemptuously to his Bolshevik dogs. I've concluded that that kind of mentality is no more expungeable than decay or cancer.

It's therefore very heartening to see the majority of Canadians supporting the Prime Minister's effort to eliminate the terroristic FLQ from the Canadian political scene. They see, even if the big-eared stalwarts of the New Democratic Party don't, just where the danger to their liberty lies and are not fearful of using those instrumentalities a liberal democracy has created for its preservation. Like myself they applaud the vigor and courage with which the Government has acted. My one regret is that it has taken the terrible death of a valued and wonderful man to alert them and the Canadian people, for the signs of the coming terror were not wanting.

May they not sink back into apathy and allow themselves to be lulled by the many boneless intellectuals who are completely isolated from the people and from the real issues of our time. Never more so than today these intellectuals are posturing in front of the cracked mirrors of their imagination; their self-congratulatory bows are to an imaginary audience made up entirely of febrile souls like themselves. It's to the great credit of Canadians that they've decided their lives and liberty are safer with Pierre Trudeau than with the degenerates of the FLQ and the bleeding heart liblabs who, no wiser than the discredited Social Democrats and Russian Mensheviks, haven't a clue to what's rising up to smash them.

Irving Layton
York University
Downsview

Writer-in-residence at York University.

Ah, Ontario

A series of television ads sponsored by the Ontario Tourism Ministry sang the question: "Ontario – is there any other place you'd rather be?"

December 3, 1970

Replying to the Ontario Government's jingle: yes, this year, this month, I would rather be in: Timbuktu, London, Paris, Athens, Barcelona, Marseilles, Aix-en-Provence, Arles, Nimes, Avignon, Two Dot, Montana, Florence, Venice, Bristol, Dublin, Stavanger, Prince Rupert, Montreal, Hull, Baie St-Paul, Halifax, Magdalen Is., Nicosia, Famagusta, Paphos, Kato Pygos, Trimithi, San Francisco, Katmandu, Davlos, Alma Ata or Erewhon.

Marian Engel
Toronto

Marian Engel won the Governor-General's Award for her novel Bear in 1976.

Ireland

March 20, 1971

It could be a much more pleasant life for the Catholics and Protestants of Ireland if they would become atheists. Then, perhaps, they could live together like Christians.

Grace Irvine
Durham

Election Time in Ontario

October 13, 1971

So we're 18. Two or three months ago we were just those dumb teen-agers. Now we're all the prodigal sons (or daughters) and do you want to know why? Because now we can vote! Everybody wants us on their side.

Pamphlets keep pouring in. "Vote Liberal, we're on your side." "The NDP are for youth." (By the way, what's an NDP?) "Vote Conservative, don't forget, we gave you the vote."

So just to prove my intelligence, I went to hear what they all had to say. From what I can figure out, the NDP want to give us free everything – which is okay if you can do it – the Liberals, when they find something they don't understand, are immediately all for it, and the Conservatives, when they don't understand something, hate it.

None of this makes too much sense to me. Whatever happened to the good old days when the King said jump and everyone asked how high? Politics, bah. Who needs 'em?

Stephanie Fulford
Grade 13, Cedarbrae CCI
Scarborough

A Pall of Professors

January 25, 1972

Fie on K. Frankum (Merit Pay – Jan. 19) for his lack of exactitude in describing professors collectively. It may be acceptable to refer in his letter to a gaggle of professors in certain very rare circumstances; it must be obvious, however, that while the genus may prate on endlessly, they must never be he(a)rd. It is far more appropriate to refer to the more verbose examples as a prattle of professors. But there are various terms which have rather specific appropriateness.

An academic procession would probably be described best as a promenade of professors, while those who have tenure might be a preserve of professors. Ones who habitually supplement their incomes by extracurricular activities, to the detriment of their teaching responsibilities, are probably a prostitution of professors; a pretension or a presumption of professors seems to be apt for those who take themselves too seriously, although it would be as apt to use pride. (In this case I am relying on Funk and Wagnalls Standard Dictionary, 1964, 1st and not 8th definition – at no time has that other book by Webster been consulted.)

For those who seem to be getting good mileage out of a variety of somewhat suspect or gimmicky theories, I suggest a pretension of professors. Schools which have large faculties but few students presumably suffer from a proliferation, profusion, progression or predicament of professors. Many classes at university survive despite the efforts of a procrastination of professors.

No, Mr. Frankum did little justice to the immense alliterative possibilities of a veritable gold mine – in fact, a provocation of professors.

Malcolm Matthew
Toronto

The Hemingway-Callaghan Fight

November 3, 1972

In his interesting article The Old Man and the Kid, William French makes one error of fact in describing the Ernest Hemingway-Morley Callaghan boxing match and its aftermath. The letter Hemingway wrote Arthur Mizener in 1951 was not the first time he had written about his sparring match with Callaghan.

The first occasion, as I noted in my recently published study of Hemingway and Callaghan, came in a letter written to Max Perkins, the New York editor who handled the work of both writers, as well as Scott Fitzgerald. The letter was dated Aug. 28, 1929, not long after the Hemingway-Callaghan bout. Hemingway and Fitzgerald had had a heavy lunch at Prunier's restaurant and hence, "on acct. of my condition" there were to be one-minute rounds with two minutes between each round. In the first round he had "slipped" to the canvas and "pulled a tendon." He did admit that he'd gotten a badly cut mouth out of the affray, and – if Callaghan could have hit hard – he "would have killed me."

Whatever version of the fight one chooses to accept – Hemingway to Perkins, Hemingway to Mizener, or Callaghan's own in That Summer in Paris – one should remember that it was not a Great Battle of the twentieth century, nor even one of Hemingway's major ones. I personally prefer the one in which he beat up the poet Wallace Stevens.

Fraser Sutherland
Montreal

Dogs

January 6, 1973

I hate dogs. Quite likely you don't care about dogs one way or another, but I hate dogs. I loathe and despise dogs. All they do is eat, defecate and bark. They eat my $200 limited-edition art books, my kid's Barbie dolls and more dinner than they weigh, then they throw it all up behind the chesterfield which weighs 900 pounds and requires my neighbor's assistance to move.

At nights, when they're young, you have to lock them in a bathroom or in the basement, right? You give them $40 worth of toys, a fur-lined doggie blasted basket, water, food, an alarm clock with a loud, comforting tick, as recommended by the best veterinarians, and a night light. My own kids don't get so much. And what do the dogs do? That's right – they eliminate all over everywhere but on the expensive doggie-dirty paper you've carefully laid out for them – they yip and howl all night – they cause the neighbor woman to miscarry, they keep the whole house awake – and when you come to release them at five a.m. they bite you.

Oh, I hate dogs! I have to tell someone, and you're it.

Paul A. Fulford
Don Mills

Investigative Reporting

February 16, 1974

My father, a great editor, 1895-1937, taught me as a cub the four great questions I might have to face in political reporting. I was never an investigative reporter, such as the great crew you now

Chapter 16

The Birth of the Coat-Hanger

February 14, 1984

I was concerned by your suggestion that the reason one always has too many coat-hangers and not enough can-openers is that the can-opener is the larval stage of the coat-hanger (Come The Evolution, We'll All Join Cells – Feb. 11).

This theory is gaining popularity, but is incorrect. Coat-hangers actually breed by spontaneous generation. Stagnant pools of phlogiston in closets crystallize and form wire coat-hangers.

Jeffrey D. Sherman
Willowdale, Ontario

◆

February 25, 1984

Jeffrey Sherman rightly points out the theory that coat-hangers are generated by crystallized phlogiston. I draw his attention, however, to the strong suspicion that coat-hangers appear in direct proportion to the number of lost left-hand woollen gloves over any given winter.

Is there an enzymatic reaction between phlogiston and wool which would account for this relationship? In addition, how does he account for the observation that in urban shopping malls, wire coat-hangers are seen to flock in large numbers with dry-cleaning plastic bags?

E. Harper
London, Ontario

◆

February 25, 1984

Jeffrey Sherman is clearly writing from the limited viewpoint of Eastern Canada. Here in the West there are no stagnant pools of phlogiston, yet the coat-hangers still breed. Another solution must be sought. Is it not time for the Government to appoint a Royal Commission to investigate the matter?

H.A. Sherman
Calgary

◆

March 3, 1984

I'm indebted to E. Harper for pointing out the relationship between coat-hangers and lost left-hand woollen gloves. It appears that this most likely results from the sinister nature of coat-hangers, rather than from any enzymatic reaction between phlogiston and wool.

E. Harper also asked how to account for the observation that in urban shopping malls, wire coat-hangers are seen to flock in large numbers with plastic dry-cleaning bags. This is easily answered. Coathangers found in plastic bags are anaerobic and belong to a different species than their phlogiston-breathing cousins. The anaerobic coat-hangers breed through the transmutation of earth, air, fire and water, and may be readily identified by small green ties around their necks.

Jeffrey D. Sherman
Willowdale, Ontario

◆

March 5, 1984

I read with interest the comments concerning the on-going problems with the proliferation of coat-hangers. Rabbits are not in it at all. This has long been an area of concern, and I am glad that at last some attention is being given to it.

I have always understood – indeed, it has been my experience – that the most massive reproduction does not depend upon the presence or absence of crystallized phlogiston; this is an understandable misinterpretation of facts. Atmospheric and environmental factors are more crucial. More and more coat-hangers will magically (well, some of us like to call it magic) appear if the conditions are right – that is to say, if they are in a dark, enclosed space, with relatively uncrowded hanging rods.

In addition, I would point out that this problem does not arise, ever, with wooden or plastic coat-hangers, nor does it occur with wire coat-hangers which are covered with anything at all – plastic foam, braided nylon, crocheted covers or plain paper. Covered wire hangers do not multiply.

Mary Lanceley
Athens, Ontario

◆

March 12, 1984

... Has E. Harper considered the ratio between such lost gloves and the regular appearance of single socks at the back of the drawers? There seems to be quite a genetic similarity between the two – digital covering, cuffs, general woolliness – and I would not be surprised if missing partners were discovered quietly reproducing in the remote corners of spare room cupboards. Anyone sighting the offspring of these possible unions, please keep in touch.

M. V. Copeland
Don Mills, Ontario

◆

March 17, 1984

Your various correspondents on the subject of wire coat-hangers seem to agree that crystallized phlogiston causes their proliferation, but no one has offered a solution to the problem.

I would like to pass on a secret I learned at my mother's knee some 70 years ago, which I have found very effective over the years. It is simple and inexpensive, and the ingredients may be obtained at the local drug store.

Purchase an adequate supply of antiphlogiston, or Zambuk; segregate the hangers to be treated and rub them all over with the preparation, being careful to include the hooks, as this seems to be the focal point of the infection.

The hangers may then be returned to the closet, but they should not be used for hanging delicate garments, as the medication may soil the fabric.

A. Gavin Hudson
Toronto

◆

March 31, 1984

... I suggest that the missing partners are indeed quietly reproducing, but not in spare room cupboards. Offspring of these unions can easily be sighted under beds and behind refrigerators, and are well known as "dust bunnies."

C.B. Ramsdale
Don Mills, Ontario

◆

March 31, 1984

In science, the best hypothesis is the one that explains the most observable facts. Therefore, while imaginative, neither can-openers nor phlogiston can be accepted as progenitors for wire coat-hangers.

Anyone who has taken clothes to a dry cleaner knows the hot, steamy conditions found there are all that is required. Coat-hangers spring to life fully grown, as evidenced by the transparent plastic afterbirth and pseudo-umbilical cords joining them at the neck.

What is not generally realized is that they are immortal if left undisturbed. They are, however, susceptible to a rare disease called Spring House Cleaning, and its obscure aberrant form, The Rent Went Up, We're Moving.

Allan Paterson
Cardigan, P.E.I.

◆

March 31, 1984

The spinning of the dryer creates a black hole that sucks single socks into nothingness.

Period.

P. Ryan
North Vancouver

Chapter 17

Life in the Fast Lane

March 5, 1974

An alternative has been suggested to a Scarborough Expressway. Improved, modernized electric street cars are all very well, trouble is you can't get your car on them.

Shea Hoffmitz
Guelph, Ontario

Whisky

March 7, 1974

Re hijackers using whisky to set aircraft afire:
  If airlines are offering whisky of quality capable of causing such flames, they should carry an equal amount of Liquor Control Board of Ontario stock to extinguish them.

Ken Morris
Lakefield, Ontario

Illegitimacy

March 14, 1974

The Ontario Law Reform Commission is proposing that the status of illegitimacy should be abolished.
  If this becomes law where will the army get its sergeant-majors?

A.G. Goodeve
Toronto

Religious Objects

March 15, 1974

I was most interested to read of the latest advances in church and religious furnishings. However, you omitted mention of such items as holy water aerosol and incense spray, or has the ecclesiastical technology still to catch up with the mid-twentieth century?

David Piggins
Guelph

Demeter Started It All

April 5, 1974

In your editorial Pretty As A Pitcher (April 1), you appear to express rather fey astonishment that females wish to encroach upon such male-oriented sports as drinking, brawling, baseball, etc. Their causative desire could have originated in the outrageous treatment received by Demeter, the Greek goddess of the soil, and the only female spectator at the first Olympic Games.

As overseer of the games, Demeter sat on a marble throne observing the naked male participants. The goddess was similarly clad, although she wore a wreath in her hair and held a symbolic sheaf of wheat, which she probably felt inclined to use as a fly swatter. After three days of dry-roasting in the blazing sun, I suspect that Demeter suffered from numerous fly-bites, a nasty dose of sunburn and a hot seat. She must have been quite relieved to return to mother naturing.

Under the circumstances, I do not find it surprising that some women seek to participate in sports, rather than retain the spectator role.

Lois E. Ladly
Islington

Inflation

April 29, 1974

The reason a dollar won't do as much for people as it once did is that people won't do as much for a dollar as they once did.

J.S. Vanderploeg
Toronto

The Jarvis-Ridout Duel

August 6, 1974

I was horrified to note that in Zena Cherry's column yesterday morning she inadvertently perpetuated some myths surrounding the Ridout-Jarvis duel. Some of these myths, I am ashamed to say, originated with those Ridouts who never want to appear in the wrong (a family failing) and continue to persist among some of my less well-informed relations despite such scholarly articles as The Duel in Early Upper Canada by Mr. Justice W.R. Riddell in the Canadian Law Times during 1915.

Whether or not Mrs. Thomas Ridout was splashed with mud by a Jarvis is really neither here nor there; mud splashing must have been an everyday occurrence in Toronto at the time, what with unpaved roads and messy spring weather. The reasons go back farther than that: Mrs. Ridout (nee Mary Campbell of Bay of Quinte, Ontario) was indeed the cause. A woman of commanding stature and countenance, likened by one of her sons to the great Mrs. Siddons in Pizarro, she was spoiling for a fight, and her animosity settled on the family of Provincial Secretary William Jarvis.

In 1815 Samuel Peters Jarvis, the Secretary's son, escorted his sister and the youngest daughter of Thomas Ridout, the Surveyor-General, to Quebec City where they were to be placed in school. Thomas G. Ridout (my great-grandfather) was living there at the time and was responsible for paying the bills of both his sister and the Jarvis girl, sending the latter's accounts back to Toronto. Mrs. Ridout got the mistaken idea that the Jarvises were not paying up and did not hesitate to say so to anyone who cared to listen. The whole business was handled so ineptly by the Ridouts, when the Jarvises protested, that a duel was arranged between George Ridout (another son of Mary Ridout's) and S.P. Jarvis. Timely intervention by Dr. John Strachan (later the bishop) saved the day. Mary Ridout was obviously not content. If her belligerent instincts were not to be satisfied by her rather temperate older boys, at least she could go to work on a younger one, John. John was a bad piece of work, short-tempered, bellicose and, from all accounts, most unpleasant, a real mother's son – of that mother at any rate. (The myth that he was so nervous that he shook during the duel is laughable.)

Without going into more details, suffice to say that the opportunity to open the old sore came when a client of lawyer George Ridout made a small claim against the Jarvis family. While George was away young John demanded payment from S.P. Jarvis in such an offensive manner that he was physically ejected from the Jarvis office. Later John attacked S.P. Jarvis in the street with a stick. John, it should be noted, was only 18 when this took place, but was a veteran of the war of 1812!

After that encounter the only way out seemed to be a duel,

which took place on the 12th of July, 1817. The duelists were to fire their pistols at the count of three; Ridout fired into the air at "two" and walked away. The seconds called him back and told him he must obey the rules. He was given his empty pistol and on "three" Jarvis fired and killed Ridout.

That was the end of the duel but Mrs. Ridout kept the old fires burning as long as she could by publishing a rather revolting libel some nine years later, and by standing on the steps of St. James Cathedral every Sunday after divine service and loudly, as only she could, cursing the Jarvis and Boulton families (D'Arcy Boulton was Jarvis' second).

Godfrey Ridout
Professor, History and Literature Department
Faculty of Music, University of Toronto

◆

August 15, 1974

I should like to pay my respects to Mr. Godfrey Ridout for his letter in your paper of Aug. 6, giving a correction of your columnist's account of the Jarvis-Ridout duel. From my family papers, I agree with Mr. Ridout's account in every detail except one small one.

I think young John Ridout was nervous enough to fire prematurely, but not into the air, as Jarvis' neck-cloth was nicked. When the referees insisted that the rules be followed, and that Jarvis should make his shot, our family story is that he meant to fire wide (as any gentleman would do in the circumstances), but that, his pistol-hand having been struck by young Ridout the day before, his shot went unintentionally to a fatal spot. No one ever really tried to *kill* a rival in a "duel of honor."

I might add that Mrs. F.C. Hood, whose maiden name was Dora Ridout, was a close and valued friend of mine for many years, but that I have not met Mr. Godfrey Ridout, whom I greatly respect.

Julia Jarvis
Toronto

Whistling for the Czar

August 14, 1974

I often wonder why John Kraglund in his always interesting music column never mentions a branch of music popular since the Stone

Age. I refer of course to whistling. It has been said: "Show me the man who whistles, and I'll show you a happy man." How true. The man who whistles while he works – or while he is doing anything else – has few worries on his mind, and little of anything else. Whistling as an art, however, is largely overlooked these days. But long ago and far away, this was not the case.

In the town of K—, in the Ukraine, when I was growing up, there lived an old man we called Uncle Vassily (the peasants called him Little Father – he was short and had nine sons). Uncle Vassily had been a concert whistler, and in his hey-day had whistled before the Czar, the Grand Duke Nicholas and Count Basie. In his ability to reach high C and stay there, he was compared to the great Ivan Peepchick.

Everyone in Uncle Vassily's family whistled or had something to do with this remarkable art. His mother was a Whistler. His father gave instructions in whistling – he told the landlord to whistle for his rent. His sister was whistled at. But while they only whistled now and then, Uncle Vassily whistled all the time.

His cheerful piping woke the neighbors long before the dawn chorus, and at dusk when the sun sank and the balloon went up, Uncle Vassily's pure notes took wing, and like blithe spirits soared to heaven.

He whistled until he died. On that sad day when the doctor drove up in his Zim to the modest little dacha and, parking on the family dog, went in and after examining Uncle Vassily told him that he was checking out, poor Uncle Vassily's whistle was the most poignant ever heard by a millionaire. (It is quite possible for doctors in Russia to make a great deal of money.)

Uncle Vassily was the last of the great whistlers, and like practitioners of other lost musical arts – drumming on the table with one's fingers while waiting for the waiter, humming through a comb and kazoo-playing – he was gone. But,

Still are thy pleasant voices, thy nightingales awake;
For Death, he taketh all away, but them he cannot take.

Dickson Russell
Toronto

Cigarets

October 12, 1974

The article Smokers' Image: Sickly, Sexual Flops, by Thomas Coleman suggests that smokers go around in a constant state of physical and spiritual detumescence. I would suggest that is snivelling propaganda on the order of that spewed by ardent vegetarians who would suggest that meat eaters are bound for baldness, business failure and early death.

I, modestly put as possible, am living proof that smoking is probably the single most beneficial pastime in the world, easily on a par with nightly readings from the scriptures and half-yearly visits to the dentist.

When I began smoking at age 15, I was sickly, short, spurned by all sexes and had a complexion to match my mean and whining personality. Suddenly, thanks to smoking Export plain ends, the only brand to smoke if you're just starting and seriously interested in improving yourself, I gained in confidence and height, and my voice changed (down) about six octaves.

No longer was my voice mistaken for my mother's on the telephone. No longer did members of the football team bring back bushels of beach sand to throw in my eyes; sand they had blithely gathered during orgies with dozens of wide-eyed little blondes in the dunes along Lake Huron while I stayed home protecting my summer pallor, knitting mufflers in the basement to try to stave off the winter colds that came week on week in phlegmy succession like breakers on a bitter coast.

No. Suddenly tall and virile youths were hovering around constantly, seeking to borrow tailor-mades. In the basement of the high school, wide-eyed little blondes with their cardigans on backwards followed me everywhere, staring in awe at the rectangular bulge in my breast pocket.

They began to take me out in their fathers' cars; forced me to smoke in the back seat at drive-ins; taught me the secrets of the universe and the proper mix of Seven-Up and cherry whisky. I became sophisticated, sought out, honored, loved and wise.

Scholarships rained on me. Powerful industrialists offered me positions as protégé. I was invited to all the best places and came to know all the best people.

Smoking, and smoking alone, made me what I am today.

Neophytes journeyed days to hear the sound of my cough.

Medical schools compete with one another for the privilege of having my lung bestowed on them.

Greatness is where you find it. Non-smokers, especially militant non-smokers, are weaklings of spirit and visionaries of mediocrity.

John Edward Slinger Jr.
Toronto

On Being Fat

January 7, 1975

A Detroit survey has revealed that fat executives are paid less than their slim colleagues to the extent of $1,000 per pound. So reports Kenneth B. Smith.

To what purpose was the fact determined? To what use will it be put? And who came up with the cash to pay for this rag-bag of trivia?

May we also question, with respect, your timing? The article plunged our New Year's Eve house-party into a deep incubus of gloom. Unslim executives sipped low-cal cordial, reneged on imported hippocras with clotted cream, and nibbled the night away on a single watercress sandwich. In periods of black despair they kept nipping off to weigh themselves in upstairs closets.

In the other corner, weighing up to 170 pounds, our fly-to-middle-weight colleagues were no less abstinent. Loaded with sub-fusc thoughts instead of brandy punch, they chatted moodily on the cost-benefit ratio of adipose tissue and plotted graphs on coasters while running an uptight eye over the girths of their erstwhile friends. We would not be surprised to have our morning desk flooded with their requests for postings to the money-pots of Detroit.

The party was dead by 11:55 p.m. Thank you, and Happy New Year to you, too.

James Barclay
Westmount, Quebec

Bad Evening

Peter Cook and his partner Dudley Moore were touring North America with their comedy show called Good Evening. While in New York, Mr. Cook was interviewed by John Hofsess for Maclean's magazine, and later by Herbert Whittaker of The Globe over the telephone from Toronto.

March 26, 1975

I trust it was a faulty telephone connection between Detroit and Toronto that made Peter Cook appear to say to Herbert Whittaker during his long-distance interview that I had presented him with a copy of The Anderson Tapes during our meeting in New York. The book he received was Alison Lurie's War Between The Tates, a marginally more distinguished selection though still far short of what I would have given Peter Cook had he showed the slightest evidence of being sentient.

John Hofsess
Toronto

◆

March 27, 1975

It was indeed The War Between The Tates that John Hofsess gave me in New York.

I found the novel so trite and tedious that I thought Alison Lurie might well be his pseudonym.

Peter Cook
Toronto

A Killer

April 12, 1975

I have been in the throes of income tax preparation for a number of hours, and I have come to the conclusion that this is a clear case of capital punishment and as such it should be abolished forthwith.

George L. Miller
Agincourt

Music on Trains

January 8, 1976

There is one curious similarity between the railway system of the Soviet Union and our own distinguished Canadian Pacific. Mind you, the Soviet trains run precisely on time, are scrupulously clean and comfortable, and provide service over an enormous variety of routes at extremely low prices, so the similarity obviously does not lie in any of these areas.

The parallel lies in the one area I can think of in which the Canadian Pacific actually outdoes the Russian trains, namely in forcing the passenger to consume vast amounts of music with which his ears are gratuitously assaulted and from which he cannot escape except by taking refuge in the rest rooms (which however may assault other sensibilities).

The Soviet trains are in fact slightly less efficient in this assault of the ear, for they give the passenger at least a slight chance to defend himself (especially if his hearing is not too good), for there is a volume control in each compartment (European trains usually consist of compartments for six to eight people).

All other countries in whose trains I have ridden are far behind the cultural level displayed by CP and their Russian colleagues; in their cultural barbarism they not only refrain from providing a homogenized background of soothing sound, they even discourage self-appointed distributors of musical art who have had the kindness to go to the trouble of bringing transistor radios with them so that they can provide entertainment to their fellow passengers. After all, no sensible person would be able to appreciate the majestic serenity of Mount Edith Cavell, or the turbulent grandeur of the Fraser Canyon, without some sweet accompanying sounds by Muzak to help make them seem real.

Anton Kuerti
Toronto

> *Mr. Kuerti, who had been called a "pianistic supernova" before he moved to Canada, achieved an artistic tour de force in 1975 by playing, in 10 concerts, all of Beethoven's 32 sonatas.*

Maureen McTeer
February 27, 1976

We have more or less got used to Margaret Trudeau's idiosyncrasies and now we have Joe Clark's wife, whatever her name is. When we had W.L.M. King and R.B. Bennett things were so peaceful. I think now it was because they didn't have wives. At the risk of being called a male chauvinist might I suggest that if we ever succeed in repatriating the constitution, we amend it to require vows of celibacy from prospective Prime Ministers.

James F. Hutchinson
Woodstock

How about the General?
March 24, 1976

It has just been announced that the tower in Tunney's Pasture, Ottawa, housing the Ministry of Health and Welfare Canada, called the General Purpose Building, is to be renamed in honor of Jeanne Mance.

While no one can object to honoring that devoted and generous person who played an important role in our early days, how about the military figure, also historical, whose name is being so lightly cast aside?

I refer to General Purpose. When the building was first opened and named in 1968 a group of enthusiasts, curious as to who this man was, investigated his career.

His early days in the Canadian West, his association there with the American military figure who became General Service, and his later rise to high rank and honor have all been recorded in a small pamphlet.

A stained-glass memorial window honoring Purpose was designed in 1968. It portrays him nude, modestly veiled with a maple leaf, capped in full beaver-pelt, astride a moose rampant. Drawings of the window exist. It has not yet been installed.

Why is Purpose being obliterated? Could it be because of his anti-Riel position in 1869-70? His long association with Protestantism? (Researches indicate that 76.9 per cent of the Methodist hospitals in Southern Ontario in 1880 had a General Purpose Committee.)

Let it not be forgotten that in 1968 the tower received a double name, General Purpose Building / Edifice Polly Valent (thus by using the name of his Outaouaise paramour of the 1890s expressing our dual nature).

Let Purpose-Valent remain honored, I say! Honor Jeanne Mance, or Marguerite Bourgeoys, or whatever historical figure can simultaneously represent womanhood and French Canada, by giving her name to the new Statistics Canada tower in Tunney's Pasture. Or to the new National Gallery.

Courtney C.J. Bond
Ottawa

◆

March 30, 1976

I must express my delight at Courtney C.J. Bond's exposition of the historical background of General Purpose, after whom so many buildings and so much equipment has been named. I trust his research may eventually shed some light on other famous military figures such as General Delivery, the father of our postal system, and that peripatetic mediator of disputes, whose record must surely be unsurpassed – could anyone ever count the number of issues settled by General Agreement?

It would be more difficult to obtain data on Major Disaster;

although his appearance on the scene is often predicted, he tends to arrive unannounced. In government circles, Major Policy Shift is continually being heralded, but many doubt his existence.

Personally, I would hope some day to see due recognition given to a humbler figure. In various parts of the world his death is repeatedly announced, yet he is expected by many observers to shoulder the burden of economic recovery. Who else but Private Enterprise?

Perhaps his low estate is due to the image suffered by all non-commissioned ranks from the bad example set by Corporal Punishment. Although banished from the education system a generation ago, he is reputed to lurk yet in various dark corners of society.

P.K. Cranston
Ottawa

◆

April 7, 1976

Recent trenchant letters have reviewed the glorious contributions made to Canadian history by General Purpose and his numerous military brothers. (Are there no sisters worthy of similar note?) I suggest that we not forget the Benedict Arnold of Canada, namely General Indifference. Perhaps some learned academic would investigate fully the General's less than glorious contributions and enlighten us all.

R.C. Spooner
Kingston

Just Call Me Joe

November 16, 1976

The Ontario Law Reform Commission has suggested many useful reforms over the past years, but I am rather dubious about its latest proposal which would allow women to retain their maiden names when they marry, among other things.

My problem is that I was born in England, where hyphenated surnames are not uncommon. My father was John Burrows-Hyde, and my mother was Jane Cholmondley-Featherstonehaugh. That made me Joseph Burrows-Hyde-Cholmondley-Featherstonehaugh when I was born.

But in 1964 my parents were divorced and my custody was awarded to my mother, who later married James Scarborough-Yoicks. Since I was still a minor at that time and my stepfather

wished to legally adopt me, my name thus became Joseph
Burrows - Hyde - Cholmondley - Featherstonehaugh - Scarbor -
ough - Yoicks.

I am now engaged to be married to a girl named Jean Gormley-
Nash - Fallingbrooke - Czyczyczynski, whose parents were also
divorced.

Do you think it would be all right if we named the child she is
expecting Jack?

Or should we stick to plain Burrows - Hyde - Cholmondley -
Featherstonehaugh - Scarborough - Yoicks - Gormley - Nash -
Fallingbrooke - Czyczyczynski?

H. W. Somerville
Toronto

The Quebec Election

*On November 15, 1976, the Separatist Parti Québécois was elected
to power in Quebec.*

November 24, 1976

Congratulations to your cartoonist Anthony Jenkins for his superb
Dismayed Beaver, surely the best of all commentaries on the issue
so dramatically pointed up by the Quebec election of the preceding
day.

It suggested to me a bit of verse which I first conceived as Con-
cise Advice to René Lévesque. However, in the light of the reac-
tions outside Quebec to the victory of the Parti Québécois, I think it
more appropriate to offer its counsel as well to Pierre Trudeau and,
indeed, to all the rest of us Canadians:

It's time to mind your P's and Q's,
    Let common sense illumine.
That wise a-P's-ment may suffuse
    Political a-Q-men.

Barney Rouillard
Toronto

Decentralizing Canada

*An article suggested that Canada be broken up into 10 separate tariff
and monetary units with total control of taxation within their borders, with a central government as a referee to prevent regional competition from hurting the Canadian economy.*

February 10, 1977

The article, Cost of Decentralizing Canada Could Be High, by Arthur Donner and Fred Lazar, raises a number of questions.

How could "regional equalization goals" be "administered regionally" in this hypothetical twentieth-century North American version of the Holy Roman Empire?

We have at present a single Canadian free trade area and monetary union. Have the authors made any estimate of the sheer dislocation costs of breaking this into 10 separate tariff units and ten separate monetary units?

How could the poorer provinces, deprived of the equalization grants and other Dominion funds they now receive, maintain anything like their present standards of public services, education, and social security? Handing over taxing powers to the rich provinces, which have plenty of tax, is one thing. Handing over the same powers to the poor provinces is very different.

The authors say the "central government would still have to act as a referee to prevent regional competition in such things as tariffs, exchange rates and monetary policies from having an aggregate negative effect on the Canadian economy."

How, precisely? The Bank of Canada, it is clear, would become a sort of miniature Bank of International Settlements. But how would the (gossamer) "central government" act as a "referee" on the provincial tariffs? And how much "Canadian economy" would be left to suffer any "aggressive effect," negative or positive? Why bother to retain a cobweb, which would be of little use to the rich mini-nations, and probably none to the poor ones?

How many would leap to their feet to sing:

O Canada! Beloved Referee
Of customs dues and banking policy!
With glowing hearts we've seen arise
Ten Norths, nor strong nor free;
But we'll stand on guard, O Canada!
To keep our Referee!
O Canada! Pale, shadowy!
O Canada! Be still our Referee!
O Canada! Long live our Referee!

But of course the Referee could still have a distinctive flag, which would surely stir the blood of every citizen of the 10 ministates: 10 jackasses eating their leaves off a single maple tree.

Senator Eugene Forsey
Ottawa

Mr. Stanfield Drives a Car

February 11, 1977

In his column this morning, Geoffrey Stevens attacks my competence as a driver, saying: "He has the reputation among his friends of being the worst driver this side of Hull."

This assertion has a false ring because my friends would never use my name in such a racist manner. Furthermore, I resent having my driving ability questioned by a columnist who, from time to time, uses the nominative case after a preposition.

I am considering suing The Globe and Mail and Mr. Stevens for several millions of dollars, and I most certainly will if his irresponsible comment should cause an increase in my insurance rates.

I wish to assure the people of Ottawa who may read The Globe and Mail that they are perfectly safe with me on their streets. I drove a car long before Geoffrey Stevens was born and my accident record is spotless.

I quite agree with Mr. Stevens, however, that Joe Clark should not drive a car. He obviously has things on his mind from time to time. I have never been accused of that.

Robert L. Stanfield
Ottawa

> *After nine years as leader of the Conservative Party, Mr. Stanfield resigned on February 22, 1976. He was replaced by Joe Clark.*

Oxygen and Heart Attacks

April 11, 1977

As an ex-Spitfire pilot and member of the Canadian Fighter Pilots' Association, I am appalled at the number of my fellow pilots that are being struck down each year with heart attacks (put me down for two); many are fatal.

I have concluded that our excessive use of oxygen during combat must have a direct bearing on the high mortality rate.

In combat we would have our control set on almost pure oxygen while flying at 20,000 feet. During combat our heights would vary from 20,000 feet to ground level. At ground level we would still be on pure oxygen. The combination of oxygen plus the added tension and excitement which already had the adrenalin flowing was too much for even the strongest hearts to take.

We were never instructed by the medical authorities as to the dangers of excessive oxygen, so we, therefore, never considered the ramifications that could be detrimental to our health.

In all fairness I must admit it was a great cure for a hangover, particularly prior to a 5 a.m. dawn patrol.

I and my remaining compatriots would like to see a published report by the medical association that would relate to my theories or any government pension data that would relate to this heart condition as a pensionable illness.

B.J. "Buzz" Hayden
Oakville

The Miniskirt

June 8, 1977

In your editorial A Leg Up you dispute the British claim to have invented the mini-skirt and give credit instead to the Scots for their kilt. Clearly, however, the British claim refers to an item of feminine attire and it is invalid for reasons that you ignore.

The truth of the matter is that the mini-skirt was a Canadian invention; it came into vogue with the womenfolk of New France in the first half of the eighteenth century.

The observant Peter Kalm, Professor of Botany at Uppsala University, during his 1749 visit to Canada in the interests of science, commented in his journal on this intriguing mode of dress. On July 25 he wrote: "Every day but Sunday they (Canadian women) wear a little neat jacket, and a short skirt which hardly reaches halfway down the leg, and sometimes not that far." A week later he noted: "Their jackets are short and so are their skirts, which scarcely reach down to the middle of their legs." He made a similar comment on Sept. 22. The testimony of this distinguished scholar, member of the Swedish Academy of Sciences, is indisputable.

It is indeed saddening that The Globe and Mail, which purports to be our "national newspaper," failed to assert Canada's rightful claim to an invention that has brought so much esthetic pleasure across the centuries to so many. Ignorance of our country's history is no excuse for this appalling lapse.

W.J. Eccles
Professor of History, University of Toronto

The Acoustic Culture

October 19, 1977

The Conference on Canadian Unity seems to have paid little attention to separatism as a world phenomenon. Horizon magazine

248

(spring, 1974) in an article on the Fourth World cited: "A host of ancient peoples is rising up to demand independence." There are six French regions seeking separatism, and also:

... French Flanders, where there exists an embryonic Flemish autonomist movement that is in touch with its ethnic analogue just across the border in Belgium.

The trend, however, is not confined to France; what one theorist calls the "regionalist revolution" is a general European phenomenon. Four revolutionary minorities already have clandestine radio stations: there is Radio Scotland, Radio Euzkadi (Basque), Radio Free Tyrol, and the Voice of Serbia. Every sizeable nation in Western Europe has its ethnic minorities, and within these minorities agitation for more self-government and cultural expression has been growing in recent years – accompanied in some cases by revolutionary violence.

The Horizon article is merely descriptive, and makes no effort to discover any underlying cause or hidden ground for this worldwide drive toward the centrifugal. In point of fact, there is only one new factor in the world environment, only one hidden ground that is exerting simultaneous pressure on all political and geographical units, regardless of their national or ethnic makeup. That "hidden ground" is the instant information environment created by telegraph, telephone, cable, radio and TV. The effect of such instant information as an environment is not to centralize power or decisions, but, on the contrary, to decentralize power and influence. When information is available everywhere at the same time, the pattern that emerges is that of the commando module, which includes the guerrilla, and the activist, and the hijacker alike.

French Canada is a deeply oral and auditory culture, much like the American South in the 1860s when the telegraph was new. The oral South wanted out of the Union because of its cultural clash with the intensely visual and literate Yankee North. When differences as deep as the oral and the literate occur, the incompatibility of such interfacing areas is great indeed. Such differences exist between the North and South of Ireland, to use the familiar case. Such a difference also exists between French and English Canada, both historically and at present. However, a new component has come into play since electronic technology has also moved the young generation of English Canadians strongly in the direction of acoustic culture. There is a large element of separatism in the TV generation which finds itself alienated from the goals and patterns of our industrial society. Our alienated TV generation shares a great deal with the French separatist. This shared alienation can become a new ground for creative understanding of each other.

Marshall McLuhan
Director, Centre for Culture and Technology
University of Toronto

CBC Soundscape

January 26, 1978

In 1974 or thereabouts, I suggested that the CBC might seriously consider the call of the loon as a spacer between all its programs and showed how this could be done by adding the announcer's voice, simply saying "This is the CBC," every 30 seconds or so over an extended loon call. The CBC needs space and air to counteract the impression that all its programs are produced in Nibelheim. But each time I reiterate the suggestion the faces of the CBC executives to whom I am speaking get strained and pureed.

The common loon is known to all parts of the country, making its summer and winter home in Canada. Variants familiar to northern listeners are the Red-Throated Loon, the Arctic Loon and the Yellow-Billed Loon. The loon is not heard in the United States (except in a few northern states); it is not heard in Brazil or Italy or the Congo. This makes the loon an uncounterfeiting and uncounterfeitable soundmark of Canada. Its haunting and lonely call strikes right to the soul of every native who has heard it on summer lakes or on the coastal ranges where it winters.

The broadcaster who begins to incorporate aspects of the Canadian soundscape into program formats will be moving a lot faster toward a distinctive Canadian radio style than is anywhere presently detectable.

R. Murray Schafer
Bancroft

> *A noted composer, Mr. Schafer published a book on sound and noise in 1977 called The Tuning of the World. In it he argued: "Wherever noise is granted immunity from human intervention, there will be found a seat of power. If quiet machinery could have been developed, the success of industrialization might not have been so total ... If cannons had been silent, they would never have been used in warfare."*

The Ten Best of CanLit

February 25, 1978

When I received a telephone call from a Kingston journalist asking my opinion of the University of Calgary Top Ten of Canadian Literature, my first response was to feel that it was one of those things in life that I was better off not to know, but on second thought I decided that I had missed the germ of brilliance in the conception.

Malcolm Ross and Jack McClelland, like many great innovators, have made the classic blunder of stopping too soon. All day I have been thinking of the categories they missed where the voting would be close, the campaigning hard and the awards worth winning.

What about Tallest Canadian Writer? Nominees: Pierre Berton, Jane Rule, Martin Myers and George Bowering. Or Shortest? Take your choice of Mordecai Richler, Adele Wiseman and Don Bailey. Most Beautiful (Female)? A hands-down win for Susan Musgrave. Most Beautiful (Male)? I'm not the best nominator, but a chance remark at a Writers' Union convention suggests that Graeme Gibson and Jim Bacque would be top contenders. For Most Battered, Milton Acorn. Longest Beard, Robertson Davies. Blondest, Sylvia Fraser vs. Andreas Schroeder.

The possibilities are endless. Hairiest Writer, Writer with Most Warts, Shortest Pencil. Then there are the national categories: Most Hungarian, George Jonas; Most Irish (Northern), a close race between the favorite, Brian Moore, and a relative unknown, George McWhirter; Most Jewish, Irving Layton; Most Homosexual, Scott Symons.

And finally, Most Embarrassed, to the begetter of the whole thing, literary critic Malcolm Ross, who, if he isn't, should be.

David Helwig
Kingston

◆

March 29, 1978

I am contemplating a series of film scripts in frank imitation of the English Carry On series, but based more on the Canadian scene in literature and politics. I have in mind the following titles:

Carry On Irving.
Carry On Surfacing.

Carry On Divining.
Carry On Riel.
Carry On Kravitz.
Carry On Manticore.
Carry On Separating
and
Carry On Up the Rideau.

So far I have been able to pick out quite easily the Canadian personalities who ought to take the parts usually assigned to the English cast, though there are some perplexities.

The Sid James parts will be played by Austin Willis; the Hattie Jacques parts by Kate Reid; the Joan Sims parts by Barbara Hamilton; the Charles Hawtrey parts by Eric House; the Kenneth Connor parts by Christopher Plummer.

I have found it difficult to spot a local counterpart for Barbara Windsor or for Bernie Bresslaw.

The Kenneth Williams parts obviously ought to be taken by René Lévesque.

Hugh Hood
Montreal

D— Right!

November 11, 1978

In a Gl... and M... article, Bermuda Meeting Attracts Allmand, Friends Via JetStar, reporter Rob... Shep... quoted Consumer and Corpo... Affairs Minister War... Allm... as saying criticism related to his Berm... trip in a governm... JetStar "is a real pain in the ..."

Did Mr. Allmand really regard it as a pain in the ...?

Or did he more realistically specify the anatomical area by calling it a pain in the ass?

I appreci... that the Gl... and M... may not wish to corr... public morals in this fash... but in the interest of accur... reporting and easier reading, I would much prefer that you call a spade a spade.

Den... McClos...
Richm... H...

An Ally

February 3, 1979

Allen Abel's alliteration assists any audience apropos ascertaining athletes' abilities and achievements. Attacking Abel's articulate anecdotes asserts an avid animosity appropriate among apes, asses, anacondas and antediluvians. Authentic aesthetes appreciate accomplished and abundant artistry.

Attaboy, Al!

H.W. Somerville
Toronto

The Best

May 8, 1979

I must take exception to D.J. MacLennan's letter, which stated Margaret Atwood "is the finest writer in Canada today."

I am the finest writer in Canada today. And one day I'll write something to prove it.

Mark Wiedmark
Port Hope

Upmanship

May 12, 1979

I was amused by what I overheard at a variety store the other day. A shopper said to the cashier, "Forget the bag, thanks. I want my neighbors to see I can afford bread and milk."

Nancy Truscott
Toronto

The Big Bang

July 21, 1979

In Glimpse Back in Time, Malcolm W. Brown writes: "Out at the observable edge of the universe, we can faintly discern fascinating objects as they were when they sent us their light more than 15 billion years ago." He goes on: "Scientists believe that the universe came into existence 15 billion to 20 billion years ago as a result of a titanic explosion, from which all the matter, energy and time in the universe have been expanding ever since."

Presumably, unless the initial rate at which matter expanded far exceeded that of light, we shall never see the Big Bang itself, even through a 10-metre telescope. But, assuming the universe to be 20 billion years old, will someone explain how these "fascinating objects" were hurled far enough in the first five billion years for the light they emitted *at that time* to have taken the next 15 billion years to reach wherever our corner of the universe has expanded to by now?

Clearly, if our own galaxy has loitered not far from the scene of the Big Bang, then their rate of recession from that primal spot must once again have far exceeded that of the speed of light for those five billion years.

If, on the other hand, we ourselves are somewhere near the outer fringes of expansion, then our own rate of recession during the subsequent 15 billion years makes the proposition slightly more credible – except that, in that case, all most distant objects should be concentrated to one side of the night sky. This I have not seen suggested anywhere.

James Harrison
Guelph

♦

July 28, 1979

There's a simple answer to the problem raised by James Harrison: it really was a *Big* Bang. Or, as Steven Weinberg puts it in his book The First Three Minutes: "(It was) not an explosion like those familiar on earth, starting from a definite centre and spreading out to engulf more and more of the circumambient air, but an explosion which occurred simultaneously everywhere, filling all space from the beginning ..."

Thus, at the stage when the material universe as we know it came into existence, different pieces of matter would already have been at astronomically large, perhaps even up to infinite distances, apart. There's no need to postulate subsequent above-light speeds to explain the separation of the galaxies we can see or the fact that we can observe radiation from the Big Bang itself.

Nevertheless, there is a paradox similar to the one suggested by Mr. Harrison. If the universe was so large to begin with – and it is much larger now as the result of expansion – then apparently much of the universe must be so far away that it is receding from us at speeds greater than that of light. Maybe this was one reason Einstein at first rejected the notion of an expanding universe when it turned up in his formulations.

However, such unbecoming behavior is not even potentially observable, however powerful our telescopes. Physicists argue that it is meaningless to attempt to apply physical concepts such as relative velocity in such circumstances. To put the matter more succinctly:

> A galaxy faster than light?
> That cannot (said Einstein) be right!
> > But further prediction
> > Belies contradiction:
> That galaxy's far out of sight.

George Rose
Weston

◆

July 28, 1979

I believe space to be gently curved (and that's why our flat earth does not fray at the edges where it rubs). Therefore, the Big Bang theory within this context should resolve James Harrison's doubts about seeing light from 15 billion years ago.

Actually, my calculations show the universe to be about 5 billion years old (give or take six months), so the 15 billion years' light is really the photons on their third (or so) trip around. In fact, were telescopes double-ended, it would be possible to see photons from the same source coming and going simultaneously.

In truth, I do not subscribe to the Big Bang theory for the simple reason that had all matter been concentrated in one place, its density would have been such as to create the biggest Black Hole you never saw. Nothing could have escaped from its gravitational clutches. Not light; not a bang; not even a squeak.

Austin Small
Oakville

The Calibre of the Mullet

August 11, 1979

I found the excerpt from The Manchester Guardian (Just What Was Said – Aug. 6) an interesting new perspective on the theories of probability.

Patrick Jeffcoate estimated the probability of the Australian golfer being struck once by a bullet falling from the beak of a seagull as one in a million. Refusing to be distracted by the intriguing question of what the seagull was doing with a bullet in its beak, I considered this estimate to be on the low side.

It was only as I read on that it became apparent that a misprint had occurred and that bullet should have read mullet. This immediately made Mr. Jeffcoate's one-in-a-million probability more reasonable. The difference in size alone would make it more likely for the golfer to be struck by a falling mullet than a falling bullet depending, of course, on the average size of a mullet and the calibre of the bullet.

A whole new area of investigation appears to be opening up for those interested in this field. We could speculate on the probability of mullet being misprinted bullet, and also on the chances of this happening again.

For instance, there are six letters in the word mullet. If the word is accidentally misprinted, there is a one-in-six probability that the initial letter would suffer. If this should happen, there remain 24 other letters in the alphabet that could replace it. The odds have now increased to 6 times 24, or 144 to one.

It is possible that the learned correspondents to The Guardian, Lord Rothschild, Mr. Jeffcoate and Professors Priestly and Flowerdew, may have some further comment.

Ernest Abbott
Scarborough

◆

August 18, 1979

There is a flaw in the reasoning of Ernest Abbott regarding the probability of a mullet (although others contend that it was a bullet) dropped by a cruising seagull, hitting a hapless Australian golfer. (Incidentally, devotees of the Royal and Ancient will recognize that the injured player could have been moved without penalty – but no nearer to the hole.)

He overlooked the far greater possibility of the gull being hit by the falling golfer and perhaps, in the collision, swallowing the mullet or biting the bullet, as the case may be. In fact, the mullet may have been shot by the bullet, thus accounting for both missiles.

As Columbus suspected (but was afraid to ask), our earth is flat. Hence those Down Under can only hang on because nature provides them with an adhesive substance on their feet to resist gravity like flies on a ceiling. (This explains most Aussies' choleric nature;

the blood rushes to their head.) Now, if this golfer were middle-aged, his natural stickiness was probably wearing thin and any unusual exertion, such as overswinging with a sand wedge, might easily launch him into space to crash on the startled seabird ... and lose two strokes.

Austin Small
Oakville

Sex as a Cure

September 15, 1979

Reports to the contrary notwithstanding, (New Help for Arthritis), sex every six hours does not relieve the pain of arthritis. You just get too tired to notice it. Besides, you can't be sure where you will be when the six hours is up. My bank manager is now very cool toward me and I owe the gift shop $129.50 for stuff that got broken one other time.

James F. Hutchinson
Woodstock

Chapter 18

Hippopotami

December 15, 1972

Your editorial concerning the Metro Toronto Zoo refers to the popularity of "lions and hippopotami."

May I point out that more than one hippopotamus (and even one hippopotamus is a lot of hippopotamus) become hippopotamusses. The name derives from potamos, Greek for river, so should not be given a Latin plural.

Ken Purvis
Toronto

◆

December 22, 1972

It was quite disappointing that you should allow yourself to be taken to task, without retort, for spelling hippopotamus in the plural with an "i."

Derivatives are subject to many eccentricities. In my Living Webster, for example, hippocampus (sea horse) is pluralized with an "i" exclusively. Hippopotamus, however, may take either the "i" or the "es." From the latter example, I conclude that the more popular the usage of a derived word, the more likely will its inflectional forms follow current rather than ancient practice.

The "es" plural of hippopotamus could be called, in this sense, more relevant, and should have been so defended. The criterion of relevance might even suggest that if hippopotamus is to be modernized, the masculinity of "us" could be occasionally adapted to circumstances by the substitution of hippopotams.

R. Durocher
Toronto

◆

December 23, 1972

Although I have good reason not to doubt Mr. Purvis' personal interest in this particular animal, I should like to correct him in the matter of their name, particularly as his interest may, at some future date, extend to more than one of the species.

The word hippopotamus is derived from the late Latin and not, I beg to differ, from the late Greek. The difference being, the Greeks spelt it hippopotamos. I am in agreement with Mr. Purvis that the Greek plural is muses; however, as we, the English, have adopted the Latin spelling it is only logical that we should not mix nationalities and adopt their plural as well, hence hippopotami.

Although this letter is written in a light vein, I, like Mr. Purvis, have a personal interest in the animal. I had to play one in a children's Christmas party recently.

A.D. Goldberg
Toronto

◆

December 29, 1972

With reference to the etymological controversy concerning the plural of hippopotamus, I submit the following suggestion. Since the word derives originally from the Greek potamos, and Greek nouns ending in os are inflected to the nominative plural oi, perhaps we could settle for hippopotamoi. Or, in deference to Hebrew readers, hippopotamim.

H.C. Hardwick
Oakville, Ontario

◆

January 4, 1973

... may I quote a rhyme written and illustrated by Oliver Herford?

> "Oh, say, what is this fearful, wild, Incorrigible cuss?"
> "This creature (don't say 'cuss,' my child;
> 'Tis slang) – This creature fierce is styled
> The Hippopotamus.
> His curious name derives its source
> From two Greek words: Hippos – a horse,
> Potamos – river, see?
> The river's plain enough, of course;
> But why they call that thing a horse,
> That's what is Greek to me."

(Miss) Amoi Bird
Toronto

January 4, 1973

A.D. Goldberg is not at his best on Greek plurals but he is correct in saying that we have taken over the Latinized form hippopotamus and if we wish to use the corresponding plural it should be hippopotami.

But would we not thereby be displaying affectation? Many years ago I learned the following verses:

The folks who live in the East End
And ride to their work in buses
Look at the pretty spring flowers
and say, "O, what lovely crocuses!"
But those who live in the West End
and would in society fly
Behold the delightful spring flowers
and exclaim, "O, what gorgeous croci!"

My sympathy in this matter has always been with the East Enders.

H.R.S. Ryan
Kingston

♦

January 9, 1973

I'm surprised – appalled, if the truth were known – at the lack of substantive research done by A.D. Goldberg, H.R.S. Ryan and other letter writers into the roots of the word hippopotamus. Without such research, all is hypothesis, and every effort at extrapolating the word's plural form will be utterly in vain.

The word hippopotamus is, of course, Early Erse, short and terse. In the primitive days of the Middle Swamp Age, that sacred beast was widely worshipped as divine, but in a curious ceremony – perhaps an early strain of the religious fanaticism which persists among many Erse descendants today – it was regularly slaughtered on its own strange altars. This may help to explain, though not entirely, the comparative rarity of the hippopotamus in Ireland today (Q. O'Gravely-Swart goes deeper into this subject in his under-appreciated work, The Incidence of the Tsetse Fly on the Upper Liffey, a volume no less penetrating for its extraordinary brevity).

Enough of the anthropological background so extravagantly missing in your readers seeking to hang Latin and Greek *derivazione* on a word antedating both cultures by at least 8,460 years. As to the word's plural, it is, as any Early Erse student will tell you at once, Hippopottopoppopommopongos.

For those who are not specialists in Early Erse (and what a treat they're missing!), I should perhaps explain that in the plural form, the "pottopoppopommopongo" is, of course, silent. The word, therefore, is pronounced "hippos" (long "o", please).

May I say how saddened I am to have to point this out?

Simon Newfeld
Toronto

◆

January 11, 1973

May I inject a note of familial dissension into the discussion about the origins and derivations of the word hippopotamus? I fear that my brother Simon Newfeld appears to be slipping up on his Early Erse. For while I agree that the plural form of hippopotamus is elliptically contracted to "hippos," the written form is simply *not* hippopottopoppopommopongos. It pains me to say so, but I think he is confusing it with the plural form of rhinoceros, which comes from Late, or Perv, Erse.

Of course the Pervs have been extinct ever since that nasty social complaint laid them waste in 1203 (1224?), so, lacking subsequent data, my brother's confusion is as understandable as, in a Ph.D., it is regrettable. Meanwhile, I hope Dr. Newfeld will now return to sources other than Quentin O'Gravely-Swart's The Incidence of the Tsetse Fly on the Upper Liffey which, while admittedly trenchant, is wildly inaccurate entymologically.

May I say how saddened I am to have to wash this dirty linen in public?

Maria Newfeld Cohen
Toronto

◆

January 15, 1973

It is past the time to end the discussion on the correct plural of Hippopotamus by sweeping aside all the false hypotheses of origin that have up till now been propagated, principally by the Newfelds whose writings contain numerous and obvious errors.

Firstly the Pervs are not extinct but left their native region on the Upper Liffey some time between 1200 and 1250. Colonies of the Pervs may yet be found in almost any city in the Western World and the Middle East.

Secondly, the Word Hippopotamus is not Erse any more than it is Greek or Latin but rather Teutonic in origin. Old Icelandic contains the word, referring to a large aquatic mammal, but not now (if ever) found in that island. The occurrence in the Erse is probably due to Viking influence as the disappearance of the animal in question from the Erse speaking areas of Europe probably coincided with the Teutonic expansion of the 10th and 11th centuries (ending with the expulsion of the Pervs from the Upper Liffey).

The correct plural of Hippopotamus is, therefore, the Old Low German Hippopotomkin.

E. A. Fuller
Barrie

◆

January 16, 1973

Good grief! All this tumult over the plural of hippopotamus.

I sincerely hope no one is rash enough to inquire about the plural of rhinoceros.

Norman A. Spears
Toronto

◆

January 18, 1973

Little did I know that when I felt compelled in the interests of pedantry to remonstrate with The Globe and Mail on its choice for a plural of "hippopotamus," I would have to take pen in hand again to defend Perv Erse. Pervosity is a subject on which I claim some expertise. In fact, our family name is reported to come from a witticism allowed himself by the Emperor Hadrian as he strolled along his wall, "Purv Erse Purus Est."

So I must emphatically declare that the roots of "hippopotamus" are Greek to me. To establish this beyond all doubt, the hippopotamus in whom I happen to own some futures, and whom I invite you to visit in the Metro Toronto Zoo, will be called Homer.

Ken Purvis
Toronto

◆

January 18, 1973

Hippostopamus!

Leon Baltas
Welland

◆

January 26, 1973

Norman Spears really didn't open a can of worms with his recent letter on the plural of rhinoceros. No problem. Rhino, of course, comes from the Greek rhis: nose. Everyone knows the plural of nose is noses. Therefore – rhinoses. OK?

Tom Feather
Toronto

Chapter 19

Who Are the Rich?

February 1, 1980

Re Vianney Carrière's article on the Communist Party of Canada (Marxist-Leninist) election rally, entitled Speakers, Sound, Slogans: Will They Make the Rich Pay?:

Would someone from the CPC(M-L) please tell us who are the rich they keep condemning?

Where is the "rich" line drawn? If the poverty level is set at $10,000 now, does that make all of us who are earning more than that rich? The article referred to "rich Canadians and corporations" – but what exactly constitutes being rich?

H. Wilson
Mississauga

◆

February 7, 1980

H. Wilson's letter raises a question which has long interested me and perhaps some of your readers can throw light on it.

A few years ago I wrote a novel in which one character described a rich man as somebody who had a yearly income of $100,000 after taxes; a man who was unquestionably rich told me later that this was inadequate because, he said, "$100,000 a year after taxes is just the income of a good corporation lawyer."

Where does wealth begin? I am not talking about health, or pleasant circumstances of work, or riches of the spirit, for these are things which the unappeasable greed of our tax gatherers is as yet unable to touch; I am talking about money. Where does wealth begin?

When I read of families who are so reduced in poverty that their children have no occupation but watching television I am astonished at the change that has taken place in our ideas of poverty since my youth. If the poverty level is anything under $10,000 a year, above what line may we place wealth? In my novelist's innocence I thought it might be $100,000 a year. Where does it truly begin?

Robertson Davies
Toronto

Master of Massey College, 1963-1981, and author of, among other books, The Deptford Trilogy.

◆

February 16, 1980

Robertson Davies asks, if $10,000 a year is the poverty line, where does wealth begin?

My guess is that those whose income is entirely paid as salary, from whose pay cheques the talons of the tax-collecting vultures have already ripped off the fruits of their labor, are today's poor. Wealthy people are those who can afford accountants to assure that none of the inviting loopholes in the law is forgotten when their tax returns are drafted. Rich people are those who can arrange for the laws to be so written that they pay no tax.

F.P. Hughes
Hawkesbury

◆

February 16, 1980

Unlike Robertson Davies, my book remains unwritten, but where wealth begins is easily put: if one must work, one is poor; if not, wealth is theirs.

John Luck
Windsor

The Olympics and Propaganda
February 16, 1980

It is my conviction that the propaganda campaign mounted by the present U.S. administration to torpedo the Summer Olympic Games in Moscow is doomed to failure.

This conviction derives from the impressions I received during a recent visit to the United States to attend the World Gymnastics

Championships. We Soviet gymnasts felt the warm attitude of Americans and saw the enthusiasm with which athletes in many countries, the United States included, are preparing for the Moscow Games. All this, I am sure, is an indication that the anti-Soviet ballyhoo raised by the official authorities does not reflect what is felt and hoped for by American athletes and, indeed, by sportsmen in other lands.

Sport is an ambassador of peace and cannot be used for political blackmail by anyone. All the more so because the drive to boycott Moscow is tending to split the Olympic movement. I am sure that the ill-wishers of the Olympiad are first of all concerned for their own political goals, rather than the interests of the Olympian athletes.

As a member of the Montreal Olympiad, I experienced myself that such international sports meets are real festivals of friendship and peace. We understood each other perfectly.

Despite language barriers, we rejoiced in our own and others' victories and felt genuinely distressed at our rivals' setbacks. This is felt by all Olympians.

So the International Olympic Organization session at Lake Placid that rejected the demand for the Olympic Games to be moved from Moscow has not come as a surprise to me. I saw once again that the noble ideas of the Olympic movement cannot be scuttled just to please a handful of politicians. As for those foreign athletes who succumbed to persuasions and promises and will not come to the Olympic competitions in the Soviet Union this summer, they will probably have only themselves to punish.

Nelli Kim
(Three Times Olympic and World Gymnastics Champion)
Moscow, U.S.S.R.

This letter, passed on to The Globe and Mail by the Soviet Embassy in Ottawa, gives rise to the amusing thought that gymnast Nelli Kim just happened to pick up a copy of The Globe and Mail in Moscow and, seeing a story on the Olympics, could not resist, like so many others, expressing her feelings about the American boycott of the Moscow Games. The Globe receives protests each time it prints letters from the Soviet Union, citing the lack of letters to the editor in Pravda as good enough reason not to print them; but it is interesting to note that the number of letters coming from Moscow seems to increase with each collapse of peace talks. It is also interesting to note Miss Kim's silence on the subject of the Olympics four

266

years later, when the Soviet bloc countries boycotted the Los Angeles Games in 1984.

Eternity

After the defeat of the short-lived Conservative Government of Joe Clark by the Liberals.

February 27, 1980

I see that nothing is changed: the government is still in the hands of the government.

John Routh
Toronto

The Tin Drum

May 3, 1980

As concerned citizens, we are writing in support of the Ontario Censor Board's decision to make cuts from The Tin Drum. To quote Donald Crosbie, deputy minister of Consumer and Commercial Relations, "Surveys show that more than 90 per cent of the Ontario population don't want to see children involved in explicit sexual acts." We feel that it is time for that majority to be heard.

If the film is really so successful and so widely acclaimed, it must be strong enough to withstand the deletion of these three distasteful minutes.

Mary Mingay
Betty Junod
Mary Godfrey
Toronto

◆

May 6, 1980

Mary Mingay, Betty Junod and Mary Godfrey refer to surveys showing that apparently more than 90 per cent of the Ontario population don't want to see children involved in explicit sex acts. They conclude that no one should be allowed to see such scenes.

That is as logical as saying that 90 per cent of the population doesn't like chocolate-covered bees, therefore no one should be allowed to eat them.

The answer for those who don't want to see something or buy something is not to see or buy. Let 10 per cent of the population see what they want and the 90 per cent, as well as Mary Mingay, Betty Junod and my mother, can read reviews to find out what films to avoid.

Anne Godfrey
Toronto

◆

May 21, 1980

It is clear that The Tin Drum controversy is having a deleterious effect on social values, most especially family relationships. What else can explain Stephen Godfrey's article on the subject (Battle Heats Up Over Censor's Decision – April 26), and the letters of Mary Godfrey and Anne Godfrey? Why can't these people simply sit down together at the family table and talk the whole thing over instead of having to tell it all to The Globe and Mail?

Dr. John F. Godfrey
President, University of King's College
Halifax

Phew!

July 4, 1980

Richard Brown, Departments of English and Social Studies, York Memorial Collegiate Institute of Toronto, puts three dots at the end of a sentence of 85 words in his letter on The McLuhan Centre.

Are these ellipses, or were three periods thought necessary to get such a sentence stopped?

Harvey H. Bowman
Islington, Ontario

The Tale of the Sasquatch

January 17, 1981

Re Robert Williamson's article, Monstrous Indulgence in the Sasquatch:

It so happened that several years ago near Seven Persons, Alta., where I farm, there were rumors of sightings of the dreaded beings. I did not know until I read Mr. Williamson's column that there could be large amounts of money involved. I must explain that since the time the Sasquatch left the egg with me, and the different times I have been involved since that day, I didn't think anyone was seriously interested in further sightings – but now a bit of it must be told.

In April (the month the egg was supposed to hatch), I kept very close watch on it. I had it in a large barn in some straw with an electric heater underneath to keep it at a steady warmth of 80 degrees F. On April 15, I noticed a purple glow coming from it, so I figured something was about to happen. I decided that it would be well to have a witness to the event, and located an Irish peasant just out of Belfast. He was part leprechaun and part from Lurgan, so he did not know much about agricultural engineering. He was a good back-up for me in case we had trouble – *and we did have trouble*.

About 8 p.m. there was suddenly a high whining sound from the egg. It turned a bright orange color; the temperature went up to 50 degrees C (and climbing), when out of nowhere came, of all things, a large Sasquatch which picked up the egg and disappeared into the night air.

My Irish peasant friend and I jumped into our 1952 Fargo half-ton with overload springs and radio (AM) and tried to follow. We could see a double trail of lights disappearing down the road allowance. The only evidence of this occurrence was large footprints about 15 feet (2.5 metres) apart.

We were indeed very unhappy. After keeping the egg warm for nearly a year, we figured the least the mother could do was let us see the newly born "Quatch" (this is what we call them).

About two weeks later, while I was working on some machinery in the late afternoon, who should come over the hill but the Sasquatch and the Quatch. This latter beast had grown to three feet, it was a purplish-orange color, with spiky hair sticking out from under a kind of motorcycle helmet, making a noise like a Volkswagen misfiring and smelling something like Chanel No. 8.

I have some pictures, so if you are interested dollar-wise, let me know.

By the way, my peasant friend will soon get his civilization papers.

James G. Pratt
Medicine Hat, Alberta

Procrastination
August 26, 1981

As a card-carrying member of The Procrastinator's Club, I must urgently protest the piece of anti-procrastination propaganda that appeared in the March 20 edition of your paper. I refer, of course, to the item titled Chronic Lateness Destructive, written by one Olive Evans in an effort to dampen the annual National Procrastination Week celebrations.

If Olive Evans must wag her finger, she should wag it at all the nags and clock-watchers who would have us reduce our lives to the efficient predictability of so many quartz crystals, under the popular modern threat of a negative psychological diagnosis ("The chronically anxious are either late or early").

National Procrastination Week is a healthy reminder to us all that it is we who wind the clocks, not the converse. It is an observance that deserves to be appreciated and enjoyed (if and when people get around to it), and your willingness to print Olive Evans' bit of wet blanketry was misguided at best.

M. A. Rothery
Toronto

Hold the Tomato
September 5, 1981

In the article Ten Winnipeg Men Face Charges Over Soliciting Of Fake Prostitutes, an angry police officer said, "It's always disgusted me that some guy can drive downtown in his big car, throw a $20 bill at some poor native girl, debauch her and drive back to his wife and a hot supper."

But what if he's not married and only wants a salad?

Austin Small
Oakville, Ontario

Square Day
September 21, 1981

The Globe and Mail, in its editorial A Day to Count On, has managed to get hold of the wrong end of yet another stick, this time with the result of taking away from us squares even that little honor we might have had.

Once every year, without fail, mothers and fathers and labor are honored, and nobody talks about mother roots, father roots or labor roots. For us squares, our day comes but nine times in most centuries – i.e. once every 11 years, on average – and then it gets called a square *root* day!

Even your definition is an oversimplification. Sure, for the last 800 years, the squares have only turned up in the last two digits of the year. But look ahead. In the twenty-second century, we'll have triple-digit squares: 10/10/100, 11/11/121, and 12/12/144. Let us hope that by then society (and even The Globe and Mail, if it's still around) will be sufficiently enlightened to give Square Day the attention it deserves.

Barbara Brougham
Toronto

A Draining Myth

September 26, 1981

Twice during the last week in your columns I have seen reference to, as fact, the hoary old myth that water running out of a plug-hole rotates in an opposite direction in the Northern and Southern hemispheres. The second occasion was Michael Valpy's report on his arrival in Australia (Just Like Home).

As L.M. Milne-Thomson points out in his classical work, Theoretical Hydrodynamics, if you have separate hot and cold taps, you can change the direction of rotation merely by changing taps. As a then young and recent graduate in physics, I conducted an experiment during the war on a long and boring voyage by troopship from Brisbane, Australia, to San Francisco. I only had one tap, but the water swirled in the same direction throughout the voyage.

The myth is interesting because it has a foundation in scientific fact – the existence of the Coriolis force due to the Earth's rotation, which is of major importance in world meteorology. The magnitude of the Coriolis effect in the bath-water case is however completely swamped by the local "viscous" or frictional forces. Several experts in fluid mechanics have conducted highly refined experiments to see if the (undoubtedly existing) Coriolis effect could be detected at all in the plug-hole context but, as far as I know, the results have been inconclusive.

J.H. Blackwell
London, Ontario

October 10, 1981

The mantle of accurate reporting needs to be restored to your two columnists who correctly reported the direction of rotation in water draining out of a plug-hole. The direction of rotation is different in the two hemispheres: clockwise in the northern.

This fact was challenged in this space, in an apparently learned opinion that reminds one of the similarly learned opinion that bumblebees are unable to fly. A novel one-tap, two-tap theory was advanced to explain the direction of rotation and this may be adequate as a first-blush observation. However, in the same terms I advance the "n" tap theory of rotation where "n" equals the number of taps filling the basin. The theory will state, "as 'n' approaches infinity, the direction of rotation will become clockwise in the northern hemisphere and anti-clockwise in the southern."

But for more ordinary folk such as myself, I can suggest that the basin be filled by whatever means with the stopper firmly in place. Then, when the water has come to a rest, pull the stopper and observe. I too have done this experiment (as described) while travelling by ship from the antipodes to North America. The motion of the ship appears to affect the direction of rotation so that near the equator, one cannot be certain of the direction of rotation. Other than that, the case appears closed.

Just in case doubters are left, I am embarking soon on another voyage to the other hemisphere. I can repeat these experiments and report again in this space in the new year. What more can you want?

L.C. Allen
Ottawa

♦

October 17, 1981

I find it regrettable that you published the letter from L.C. Allen since it is quite apparent that he doesn't know what he is talking about but is instead allowing his prejudices to perpetuate an old myth. Perhaps neither you nor Mr. Allen recognized that the writer, J.H. Blackwell of London, Ont., is (or was) a professor of both mathematics and physics at the University of Western Ontario and is supremely well qualified to comment on the matter. His remarks were comprehensive yet brief, and absolutely correct.

Questions about the same myth have turned up many times over the years in a number of books and periodicals. I would like to quote one which appeared in the periodical The Physics Teacher in the 1976 January issue. The answer was provided by Malcolm Correll of the University of Colorado and concludes as follows: "If a drain orifice is carefully opened at the bottom of a basin of undisturbed water, we might expect to see the existing water rotate counterclockwise in the northern hemisphere and clockwise in the southern. However, to produce the effect requires very elaborate controlled conditions. Vanes, roughnesses, or other deflecting elements and initial residual motion of the water, including any stirring as the plug is removed, will almost certainly mask the comparatively tiny Coriolis effect. Bowls of water have memories of the direction of initial rotation that may last for hours. Toilets usually introduce flushing water from the top rim and some have a jet that enters from below. These violent effects can easily mask the weak Coriolis force, and the true effect is never seen with household devices."

Robert E. Heath
Sault Ste. Marie, Ontario

◆

October 17, 1981

The diverting arguments on the direction of rotation of water draining from a basin in the northern or southern hemispheres are all very well, but as I have digital timekeepers, will someone please explain to me what "clockwise" means?

Furthermore, if you are in outer space, the water will not rotate at all when you unplug the basin but will rise straight up and hit you in the face.

Austin Small
Oakville, Ontario

The Centre of Canada

January 16, 1982

I must take issue with the editor of the Edmonton Journal quoted by Richard Needham, who holds that the geographic centre of Canada lies as far north and west as Baker Lake in the Northwest Territories (64°N, 96°W).

Even on a Mercator's projection (which, by opening out the globe, exaggerates northern areas) the geographic centre of Canada lies well to the south, and in global terms probably lies near the Nelson River in Manitoba (57°N, 93°W).

More important, however, my research suggests that the population centre of Canada is about 45°N, 80°W, or about 100 miles north of Toronto on Georgian Bay, with the average Canadian living about 90 miles from the border. This has considerable implications in that this is just as much a southern nation as a northern, and its population centre still lies toward the east, though shifting slowly west and north.

D.J. Reynolds
Kanata, Ontario

Sprucing Down

February 23, 1982

Last spring, I built a windowbox and varnished the front door, bravely attempting to make our scruffy house less of an eyesore in a pretty street. This tarting-up was my entire renovation effort – inside, the house retains all of its ex-roominghouse charm.

Imagine my surprise to receive a 270 per cent increase in tax assessment. The cosmetic job is costing me an additional $1,000 a year. I had intended to change the washers in the taps, but fearing it might mean taking out a bank loan, I called the area assessor.

Is there a pro-rata scale, I asked, $30 per foot of weatherstrip, $250 for a kitchen shelf, with a complete renovation financing the Scarborough Expressway? Not exactly, said the gentleman, it's simply that we are testing a novel way of assessing house values. It all depends on how the house looks from the outside.

Well, I'm flooded with admiration for this stroke of ergonomic genius: all those tedious man-hours saved visiting each house individually. But on reflection, I think we can beat them at this game, so here's my advice on how to keep your rates down. Renovate your house entirely – triple-glaze, insulate, cram Jacuzzis in every corner, make every room a bathroom if you wish. Turn it into a palace of comfort. Then, nail up some torn drapes, break a few windows, spray-paint slogans on the walls, tie a mutt to the porch and strew some garbage about.

The next time our overworked provincial assessors cruise your neighborhood, they won't give you a second glance. Your house won't *look* renovated.

Annie Massey
Toronto

Gobbledygook

July 10, 1982

A letter complained about your music reviews, lamenting both the presence of gobbledygook and the lack of respect for the audience's intelligence. This letter is to urge you to be cautious in any action that would eliminate gobbledygook from your pages since the results would be very serious, perhaps terminal.

If he were denied the use of gobbledygook, how would your art critic describe the contents of our most progressive art galleries? What would happen to your economics commentators if they were forced into the use of precise language? Could there ever be an article on the stock market?

Hammond Dugan
Thornhill, Ontario

Those TV Ads Must Be Working

October 30, 1982

In this time of emphasis on energy conservation, there is an obvious, simple and practical explanation of why the star Epsilon Aurigae disappears every 27 years (Mysterious Star Fades from View Every 27 Years). God simply turns out the light for one year out of 27 to save power.

H. Francis
London, Ontario

In Suspense

December 8, 1982

In connection with the story Sex and the Aged, about the sexual trials and tribulations of 73-year-old Albert, I strenuously object to being left in suspense. We never do find out whether Albert finally achieved success or not.

We meet Albert, a "sexual virtuoso," who has fallen from grace. His girl friend has rejected him because he can't perform. Ostensibly to cure the condition, the doctors inflated his penis. Albert was jubilantly looking forward to testing himself again. And there the story ends. This is like having your TV set conk out in the middle of a Dallas episode. I demand to know what happened.

Marvin Fremes
Toronto

The Post Office

January 6, 1983

Re Is Mail Service Really Faster?:
  Yes.
  On Nov. 23, I received, at my office, a personal letter from the Chief Justice of Canada, posted at the Supreme Court on Nov. 17. It was correctly addressed, postal code and all, and typewritten. The distance is seven blocks.
  In 1967, I had a personal letter from the then Minister of Justice, correctly addressed, posted at the West Block of the Parliament Buildings, to my then office at the Ottawa Electric Building. The distance is three blocks. It took nine days.
  Seven blocks in eight days is certainly a notable improvement over three blocks in nine days.
  There has also been a great improvement over 1977. On Nov. 11 of that year, I sent a letter, correctly addressed, to a well-known private citizen, from the Civic Hospital to his address, 200 Rideau Terrace, Ottawa. He received it on March 26, 1978.

Eugene Forsey
Ottawa

The First Baby

January 15, 1983

It was reported that a baby delivered at Doctors Hospital in Toronto was the first born in Canada in 1983. While I regard the so-called competition between Canadian hospitals for the honor of delivering the year's first baby as rather inconsequential claptrap, nevertheless, in the interests of scientific truth, I would like to draw your attention to an error.
  The baby born at Doctors Hospital in Toronto was said to have beaten out a baby born at St. Mary's Hospital in Montreal, the former having been born at the stroke of midnight, where the latter was born one-hundredth of a second past midnight. Without wishing to contribute further to English-French tension, it should be noted that the Montreal baby is in fact the victor. A baby born at exactly midnight, 2400 hours, is really born on Dec. 31 and not Jan. 1, midnight, 2400 hours, being the very end of a day and not the start of a new day.
  "Trivial Pursuit" buffs take note.

P.W. Young
Guelph, Ontario

January 15, 1983

I wholeheartedly agree with your suggestion of a committee to regulate the birth of the first baby in Canada of the New Year.

One sticky question I am sure would be on top of the agenda is: what about the baby born in Victoria at 9 p.m. local time, 12 midnight Toronto time? Does this baby qualify? Or do we end up with regional First Babies (New Year Baby Newfoundland, New Year Baby Central Canada, New Year Baby Prairies, etc.)?

Kara Kieferle
Ottawa

In Metric

February 8, 1983

Re the article Tory MPs Sell Gas by the Gallon, Say They Are Ready to Go to Jail:

I suppose after the Tory caucus, anything is preferable.

Keith Davey
The Senate
Ottawa

Goodbye, Mr. Zzzzyzka

April 23, 1983

In the course of human events, no one can ignore the procession of special people who pass through the doors of fame. It comes, then, as a sober reminder to all of us that another popular milestone has been toppled on the road to stardom.

The 1983 Toronto phone books have been delivered, and a fast sweep of the spotlight to page 1784 reveals that Z. Zzzzyzka, our anchor person for the last year, has relinquished the post.

In an alphabetical world where the last one in is a rotten egg and the last one out turns off the lights, I believe Z. Zzzzyzka has finally tired of waiting.

Phil Brown
Brampton, Ontario

> *Z. Zzzzyzka's treasured place in the Toronto directory was, alas, a victim of corporate takeover. The last-place finisher in 1983 was Zyzosner Productions and, in 1984, Zz International.*

French on Cereal Boxes

September 17, 1983

Re your editorial, There Is Another Side:

Major Dunsheath is right: someone is turning the products French-side-out in the supermarkets. However, he is wrong about who and why. The person who does this (and every supermarket has one) is the same person who makes sure the package of pork chops you want is at the bottom of the heap; ditto the steaks; goes around the produce department with a little hammer putting one tiny bruise on each piece of otherwise perfect fruit; hides the kind of soup you like on the bottom shelf at the far end of the display; places your dog's favorite brand of food (a large, heavy box) on the top shelf of the display; and sends a telepathic message to the clerk at the delicatessen counter to start slicing a three-week supply of cooked meats (and / or clean the slicing machine and everything else in the department) just as you arrive to buy your weekly four slices of ham. The clerk ignores you because you're the only person at the counter.

So now we have the "who." The "why" is easy: because they hate us, that's why.

Dorothy Coaker
Don Mills, Ontario

Divorce Statistic

October 8, 1983

Re your headline, Parents of 65,000 Divorced Last Year:
Wouldn't you?

M.F. Yalden
Ottawa

Commissioner of Official Languages.

Rebirth

November 19, 1983

The other day I received one of the strangest phone calls ever. It seemed, according to this all-too-pleasant voice, that my beautiful 5-year-old son had been "eradicated" – he was one of the "3 per cent lost in the computer."

Aside from being irritated by this person's patronizing manner – as though I were entirely without wit – she felt compelled to explain to me that, although she had found the necessary information in a filing cabinet, she was going to have to "create" my son. Well, I thought that was jolly kind of her, but I thought I had already done that.

You can imagine that I was not too tickled – nor even slightly amused – at my son's death and resurrection, nor was I even faintly sympathetic to this person's predicament. As well, I wish to God that people would stop assuming that the housewife on the other end is a mental midget.

Today all is well – my son is alive, thriving and bursting with unknown sources of energy. I've no idea whether his "creation" has occurred – nor do I give a damn.

Michele Patterson
Toronto

Too Hard by Half

November 30, 1983

The letter fired off by Gen. Viktor G. Kulikov, Commander-in-Chief of the Warsaw Pact Forces, along with other letters from Soviet officials which have appeared recently, indicates that The Globe and Mail is becoming popular in the Kremlin.

I shouldn't be surprised one morning to read a letter from himself complaining – like many of your readers – that the Cryptic Crossword is too cryptic by half.

Dickson Russell
Toronto

This Is It

December 19, 1983

My friends are expecting me to write a strong letter on the subject of the Canada Health Act. This is that letter. Please print it, as I hate to disappoint my friends.

Morton S. Rapp, MD
Toronto

Nipples

February 11, 1984

With regard to the headline Federal Limit Is Expected on Nipples:

Until today, I had been under the impression that there already was a limit of two per person.

Mary E. Hofstetter
Kitchener, Ontario

The Accused's Condition

February 11, 1984

I was intrigued by your story about the former head of the Montreal police drug squad who was found guilty of trafficking.

I note that the accused "crumbled onto a chair" when he heard the verdict. Surely we deserve more elucidation. Would he be reassembled before being taken off to jail? And once incarcerated, how would a person possessed of this artifice be securely contained? More important, is this condition genetic or can it be learned? Please tell us more.

E.W. Kortes
Edmonton

◆

February 18, 1984

I cannot understand why your Edmonton correspondent needs elucidation of the statement "crumbled onto a chair," unless of course he is totally unfamiliar with the judicial process. I have frequently observed an accused "go all to pieces" when sentenced, only "to pull himself together again" before being led away. Once in the cell block, of course, containment is no problem since convicts always "stick together."

What word other than "crumbled" could have conveyed all these insights with such eloquence and brevity?

T.R. Priddle
Oldcastle, Ontario

Chapter 20

A Prophecy

February 29, 1984

It appears that renowned sixteenth-century seer Michel Nostradamus clearly envisioned the birth and career of Pierre Elliott Trudeau – from his first home on Durocher Street to his handling of the FLQ Crisis – when he chose to include the following in his illustrious book of prophecies (Chapter VII, Stanza 32):

> Du Mont Royal naistra d'une casane,
> Qui duc, & compte viendra tyranniser,
> Dresser copie de la marche Millane,
> Favence, Florence d'or & gens espuiser.

> (Out of Montreal shall be born in a cottage,
> One that shall tyrannize over duke and earl,
> He shall raise an army in the land of the rebellion,
> He shall empty Favence and Florence of their gold.)

> – Translation by H.C. Roberts

As to the apparently ambiguous reference in the final line of this quatrain, one could only speculate at present; unless of course, our Prime Minister is indeed contemplating further manoeuvres.

P.D. Caughill
Weston, Ontario

Later that same day, Pierre Trudeau tendered his resignation as Prime Minister of Canada.

Index of Writers

A.B.C., 10-11
A.B.C., 133-4
Abbott, Ernest, 255-6
Adams, W.H., 87
Allen, L.C., 272
Amateur Astrologist, 141
Armstrong, J.E., 134
Armstrong, Joseph A., 30-1
'Arris, Mrs., 135
Ashley, C.A., 229
Axworthy, Lloyd, 210-1

Bain, George, 222
Baldwin, Harry, 81-2
Baltas, Leon, 263
Barclay, Geo. J., 34
Barclay, James, 240
Barker, W.E., 88
Barque, Graeme, 201-2
Bengough, Elven, 55-6
Berlin Readers, 76
Berry, Reginald, 196-7
Berton, Pierre, 193-5
Big White Owl (Jasper Hill), 145-6
Bigras, Jean Guy, 167-8
Bird, Amoi, 259
Bird, John, 126
Black, D.C., 32-3
Black, Will, 164
Blackwell, J.H., 271
Boa, Jim, 166
Bocock, John Paul, 19-20
Bond, Courtney C.J., 242-3
Bonwick, Gerald, 169-70
Bowman, Harvey H., 268

Brant-Sero, J. Ojijatekha, 51-2
Brett, R. de R., 188
Bridgen, Bridget, 121
Brighty, Isabel McComb, 122
Brisebois, Jos. E., 114-5
Britt, Wm. E., 84-5
Brougham, Barbara, 270-1
Brown, J.R., 54
Brown, Margaret A., 112-3
Brown, Phil, 277
Brownrigg, Peter, 219
Bruyns, A.G.M., 179-80

Cameron, J.H., 113-4
Campbell, Wm., 49-50
Canham, Arthur, 109-11
Carmichael, W., 85-6
Carnochan, A.R., 48-9
Carr, William Guy, 181
Carson, Chester, 99
Caswell, E.S., 191
Caughill, P.D., 281
Chandler, (Mrs.) R., 129
Chellew, A., 28
Civis, 44
Clark, Gregory, 227-8
Clark, V.M., 200-1
Clarke, George Frederick, 102
Coaker, Dorothy, 278
Cohen, Maria Newfeld, 261
Cook, Peter, 241
Cooper, R., 199
Copeland, Agnes Grote, 37-8
Copeland, M.V., 232
Corsan, George Hebden, 176

Index of Subjects

abdication, King Edward and, 133
accent, Canadian, 198
advertising: answered, 224;
  interruptions by in hockey,
  219-21
Agamemnon, quoted, 117
airport, troubles in, 193-5
Alberta, drinking laws in, 96-7
Algonquin Group (Group of
  Seven), 66
Algonquin Park, 128
alliteration, 252-3
alphabet, creation of Cherokee,
  19-20
anthem, French and English
  versions of, 217
Arabi Pasha, 7
arthritis, cure for, 257
astrology, King Edward and, 133
astronomy: Big Bang Theory,
  253-5; January sky, 28-30; new
  satellite, 30-1
atheism, in Ireland, 225
atom, splitting of, 171
atomic warfare: against Japan,
  169-70; defence against, 177;
  defence of Toronto, 188-9; on
  moon, 183
attorney-general, application for,
  115-16
Atwood, Margaret, 253
Audubon, John James, 32
Australia, emigration to, 108-9
automobiles: driving of, 247;
  speed of, 53-4
averages, laws of, 121

baby: first of new year, 276-7;
  view of life by, 144
Balaclava, battle of, 54
bank robberies, defence against,
  185-6
barking, lessons from, 151-2
baseball: memories of in 1866,
  95-6; popularity of, 64
bat (as bird), 101
Batoche, 4
Battleford, 5
beards, 206-9
beaver, as symbol, 76; 105
beer, and singing, 147-8
Bennett, George, and George
  Brown, 49-50
Bethell, Sir Richard, 21
Bible: cocktails and, 133-4; effect
  of moon on, 143
bilingualism: on cereal box, 278;
  on pill box, 63
bird: group-soul of, 51; national
  symbol, 98-107; teaching to
  talk, 26-8
Bismarck, Otto von, 6
black man, birth of, 145-6
blasphemy, on trains, 72-3
blue jay (bird): 98; 106; as whiskey
  jack, 104
boogie-woogie, denunciation of,
  161
books, censorship of, 189-90
Borden, Sir Robert, 78
boxing: Dempsey and Gibbons,
  90-2; Hemingway and
  Callaghan, 226-7

Boys, Thomas T.A., 36
bradyarthia (speech disorder), 154
brain fever, 25
Brant, Joseph, memorial for, 51-2
bridge (game), perfect hand dealt, 121
bridge, Windsor to Detroit, 88
British ideals, 159-60
British National Canine Defence League, 185
Brock, Gen. Isaac, 51
Brown, George: candidature of, 38; shooting of, 49-50
Buffalo, police tactics in, 171-2
bullfrogs, 134
Bunyan, John, 19
Burke's Peerage (book), 188
Burns, Robert, celebrated by Russia, 200
bus, plural of, 1
Bystander (journal), 21

Cabbagetown, location of, 197
Cadmus the Phoenician, 19
Calgary, spelling of, 85-8
Callaghan, Morley, 226-7
Canada: centre of, 273-4; colonial status of, 13; 144-5; cuisine, 198; culture of, 180; 186-7; decentralization of, 245-6; division between English and French in, 152; economic domination of, 212; education in, 39-41; employment in, 210-11; George Bernard Shaw and, 124-5; immigration to, 108-9; 159-60; national colors of, 78; no literature in, 12-14; origin of name, 31-2; privileged classes in, 188; union with United States, 183; 205; 213-4
Canada goose (bird), 99; 101-6
Canada Health Act, 279

Canadian Authors' Association, 124-5
Canadian Broadcasting Corporation: Gladstone Murray and, 153-4; station breaks on, 250
Canadian Corps Association, 159-60
Canadian Fighter Pilots' Association, 247
Canadian Monthly and National Review (journal), 21
Canadian Pacific Railway, immigrants aboard, 108-9
Canadians: health of, 50-1; typical, 74-5
cancer, in English and French, 114-5
cards, chewing gum, 173-5
Carman, Bliss, 98; 103; celebrated by Russians, 199-200
cats: and war, 72; snowshoes on, 132-3
cellars, as bomb-shelters, 177
censorship: films, 267-8; expletives, 252; literature, 189-90; wartime, 146-7
century, beginning of, 34-5
chain-shot, as weapon, 64-5
chairs, as weapons, 41-2
Charlesworth, Hector, 66
cheerfulness, laughter and, 122-3
Cherokee, alphabet of, 19-20
Chesterton, Gilbert Keith, quoted, 82
chewing gum cards, 173-5
chickadee (bird), 100-1
Church of England, 16
church, reasons for going to, 148-9
Cincinnatti Zoological Garden, 32
civilization, of Canada and United States, 39-41

Clark, Joe: beard and, 208; 209; defeat of, 267; driving a car, 247

Clarke, George Frederick, 98

clay, making humans of, 145-6

Clemenceau, Georges, 160

Clouds Across the Canyon (painting), 69-72

coat of arms: Canadian, 78-9; of Ottawa, 179-80

coat-hanger, origin of, 230-3

cocktails, invention of, 133-4

College of Arms, 78

communism, effect of moon on, 143

Communist Party of Canada (Marxist-Leninist), 264

commuting, 181-3

compass, Ottawa's coat of arms and, 179

computers, destruction of data in, 278-9

Cook, Dr. Frederick A., 55

Coriolis effect, 271-3

cosmonauts, Russian, 199

cows: getting up, 134-5; music and milk production of, 170-1; newspapers as fodder for, 166-7

critics of art, 66-8

crooners, on radio, 119-21; 176

cross, seen on moon, 138-43

crow (bird) 26-8; as Bolshevik, 106

Cruel Sea (book), 215

crumbling, act of, 280

culture, oral and written, 248-50

Curtis, Smith, 41-2

dancing, in Egypt, 23-5

Davis, Jefferson, 6

de Gaulle, Charles, 215-7

Demeter (goddess), 235

Demosthenes, 7; 154

Dempsey, Jack, 90-2

Department of National Revenue, 229

Department of Soldiers' Civil Re-establishment, 91

diamonds, in Northern Ontario, 117-9

dictionary, brief edition, 10-11

Diefenbaker, John, 79; 203-4

divorce, statistics of, 278

dog: as sheep-killer, 126; hatred of, 227; in Sputnik, 184-5; lessons from, 151

Douglas, Tommy, 223

dove (bird), 103; 105

Drew, George, 176

drinking: and drunkenness, 96-7; behavior on V-Day and, 161; moderation in, 150-1

Duck Lake, 6

Earles, Maude, 36

Earth: as moon's moon, 30-1; mass of, 110; roundness debated, 82-5

elections: no change in, 267; voting in, 225; women and, 9

electricity: and ouija boards, 73; dangers of, 44; failure of, 212

Elegy Written in a Country Churchyard (poem), 149-50

elephant, in Sputnik, 185

ellipses, use of, 268

Employment Service of Canada, 132

English people, incidence of cancer in, 114-5

Epsilon Aurigae, disappearance of, 275

Euclid, 44-6

Evening Telegram (newspaper), 21

farm life, spring and, 172-3

fascism, effect of moon on, 143

fatness, 240

Martin, Joseph, 41-2
Masonic Order, 122
McAree, J.V., 2
McBride, Richard, 41-2
McCullagh, George, 2
McGee, Thomas D'Arcy, shooting of, 9-10
McGill Daily (newspaper), 153
McTeer, Maureen, 242
medium (spiritualist), 10
Métis, 4
metric, conversion to, 277
Metro Toronto Zoo, 258; 263
Middleton, Gen. Frederick, 4
milk, effect on production of, 170-1
millennium, coming of, 16
Miner, Jack, 90; 98; 105; 127
miniskirt, 218; origin of, 248
Mizener, Arthur, 226-7
modernism, in art, 80-1
Mohawks: 52; 65; 204-5; origin of Yankee and, 113-4; 204-5
money, red leaves on, 77-9
Montreal Canadiens, 219-21
moon: as atomic testing site, 183-4; as inspiration, 30; cross seen on, 138-43; effect of on abdication, 133; effect of on tides, 110
moonshine, effect of on moon, 140-1
Morgan (ghost), 122
mullet, falling from sky, 255-7
Murray, Maj. Gladstone, 153-4
music: beer parlors and, 147-8; effect of on milk, 170-1; from stove, 128; on Soviet trains, 241-2

names: and numerology, 229; change of in marriage, 22; hyphenation of, 244-5

Napoléon Bonaparte, 6
National Federation of Christian Laymen, 181
National Film Board, 155-6
Nazarene Gospel, 215
nazism, effect of moon on, 143
Neptune, effect of in astrology, 133
New Democratic Party, 223; 225
Newfoundland, 214
newsboys, 163
newspapers: errors in, 156; 162-8; habit of reading, 162; reporting in, 227-8
Niagara Gleaner (newspaper), 122
Nightingale, Florence, 54
nipples, 279-80
North Pole: cold weather from, 60; discovery of, 55; gravity at, 110
Northern Ontario: development of, 117-9; where to plug vacuum in, 166
Northwest Rebellion, 4-7
Nostradamus, Michel de, quoted, 281
numerology, war and, 71-2; 126

O Canada (song): French and English versions of, 217-8; lacking reverence, 77; rewritten, 246
obesity, 240
obey, as marriage vow, 15-16
obituary, wrongly noted in, 223
odds, in bridge hands, 121
Ode on the Mammoth Cheese (poem), 12
Ogopogo, in Okanagan, 111-2
oh, oh, spoken in Parliament, 221-2
Olympic Games: original, 235; participation in, 265-6

Ontario: advertising for, 224; as tourist attraction, 127-8; ode to, 11-12; wealth of, 117-9

Ontario (poem), 191

Ontario Society of Artists, 66

Orange Order, goat and, 164

ouija boards, 73

owl (bird), 99-100; 106

oxygen, and heart attacks, 247

panhandling, 131-2

Papineau, Louis-Joseph, 6

Parallax (Samuel B. Rowbotham), 82-4

Parti Québécois, 245

partridge (bird), 103

passenger pigeons, disappearance of, 32-3

peace: Indians as an example of, 204-5; with United States, 202-3

Pearson, Lester B., 79; 217; 219

Peary, Robert Edwin, 55; 60

Perkins, Maxwell, 226

phlogiston, 230-3

pigeon (bird), 176-7

Pike, General, monument to, 123-4

pill, as substitute for lunch, 47-8

Pluto, effect of in astrology, 133

poetry: badness in, 16-19; modernism in, 68-71

poker, Adolf Hitler and, 137

police, behavior of in Buffalo, 171-2

Port Dalhousie, 83

Port Said, 23-5

postal service, speed of, 276

Poundmaker, Chief, 5

poverty, definition of, 264-5

procrastination, 270

professors, in groups, 225-6

Progressive Conservative Party: campaigning, 225; caucus of, 277; defeat of, 203-4; loss of leadership of, 175

prohibition, attacks on, 81-2

promises, in marriage vows, 15-16

pronunciation: American, 160; 222-3; 222-3; Canadian accent, 198; lessons from dog on, 151-2; of Pied Piper, 130-1; on radio, 158

prostitution, 270

Protestants, threatened, 26

punch, recipe for, 88

Pythagoras, 143

Quebec, and war effort, 152

Queen Elizabeth, Satan in hair, 180-1; and stockings, 200-1

Queen Street, condition of, 59-60

Queen Victoria, death of, 37-8

radio: crooners on, 119-21; culture contained in, 117; permits for, 176; quality of language on, 157-8; received by stove, 129; uncertain reception, 129-30

RCMP Museum, 8

rebirth, in computers, 278-9

red man, birth of, 145-6

Redford Canal, 82-4

Reform Government, election of, 28

religious objects, 234-5

renovations, taxation and, 274

rhinoceros, 262; 263

Riders of the Plains (poem), 36

Ridout, John and Mary, 235-7

Riel, Louis, 4-8; hair of, 8

Roberts, Charles G.D., 98

robin (bird), 98-9